This work is a celebration of demographic workmanship. Todd Johnson has spent his life building an authentic village of craftsmen and craftswomen, mentoring many young scholars in World Christianity and missiology with skill and patience. As an immigrant, otherwise gleaning only on the margins, I consider myself grateful for the multiple doors he helped open for me in mission and academia. This book is for all who aspire to do the same.

WANJIRU M. GITAU, PHD
Assistant Professor, World Christianity and Practical Theology,
Palm Beach Atlantic University

This volume is not only a powerful testimony of Dr. Todd Johnson's well-recognized status, rich accomplishments, and muti-dimensional global influence as the authority on Christian demography, but also a very valuable source for the study of World Christianity in the past and present centuries.

KEVIN XIYI YAO, PHD
Professor, World Christianity and Asian Studies,
Gordon-Conwell Theological Seminary

This volume is a fitting tribute to the bespoke Dr. Todd Johnson. One who is always keen to see not just the trees but the forest, he embodies a meta-analytical skill set which this book stays true to. Christianity should be for and by everyone, and Todd is one of the chief catalysts to bring it all together so beautifully. He is a storyteller and mentor par excellence, both in his writings and to all those he encounters personally, as exemplified by the magisterial data and moving testimonies that lie herein.

ALLEN YEH, DPHIL
Professor, Intercultural Studies & Missiology,
Biola University, Cook School of Intercultural Studies

# Portraits of Global Christianity

Research and Reflections in Honor of Todd M. Johnson

Gina A. Zurlo, Editor

visit us at missionbooks.org

*Portraits of Global Christianity: Research and Reflections in Honor of Todd M. Johnson*
© 2023 by Gina A. Zurlo. All rights reserved.

No part of this book may be reproduced, stored in a retrieval system, or transmitted in any form or by any means—electronic, mechanical, photocopy, recording, or otherwise—without prior written permission from the publisher, except brief quotations used in connection with reviews in magazines or newspapers. For permission, email permissions@wclbooks.com. For corrections, email editor@wclbooks.com.

Scripture quotations marked (NIV) are taken from the Holy Bible, New International Version®, NIV®. Copyright © 1973, 1978, 1984, 2011 by Biblica, Inc.™ Used by permission of Zondervan. All rights reserved worldwide. www.zondervan.com. The "NIV" and "New International Version" are trademarks registered in the United States Patent and Trademark Office by Biblica, Inc.™

Published by William Carey Publishing
10 W. Dry Creek Cir
Littleton, CO 80120 | www.missionbooks.org

William Carey Publishing is a ministry of Frontier Ventures
Pasadena, CA | www.frontierventures.org

Cover Design: Mike Riester

ISBNs: 978-1-64508-461-7 (paperback)
       978-1-64508-463-1 (epub)
       978-1-64508-490-7 (hardback)

Printed Worldwide
27 26 25 24 23   1 2 3 4 5   IN

Library of Congress data on file with the publisher.

# Contents

| | |
|---|---|
| Preface | viii |
| Introduction, *Gina A. Zurlo* | xi |

## Part I: Partnership in World Christianity and Mission Research — 1

Chapter 1: Trends in Global Christianity Through Design — 2
*Gina A. Zurlo and Peter F. Crossing*

Chapter 2: 1993: A Seminal Year — 26
*Patrick Johnstone*

Chapter 3: Partnership in Quantitative Research on World Christianity — 32
*Jason Mandryk and Molly Wall*

## Part II: Lived Global Christianity — 47

Chapter 4: Invitation to the Kitchen, Not Just to the Table: Todd M. Johnson's Motif of Global Christianity — 48
*Uchenna D. Anyanwu*

Chapter 5: Reflections and Lessons from Massachusetts to Uganda — 62
*Joseph Byamukama*

Chapter 6: Moments in Time: Challenging the Fabric of Faith — 68
*Jane Kyong Chun*

Chapter 7: Dismantling the Ethnic Foods Aisle in Theological Libraries — 70
*James Marion Darlack*

Chapter 8: Who *Are* These People? A Rediscovery from Ephesians 3 and 4 — 75
*Darrell Dorr*

Chapter 9: Story as a Bridge to Understanding: The Role of Narrative in Creating Global Empathy — 80
*Sharon Ellis*

Chapter 10: A Missiological Hermitage: Representing Jesus Across Cultures — 84
*Jarrett Fontenot*

Chapter 11: What Is the Posthuman Gospel? — 86
*Michael Hahn*

Chapter 12: Many Books  93
　Richard L. Haney

Chapter 13: Global Hermeneutics and the Ethical Potency of Scholarship:
　Reflections on the Character and Expertise of a Religious
　Demographer from an Aspiring Biblical Scholar  101
　David A. Hannan

Chapter 14: I Am Where I Am Today Because of Todd Johnson  106
　Bert Hickman

Chapter 15: Lessons and Gifts of Interreligious Encounters  109
　Daryl R. Ireland

Chapter 16: Capacious Faith  111
　S. Kyle Johnson

Chapter 17: An Appreciation for Todd Johnson: A Personal Reflection  117
　Grace Ji-Sun Kim

Chapter 18: How Are You? What Is Your Name?
　Hospitality and Friendship in Mission and World Christianity  120
　Feruza Krason

Chapter 19: The Power of Curiosity and Generosity  123
　Sandra S.K. Lee

Chapter 20: Intellectual Work:
　Reflections on 30 Years of Mission Research  127
　Justin Long

Chapter 21: The Transforming Power of Images, Memories,
　and Words on Local Church Mission  132
　Brian McAtee

Chapter 22: A Collaborative Approach  137
　Bryan Nicholson

Chapter 23: Fairest Lord Jesus, Ruler of the Nations  139
　Sujin Park

Chapter 24: Living Global Christianity in Thailand  144
　Eva M. Pascal

Chapter 25: Working on Religious Demography with Todd M. Johnson:
　Not Only Quantities but Quality and Values  147
　Kenneth R. Ross

Chapter 26: Listen, Empower, Enjoy, and Think  157
　Justin Schell

| | |
|---|---|
| Chapter 27: Humility, Kindness, and Music:<br>Reflection for Todd Johnson<br>*Jennifer Lee Shin* | 161 |
| Chapter 28: Confronted with the Facts: 86% of Hindus, Buddhists, and Muslims Have Relatively Little Contact with Christians<br>*Benjamin P. Thomas* | 163 |
| Chapter 29: "One of the Excellent People Struggling for the Faith":<br>A Personal Reflection on the Life of Todd Johnson<br>*Charles Tieszen* | 165 |
| Chapter 30: By the Numbers<br>*Cindy M. Wu* | 170 |
| Chapter 31: Belonging<br>*Kenneth Young* | 176 |
| **Part III: The Work of Todd M. Johnson: Data** | **179** |
|     Martyrdom | 181 |
|     General Country Data | 183 |
|     World Religions | 184 |
|     Major Christian Traditions and Movements | 194 |
|     Christian Mission | 201 |
|     Denominations | 203 |
|     Peoples | 207 |
|     Evangelization by Peoples | 212 |
|     Bible Translation | 214 |
|     Cities | 216 |
|     Country Indicators | 218 |
| Acknowledgments | 222 |
| Contributors | 223 |

# Preface

Since moving to Gordon-Conwell Theological Seminary in 2003, Dr. Todd M. Johnson has insisted that Boston is one of the best places in the United States to study World Christianity. Home to dozens of colleges and universities, tens of thousands of international students, and scholars from every academic discipline imaginable, there is no shortage of opportunities for high-level engagement, ecumenical relationships, and interfaith activism. It is appropriate that a book in honor of Todd's life and work begins with words from his friends: Margaret Guider, Dana Robert, and Luke Veronis, his long-time colleagues at Boston College, Boston University, and Holy Cross Greek Orthodox School of Theology. This party of four has been meeting nearly monthly for the last 18 years through the Mission and Ecumenism Committee of the Boston Theological Interreligious Consortium. Together, they share a spirit of friendship and common sense of duty to advance scholarship in global Christianity and mission.

---

At a time when, for many, the Gospel-based ecumenical commitment "that all may be one" (John 17:22) seems to have lost its urgency and significance, Todd Johnson stands out as an unrelenting witness to the Johannine vision of unity among the followers of Jesus Christ. Deliberate, astute, and humble in his way of proceeding, Todd creates and cultivates the conditions for mutual recognition and respect in service of the Reign of God. As teacher and mentor, he has devoted himself to broadening the confessional and religious horizons of his students as well as his colleagues. In the process, his inter-continental research on global Christianity has provided insight into both the demographics and the dynamics of Christian identity and influence in a religiously pluralistic world. Todd's genuine interest in the traditions and cultures that have shaped Christian life and practice in countless contexts is driven by his tireless enthusiasm for pursuing and sustaining networks of relationships and collaborative efforts in mission. Viewed from a Roman Catholic perspective that is informed by the example and hopefulness of Pope Francis, Todd is an exemplary model of what it takes to foster an enduring culture of encounter amidst the divisions, polarizations, and hostilities that have become all too familiar in every corner of our common home.

*Margaret E. Guider, OSF, PhD*
*Associate Professor of Missiology*
*Boston College*

As the tributes in this book show, Dr. Todd Johnson is the rare person who is both an imaginative visionary and a meticulous analyst, a prophet, and a prolific scholar. Through his pioneer work in religious demography, he charts and shapes the field of World Christianity. By so doing, he renders service to Christian movements around the world. For decades, Todd has represented Gordon-Conwell Theological Seminary on the Mission and Ecumenism Committee of the Boston Theological Interreligious Consortium. As fellow committee members, we have been privileged to meet monthly during the academic year, as we plan Boston-area and regional events in mission studies and World Christianity. Our committee planned and carried out the Boston meetings of the Edinburgh 2010 process, through which seminarians from around the region experienced a truly ecumenical academic festival of rich learning, meaningful worship, and fresh missiological insights. Much of the success of that event was due to Todd's unique contributions.

Through working together for God's mission in the world, Todd Johnson has become a faithful friend. Todd and I have taught courses and mentored students together. We have cried together and prayed together. Although this Festschrift celebrates his many accomplishments over decades of hard work, it also provides a foundation for the new possibilities that await him as he enters the next phase of professional life. As with other readers of this volume, I give thanks for Todd Johnson—for consistent and creative work over many decades, and for hope-filled horizons in the future.

*Dana L. Robert*, PhD
*William Fairfield Warren Distinguished Professor*
*Boston University*

---

Todd has acted as a wonderful peacemaker and bridge to Christian unity by trying to value and understand the many expressions of global Christianity. His meticulous work in researching and collecting the most up-to-date demographic information, while always respecting each church tradition's own perspective, sets an admirable example of how we should encounter one another. Christians throughout the world use and appreciate Todd's data to better understand the changing global reality of Christianity. For me personally, what stands beyond Todd's scholarly work is his authentic witness as a follower of Jesus Christ. I've been blessed to meet with Todd once a month, along with other colleagues in the Boston Theological Interreligious Consortium, for the past 18 years. Todd has richly blessed me with his sincere friendship and love. His faith and commitment have inspired and pushed me to grow in my own faith. I've appreciated when he enthusiastically visited the Saints Constantine and Helen Greek Orthodox Church I serve in Webster, Massachusetts or when he attentively listened to stories about the mission work I engaged in the Orthodox Church of Albania. He takes a keen interest in better understanding the ancient and timeless form of Orthodox Christianity, as well as any other form of Christianity he encounters, while learning and growing himself. It's most appropriate to honor this good and faithful steward of the global Christian church.

*Fr. Luke Veronis*, PhD
*Director of the Missions Institute of Orthodox Christianity*
*Holy Cross Greek Orthodox School of Theology*

# Introduction

*Gina A. Zurlo*

On the day Dr. Todd M. Johnson was born in Fridley, Minnesota on June 9, 1958, the cover of LIFE Magazine included the following teaser: "Adventists to Pentecostals: Fastest-Growing Church Movement." It is hardly believable that the article titled, "The Third Force in Christendom" contained descriptions, photos, and commentary on newly emerging and quickly growing Pentecostal and Charismatic movements worldwide. It even included a table of "U.S. Third Force Groups" with *quantitative data* from Churches of Christ to the Pentecostal Holiness Church.

Nothing could be more prophetic.

Todd Johnson is part of a research legacy that stretches back to at least 1957, when the progenitor of the work, Rev. Dr. David B. Barrett, arrived in Nyanza Province, Kenya, with the Church Missionary Society. As a trained aeronautical engineer, David wanted to use his mathematical and scientific gifts for the world mission of the church, but thought the church had no need for someone who knew how to fly airplanes. He received a PhD in religion from Columbia University and Union Theological Seminary in New York. He then embarked on his life's work of quantifying Christianity first in Kenya, then sub-Saharan Africa, then the world. His personal experience of African-led breakaway movements from mission-founded churches compelled him to seek other such movements worldwide. He discovered that nearly all previously published data on Christian affiliation worldwide overlooked numerous grassroots movements and on-the-ground realities of Christian change. In 1965, he established the Unit of Research of the Church of the Province of Kenya, Act I of what is now the Center for the Study of Global Christianity (CSGC). Seventeen years later and after conducting research in 212 countries, David published the *World Christian Encyclopedia* (Oxford University Press, 1982), which was the first attempt to put all the world's Christians equally together in a single book. It was praised as a "miracle from Nairobi" and had a massive influence on academic and mission circles alike.[1]

    David and his family—his wife, Pam, and their three children, Claire, Luke, and Timothy—moved to Richmond, Virginia in 1985 to work with the Foreign (now International) Mission Board of the Southern Baptist Convention. David also formed the independent World Evangelization Research Center

---

1 See Gina A. Zurlo, *From Nairobi to the World: David B. Barrett and the Re-Imagining of World Christianity* (Leiden/Boston: Brill, 2023).

(WERC), Act II of the current CSGC. Todd Johnson, a YWAM missionary and doctoral candidate at William Carey University, joined David in 1989 after five years working at the U.S. Center for World Mission, founded by his in-laws, Ralph and Roberta Winter. Their team in Richmond consisted of, at varying times, Bill Shumaker, Justin Long, and Peter Crossing (systems and data analysis), Kimberly D. Doyle, Jeanine Guidry, and Christopher Guidry (desktop publishing and design), Michael Jaffarian (research), and Judy Alexanian, Carol Vanlandingham, and Sondra Stephens (word and number processing). During the 1980s and 1990s, David and Todd built an extensive research agenda for WERC, expanding into analyses of evangelization among the world's peoples and languages, cities, and provinces. Their numerous publications partly fueled the movement focused on the year 2000 as a goal for world evangelization, inspiring concerted efforts but with a healthy dose of cautionary notes from history and statistics. The team was fully aware, informed by the data, that world evangelization would not be achieved by the year 2000, given that most evangelistic work was being directed at already Christian places, not the least reached.[2]

In 2001, David and Todd released the *World Christian Encyclopedia* 2nd edition (Oxford University Press) and its corresponding technical volume, *World Christian Trends* (William Carey Library). These reference works became indispensable resources for mission organizations attempting to re-frame their understanding of how Christianity had spread around the world and how to engage peoples with the least access to the gospel. While in Richmond, Todd had a vision of Act III of the research legacy: a center full of students working away on computers. In 2003, with assistance from Richard Haney of Frontier Fellowship and Doug Birdsall of the Lausanne Movement, Todd moved to Gordon-Conwell Theological Seminary (South Hamilton, Massachusetts) and re-named WERC the Center for the Study of Global Christianity. Todd's vision was fulfilled on the first floor of a student apartment building and in a former preschool; the CSGC was finally situated in a proper academic setting. Perhaps the single greatest benefit of the move from Richmond to South Hamilton was the ability to employ graduate student researchers, who work diligently to keep the research going.

As director of the CSGC, Todd knew the future would be in the digital realm, and thus launched the *World Christian Database* (Brill) in 2003 and the *World Religion Database* (Brill, in partnership with Boston University) in 2007, and in doing so, fulfilled David's long-standing desire to produce publicly available religion databases. Under Todd's leadership, and now with

---

2 See, for example, E. Michael Jaffarian, "World Evangelization by A.D. 2000: Will We Make It?" *Evangelical Missions Quarterly* 30, no. 1 (January 1994): 18–26.

co-director Gina Zurlo, the CSGC has produced numerous reference works that appear throughout this volume, such as the *Atlas of Global Christianity* (Edinburgh University Press, 2009), the *World Christian Encyclopedia*, 3rd edition (Edinburgh University Press, 2019), and the 10-volume Edinburgh Companions to Global Christianity series (Edinburgh University Press, 2017–2025).

**Contents of This Book**

The Center for the Study of Global Christianity is framed by four primary areas:

1. **Global**. The CSGC studies every country in the world and every form of Christianity. Here, "global" means that all forms of Christianity have an equal say in defining the contours of Christian faith. The CSGC is particularly committed to decentering Western or White Christianity as the standard for Christian theology, ecclesiology, and mission. The CSGC follows historian Andrew Walls' dictum that Christianity is both fully indigenous and fully universal.[3]

2. **Ecumenical**. The CSGC holds that all Christian traditions should work closely together. Since its founding in 1965, researchers have collaborated with Christians across the theological and ecclesiological spectrum, including Catholics, Orthodox, Protestants, Pentecostals, Independents, Pentecostals/Charismatics, and Evangelicals.

3. **Interreligious**. The CSGC has always had a close working relationship with people who study world religions and those who work in headquarters of religious organizations. Close attention has been given to smaller religions such as the Baha'i and the Jewish communities. The *World Religion Database* (Brill) is the only comprehensive quantitative resource that includes estimates for the size of smaller world religions.

4. **Social justice**. Familiarity with events worldwide has strongly motivated the CSGC to stand up on behalf of the oppressed. Researchers are particularly concerned about gender inequality and the poor treatment of women and girls worldwide, as well as combatting racism, antisemitism, and other forms of injustice.

---

3 Andrew Walls, *The Cross-Cultural Process in Christian History: Studies in the Transmission and Appropriation of Faith* (Maryknoll, NY: Orbis Books, 1996).

The contents of this book reflect each of these pillars in extraordinary ways. This book was produced in partnership between Peter Crossing and Christopher Guidry, long-time colleagues in data analytics, desktop publishing, and design. The overarching theme of Part I is partnership in global Christianity and mission, with contributions from Gina Zurlo and Peter Crossing on data visualization, Patrick Johnstone on the historical connection between David Barrett and Operation World (OW), and the contemporary relationship between the CSGC and OW by Jason Mandryk and Molly Wall. Each of these chapters reflects a core philosophy of Todd Johnson: that research is better done in community than in a silo. Part II includes contributions from 28 of Todd's students, research assistants, colleagues, and friends with reflections on the impact of his scholarship, Christian witness, spiritual life, and friendship. Contributors describe Todd's encouragement to expand their worldviews to become more global, ecumenical, interfaith, and justice-oriented for the sake of living harmoniously within both their global and Christian families. Part III contains 185—yes, 185!—"top 10 tables" with color graphs featuring the results of Todd's labor over the past several decades. No book about the work of Todd Johnson is complete without data.

**Lived Global Christianity**

The concept of "lived religion" began with Harvard historian David Hall in the 1990s to investigate how religion is experienced and practiced in people's everyday lives, outside of formal religious institutions.[4] Sociologist Nancy Ammerman has drawn significant attention to this concept, which is centered around documenting and analyzing "the social dynamics of religion in ordinary everyday life."[5] Lived religion is about studying, for example, what religious practices people do in their particular cultural contexts, their connection to spiritual realities, the rituals they partake in, what material objects they use, and influences in their religious lives.[6]

Although this is a book in honor of Todd Johnson, as the reflections will indicate, working with Todd is more than just data and numbers, facts and figures. Todd embodies the concept of lived World (or global) Christianity, where Christians live, think, and act according to global realities in their everyday lives, not simply amass knowledge for the sake of knowledge.[7]

---

[4] David Hall, *Lived Religion in America: Toward a History of Practice* (Princeton: Princeton University Press, 1997).
[5] Nancy T. Ammerman, *Sacred Stories: Spiritual Tribes: Finding Religion in Everyday Life* (New York: Oxford University Press, 2013), xiii.
[6] Nancy T. Ammerman, *Studying Lived Religion: Contexts and Practices* (New York: New York University Press, 2021).
[7] The terms World Christianity and global Christianity are used interchangeably in this volume.

As many attest, Todd both "walks the walk" and "talks the talk" of global Christianity in his interactions with others, especially people at the margins and those who have been overlooked. Many have studied under Todd at Gordon-Conwell Theological Seminary expecting to learn history, trends in mission, and the current status of Christianity worldwide; most do not expect to be fundamentally changed as a result. But this is a critical aspect of Todd's teaching philosophy: for you to master a subject, it must first master you. Personal transformation is at the heart of learning to love others more fully. Todd can guide others into lived World Christianity because he has experienced it himself: at the Khao-I-Dang refugee camp in Cambodia (1980), and while living in Singapore (1988–1989; 2002–2003) and in Thailand (2009–2010; 2016–2017). But even in other places he has called home—Minneapolis, Tacoma, Pasadena, Richmond, Boston—he knows that living global Christianity means extending hospitality and friendship to everyone, not just those who look or think like you. This is, in fact, the way of Jesus that Todd has walked his entire life.

Several core themes emerge from the reflections in this book, each important for lived global Christianity, and all exemplified in Todd's life and work. Perhaps chief among them is knowledge. Data, facts, and figures are the starting place to realize the world is bigger, more diverse, more beautiful, and perhaps more troubled than previously thought. Good data provide the solid foundation to live into the realities of World Christianity. It is humbling to learn that your Christian story is just one of 2.6 billion, and each Christian has experienced Jesus and the church differently across time, location, language, and social context. Humility is needed to live global Christianity, which requires putting others before yourself, ceding the stage to underrepresented voices, and giving opportunities away, not always taking them. Non-judgmental faithful witness allows you to more authentically experience other people, cultures, and contexts. Any world traveler has likely experienced the generous hospitality of others. Todd and his wife, Tricia, have made hospitality a cornerstone of their Christian witness, and as many describe in this book, fondly recall dinners at the Johnson home with Tricia's apple pie and scintillating conversation in the sitting room, surrounded by precious artifacts from decades of global travel.

Living World Christianity is not a mere knowledge experiment, it is an exercise in building personal relationships. It is clear these students, colleagues, and friends truly know Todd, because Todd made the concerted effort to build relationships with them, no matter if he knew them for two years or twenty. Everyone knows that for many years Todd's day began at 5am at Starbucks and that he loves science fiction, running, and New England lobster; they know he listens to a huge diversity of musical genres and enjoys collecting Christian art from around the world. Finally, everyone has permission to call him either

Todd or Dr. Johnson as they prefer, because he is always your equal, no matter who you are.

**Works Cited**

Ammerman, Nancy T. *Sacred Stories: Spiritual Tribes: Finding Religion in Everyday Life.* New York: Oxford University Press, 2013.

Ammerman, Nancy T. *Studying Lived Religion: Contexts and Practices.* New York: New York University Press, 2021.

Hall, David D. *Lived Religion in America: Toward a History of Practice.* Princeton: Princeton University Press, 1997.

Jaffarian, E. Michael. "World Evangelization by A.D. 2000: Will We Make It?" *Evangelical Missions Quarterly* 30, no.1 (January 1994): 18–26.

Walls, Andrew. *The Cross-Cultural Process in Christian History: Studies in the Transmission and Appropriation of Faith.* Maryknoll, NY: Orbis Books, 1996.

Zurlo, Gina A. *From Nairobi to the World: David B. Barrett and the Re-Imagining of World Christianity.* Leiden/Boston: Brill, 2023.

# Part I

# Partnership in World Christianity and Mission Research

Nalini Jayasuriya (1927–2014), *Creation*, courtesy of the Overseas Ministries Study Center at Princeton Theological Seminary, Princeton, New Jersey, USA.

# Chapter 1:
# Trends in Global Christianity Through Design

*Gina A. Zurlo and Peter F. Crossing*

Sociologist Peter Berger (1929–2017) wrote the foreword to Todd Johnson and Brian Grim's methodological volume on religious demography, *The World's Religions in Figures: An Introduction to International Religious Demography*. In classic Berger fashion, he told a joke:

> As an old joke has it: as the lady said to the insect specialist after sitting next to him at a dinner party, during which he told her endlessly about his beloved insects—"This is very interesting, if you are interested in it."[1]

Quantitative data on religion has the propensity toward the same—it is interesting, if you are interested in it. Historically, number-crunching in religious communities took the form of counting heads via births, baptisms, and deaths, laying the foundation for what would become national censuses. Also, missionaries created population ledgers for the sake of evangelization, proto-social scientific discovery, and the creation of historical datasets. Over time, quantification became the gold standard for social scientific investigation, where human behavior could be described in terms of facts, figures, and discernable trends.

The structural origins of the *World Christian Database* (Brill) began in the 1960s with David Barrett's 10,000 IBM punch cards and 2,500 paper tapes to feed what he called his first "databank." The trajectory of the research legacy weaves in and out of advances in computing technology, beginning with the Wang 2200 WCS/30 C-6 minicomputer in 1978 at the hefty price tag of roughly $111,000 (around $394,000 today). The first *World Christian Encyclopedia* (Oxford University Press, 1982) partially took so long to complete (14 years) because of the book's intricate design with 700 photographs, 500 statistical tables, a full-color atlas, 15 different fonts, and hundreds of flags, maps, and line graphs. Most readers of the *Encyclopedia* were simply overwhelmed by the amount of data in the book, where Barrett suggested tables should be read with a ruler because of their massive width and small font size. For Barrett, and indeed for today, obtaining the best data was the most important part of the work, but what good is good data if it is communicated poorly? Layout, design,

---

[1] Todd M. Johnson and Brian J. Grim, *The World's Religions in Figures: An Introduction to International Religious Demography* (Malden, MA: Wiley-Blackwell, 2013), xxii.

and the presentation of quantitative data has always been a critical feature of this kind of work to ensure the data are, well, interesting.

It is not natural for most people to get excited about databases, large tables full of numbers, and spreadsheets with many thousands of lines (present company excluded). Quantitative research on religion is far more interesting if it is presented in an accessible way to a broad audience. Creative design not only helps make data more palatable, but it also makes data come alive, reach more people, and tell new stories. This chapter journeys through the history of the Center for the Study of Global Christianity (CSGC) in a new way—through design. From the 1950s to today, David Barrett, Todd Johnson, and now Gina Zurlo and their team (Christopher Guidry, Brad Coon, Justin Long, Bryan Nicholson, Nana Bin, Amanda Perkins, and others) have been experimenting with new ways to show global Christian trends through diagrams, infographics, maps, charts, and graphs. This chapter is organized by decade, from the 1950s to the 2020s, and includes representative graphics from each to show the evolution of design and the communication of quantitative data on religion.

The CSGC's research agenda centers around three core pillars, which are illustrated throughout the designs presented in this chapter: ecumenical Christianity, world religions, and Christian activities.

1. **Ecumenical Christianity.** David Barrett was the first person to include all the world's Christians equally in a single book, with no theological or exclusionary boundaries among Catholics, Orthodox, Protestants, Evangelicals, Pentecostals, Latter-day Saints, or Jehovah's Witnesses. For example, Barrett was the first person to quantify newly formed African Independent Churches (24 million in 1980) in the *Encyclopedia*. As such, graphs that depict global Christianity have always been ecumenical and include all the world's Christians.

2. **World religions.** Barrett's *Encyclopedia* was also the first place to quantify adherents of every major world religion, including separate categories for atheists and agnostics. He was the first to estimate the size of non-religious populations worldwide (16.6% in 1980). In doing so, Barrett set the stage for considering Christianity in the context of other world religions, a major feature of the CSGC's research over time. Today, the CSGC tracks 18 categories of religion and non-religion (in order of size in 2020): Christians, Muslims, Hindus, agnostics, Buddhists, Chinese folk-religionists, ethnic religionists, atheists, New religionists, Sikhs, Jews, Spiritists, Daoists, Confucianists, Baha'is, Jains, Shintoists, and Zoroastrians.

3. **Christian activities**. The CSGC has always tracked trends in activities of Christians worldwide, including missionary sending and receiving, national workers, Bible translation and distribution, evangelization (gospel access), martyrdom, and ecclesiastical crime. Also included here are analyses of Christianity by city, province, and ethnolinguistic people groups.

## Design Through the Decades

*1950s*

From 1952–1954, David Barrett was a Master of Divinity student at Ridley Hall, University of Cambridge. Ridley Hall opened in 1882 as a training center for Evangelicals in Church of England ministry, and many Ridleians, like Barrett, served abroad as missionaries with the Church Missionary Society.[2] He took courses in Old and New Testament, systematic theology, philosophy of religion, psychology, Christian ethics, Anglican ordination, church history, ministry, worship, and evangelism. The pursuit of theological training at Ridley involved a quest for deep faith and understanding, self-awareness through prayer, discernment toward serving in overseas mission, and the importance of Christian community. In the 1950s, Ridley trained students to be foremost a Christian, able to cooperate across Christian traditions. A high proportion of Ridley men (the school was mostly single, middle-class White men) became cross-cultural missionaries.[3]

In 1953, Barrett created a draft of his first global diagram, which was a theological representation of the drama of God (figure 1). This graph illustrates two important parts of what became his career in quantifying religion. First, as an aspiring missionary, Barrett was invested in understanding systematic theology, God's salvific plan for the world, and the theological concepts of atonement, sin, and redemption. Part of Barrett's motivation for quantifying every religion and Christian denomination was evangelistic. Throughout church history, it was always missionaries that cared about who adhered to what religion for the purpose of personnel deployment. Part of Barrett's motivation to quantify the world was to know how many non-Christians there were and where to reach them with the Christian message. This graph from 1953 is the first of what would become many such global diagrams, where Barrett attempted to succinctly summarize complex concepts. The shape and style of this diagram—a large outer circle with numerous details within it—is featured throughout his 2001 *World Christian Trends*.

---

[2] See Michael H. Botting, *Fanning the Flame: The Story of Ridley Hall Cambridge. Volume 3: 1951–2001* (Cambridge: Hassall & Lucking Ltd, 2006).

[3] F.W.B. Bullock, *The History of Ridley Hall Cambridge. Volume 1: To the End of AD 1907* (Cambridge: Cambridge University Press, 1941).

*Figure 1. David Barrett's theology global diagram, 1953*

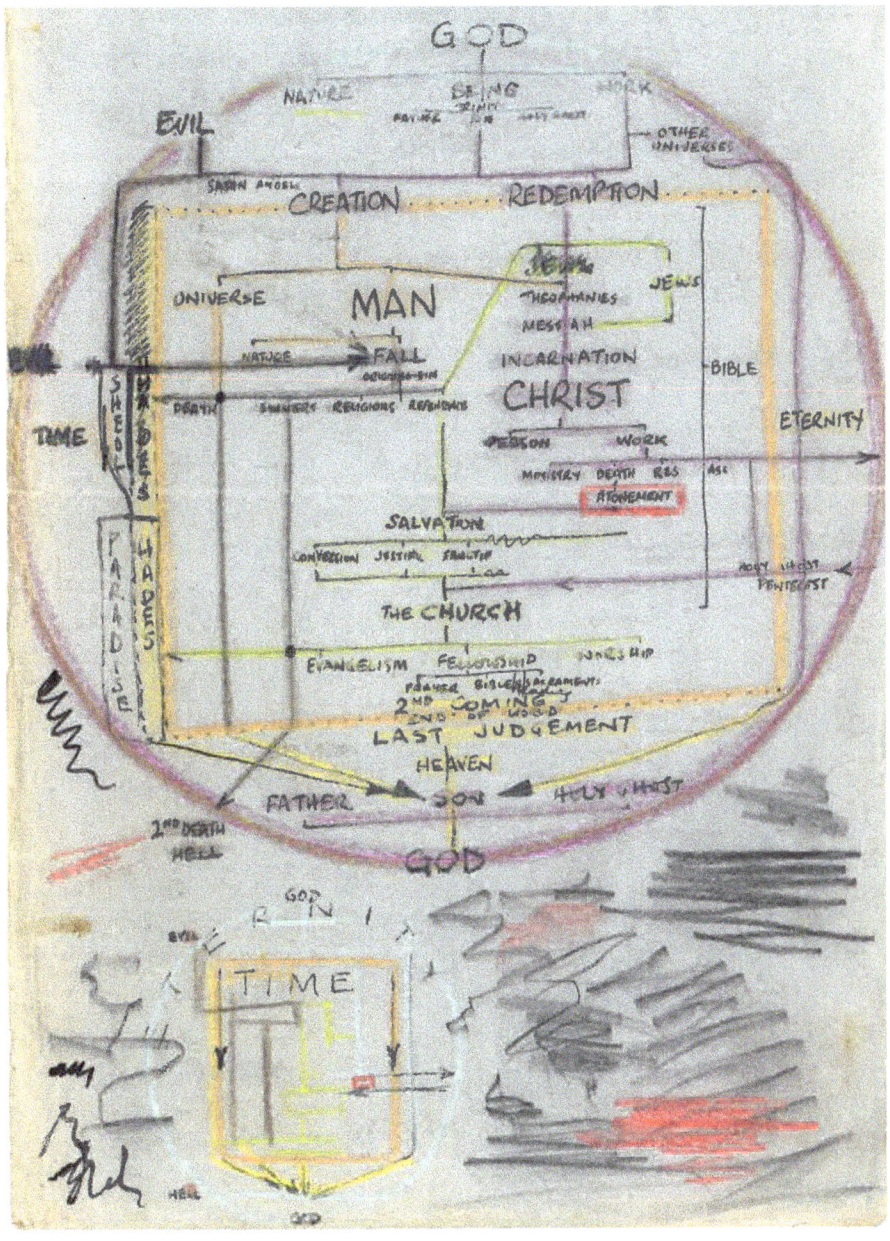

Source: David B. Barrett Papers 1957–1985, Center for the Study of Global Christianity, Gordon-Conwell Theological Seminary (South Hamilton, MA, USA).

## 1960s

The 1960s was a busy decade for Barrett. From 1957–1961, he served his first missionary tour in Kisii, Kenya with the Church Missionary Society, after which he headed to New York City to pursue doctoral work at Union Theological Seminary and Columbia University. In 1965, he participated in a 21-country survey of evangelization in West Africa in cooperation with the World Council of Churches and the All Africa Council of Churches. That year he also established the Unit of Research of the Church of the Province of Kenya, the first iteration of what is now the Center for the Study of Global Christianity. He took a sabbatical in New York City from 1968–1969 as a visiting professor of religion and African studies at Columbia University, and published his dissertation as *Schism and Renewal in Africa* (Oxford University Press). In the 1960s, Barrett was handed the *World Christian Handbook*, the predecessor of what would become the the *World Christian Encyclopedia*. All of these experiences, appointments, studies, and publications influenced Barrett's thinking about the social scientific study of Christianity and mission, in particular, how Christianity spread among indigenous communities around the world.

Barrett's hand-drawn missionary deployment map illustrates numerous aspects of his evangelistic drive as a missionary and his academic background (figure 2). He was keenly aware of the importance of history in missions. His preparation for missionary work in Kisii included learning about the history of Christianity in East Africa and to what extent the gospel had been spread and by whom. This map is ecumenical in that it includes the movements of Catholics (R.C.), Anglicans, Lutherans, Presbyterians, Africa Inland Mission (A.I.M.), and the Church Missionary Society (CMS). For Barrett, these were all equally valid expressions of Christianity, and each made contributions to gospel access. Furthermore, this map includes the names of people groups in the region, illustrating that the people group thinking of the global missions movement that took off in earnest in the 1970s had already begun in the decade prior.

*1970s*

An explosion of number-crunching in missions occurred in the 1970s, but it certainly was not new to that decade. In 1792, British Baptist missionary William Carey produced estimates of adherents to the world's religions in his *Enquiry into the Obligations of Christians to use Means for the Conversion of the Heathen*—the first to do so. Throughout the 19th century, quantitative perspectives on mission grew in importance as mission advocates encouraged Christians to think differently, and more critically, about needs abroad. Numbers were used to shock readers and compel them to serve abroad or give financially to missionary efforts. The 19th and early 20th centuries were full of books and pamphlets that described the fate of the world's unevangelized millions and the obligations of Christians to reach them, many utilizing facts, figures, charts, and maps. As a missionary, Barrett was immersed in this kind of popular writing on missions and worked to inform the church of global missions. As an academic, he operated from a scientific perspective and was aware of the literature in demographic studies, atlases, and encyclopedias of world religions. He also believed that numbers provided "objective facts" to help spur the church to send more missionaries abroad.

*Figure 2. Missionary deployment map up to 1914*

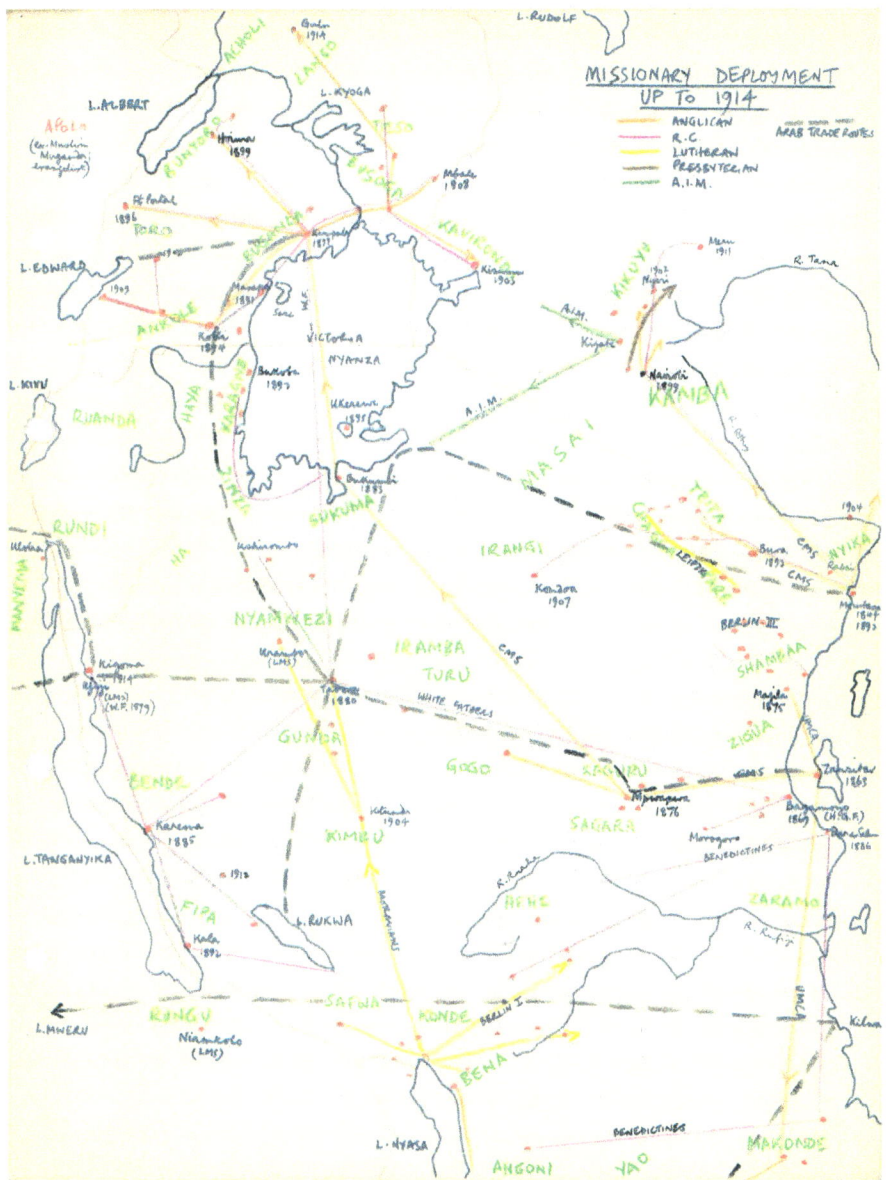

Source: David B. Barrett Papers 1957–1985, Center for the Study of Global Christianity, Gordon-Conwell Theological Seminary (South Hamilton, MA, USA).

In 1970, Barrett produced an article in the *International Review of Mission* that estimated there would be 350 million Christians in Africa by the year 2000. This stood in contrast to other scholars who believed religion was dying and would be nearly extinct by the turn of the 21st century. His growing research on global evangelization and his connection to the Lausanne Committee for World Evangelization launched Barrett into the middle of the missiometric movement within Western missions. His work on ethnolinguistic people groups was part of the emerging people group movement sparked by Donald McGavran in the 1950s and popularized by Ralph Winter at the 1974 meeting in Lausanne, Switzerland. This seismic shift in Protestant missiological thinking reimagined the definition of "nation" away from geopolitical boundaries and toward homogenous people groups. The world was not a couple of hundred nations, it was actually tens of thousands of unique peoples, many of whom had no access to the Christian gospel.

Figure 3 illustrated a new way of looking at Christianity in Africa, not by nation, but by peoples. This map was innovative in that it showed, for the first time, the emerging African Independent movement that would become both a cornerstone of Barrett's research as the first to quantify these churches, but also central to what would become the entire academic disciple of World Christianity by the end of the 20th century.

Figure 4, Christianity in Tivland, was published in *The Gospel and Frontier Peoples*, a text that informed readers of the new, emerging people-centric perspective in missions. Barrett and his colleagues contributed a chapter with in-depth research of Christianity among the ethnolinguistic peoples in Africa. This graph gave detailed information on Tivland (modern-day Nigeria and Cameroon), utilizing a hand drawn logarithmic scale graph to show Tivland's number of total Christians, number of Catholics and Protestants, and church attendance in the context of national census data. This graph is reminiscent of the kinds of visualizations Barrett encountered in his scientific studies, as well as popular writing on missions.

*1980s*

The key to Barrett's research on mission, evangelization, and religion was his ability to piece together local knowledge into a global story; he paid attention to minute details to communicate the big picture. Nothing is more emblematic of this than the *World Christian Encyclopedia: A Comparative Survey of Churches and Religions in the Modern World, A.D. 1900–2000* (Oxford University Press, 1982), which contained information on 20,800 Christian denominations in 238 countries, plus Christianity among 8,990 people groups who spoke 7,010 languages. This text presented, for the first time, a comprehensive quantitative

*Figure 3. Religious independency in Africa, 1967*

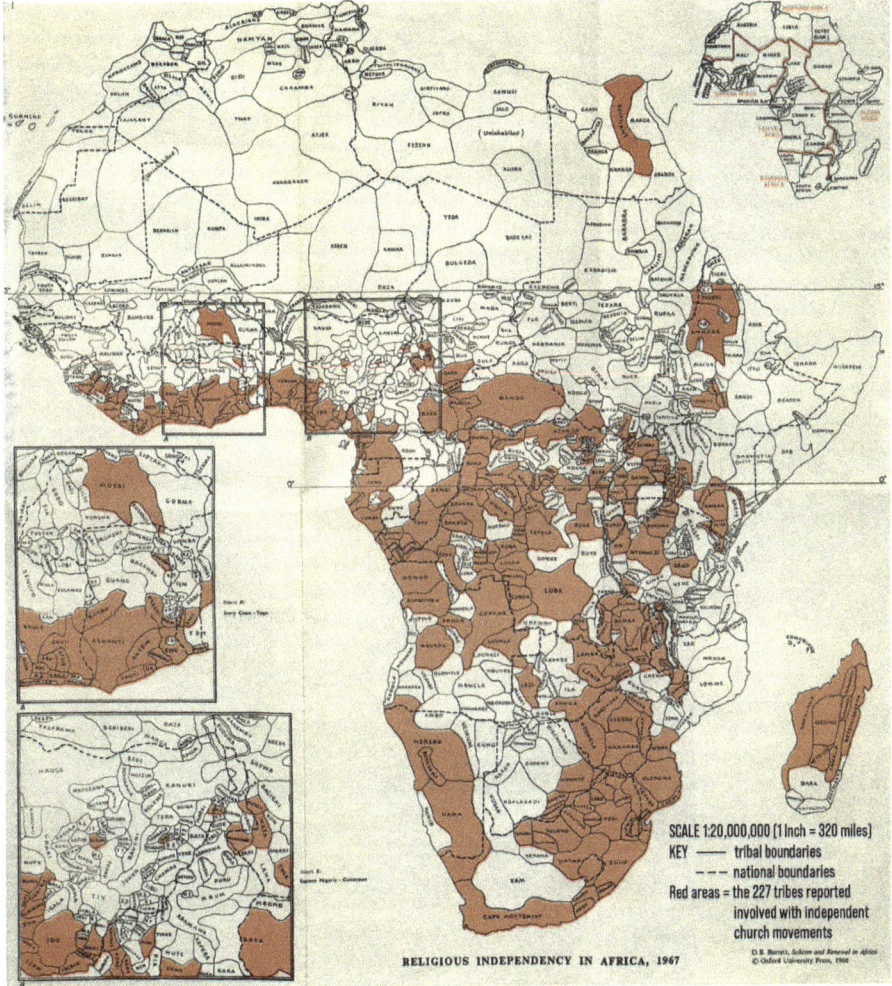

Source: David B. Barrett, *Schism and Renewal in Africa: An Analysis of Six Thousand Contemporary Religious Movements* (Nairobi: Oxford University Press, 1968).

assessment of all branches of global Christianity. The media, scholars, and mission researchers hailed it as a vital resource, and it had a tremendous impact in both scholarly and missiological circles. The *Encyclopedia* presented a picture of World Christianity that was diverse and fragmented, not unified and cooperative, held together by Christian self-identification within the church. His motivation for the *Encyclopedia* was two-fold. He believed that in the age of increased technological advancement, ease of travel, and advances in computer analysis, questions about global religious adherence should not be matters of faith but matters of fact. He wanted to answer previously unanswerable questions about the status of world religions in the 20th century,

10    Portraits of Global Christianity

*Figure 4. Christianity in Tivland, 1967*

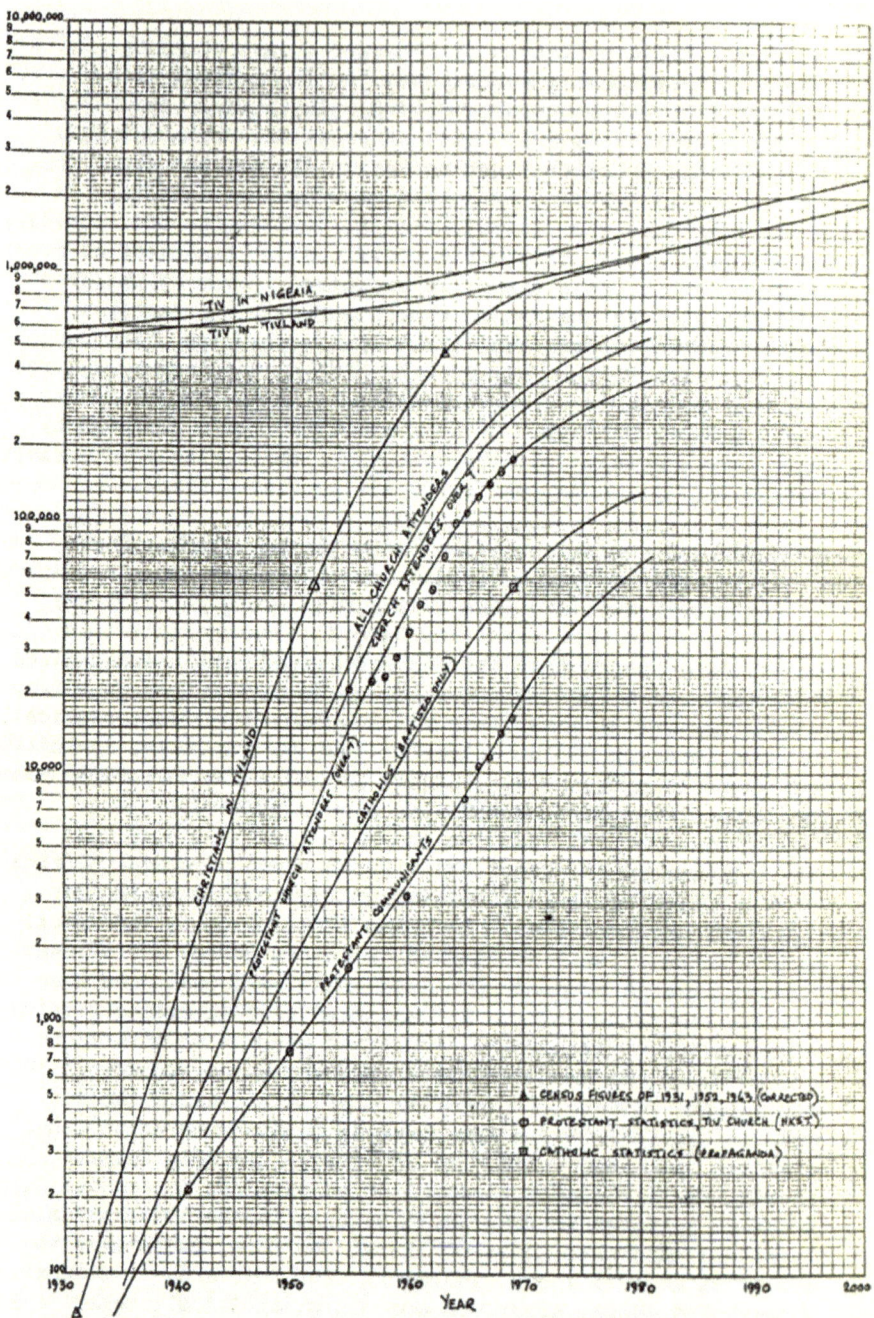

Source: David B. Barrett, Mary Linda Hronek, George K. Mambo, John S. Mbiti, Malcolm J. McVeigh, "Frontier Situations for Evangelism in Africa, 1972, a Survey Report," in *The Gospel and Frontier Peoples: A Report of a Consultation December 1972*, ed. R. Pierce Beaver (Pasadena, CA: William Carey Library, 1973), 264.

but he also wanted to provide tools and resources to help missionaries more effectively communicate the gospel among the world's peoples.[4]

Figure 5 was Barrett's illustration of the ecumenical spirit of the *World Christian Encyclopedia*—all Christian traditions, despite their theological differences, historically led back to Jesus Christ. Considering all expressions of Christianity equally was a truly unique contribution of his work, and the *Encyclopedia* expressed the unity in diversity that would come to characterize the world Christian movement. This perspective put Barrett at odds with many Evangelical missions-minded Christians, who would not consider his category of "marginal Protestants" to be "real" Christians, such as the Church of Jesus Christ of Latter-day Saints and Jehovah's Witnesses. Yet, including them was important to maintain the social scientific gold standard of self-identification: if you consider yourself a Christian, then you are counted as a Christian.

Figure 6 illustrates two features of his work that continue today: change over time and access to the Christian gospel. A major contribution of the *Encyclopedia* was the inclusion of historical data on religious adherence to the year 1900. Barrett used his historical research to not only report on the size of all world religions at the start of the 20th century, but also to estimate world evangelization at that time and compare it with the contemporary situation of 1980. Change over time continues to be a unique feature of the work of the Center for the Study of Global Christianity, which is the only research center with historical estimates for adherence to every religion in every country of the world throughout the 20th century.

*1990s*

After the publication of the *World Christian Encyclopedia*, Barrett turned his attention toward the continuation of data science in service of world mission and evangelization. He left Kenya in 1985 to work at the Southern Baptist Foreign (now International) Mission Board—though remained a life-long Anglican—and reframed his research as the World Evangelization Research Center (WERC). Todd Johnson, a missionary researcher and doctoral candidate, joined WERC in 1989 to learn under Barrett. Together, they authored the second edition of the *World Christian Encyclopedia* (Oxford University Press) and its companion text, *World Christian Trends* (William Carey Library) in 2001. The 1990s was an intense time for world missions as Christians looked toward the year 2000 as a target date to complete world evangelization. A proliferation of denominational and agency plans emerged, and virtually all

---

4  See Gina A. Zurlo, *From Nairobi to the World: David B. Barrett and the Re-imagining of World Christianity* (Leiden/Boston: Brill, 2023).

*Figure 5. Fission and fusion in world Christian traditions, 30–1985*

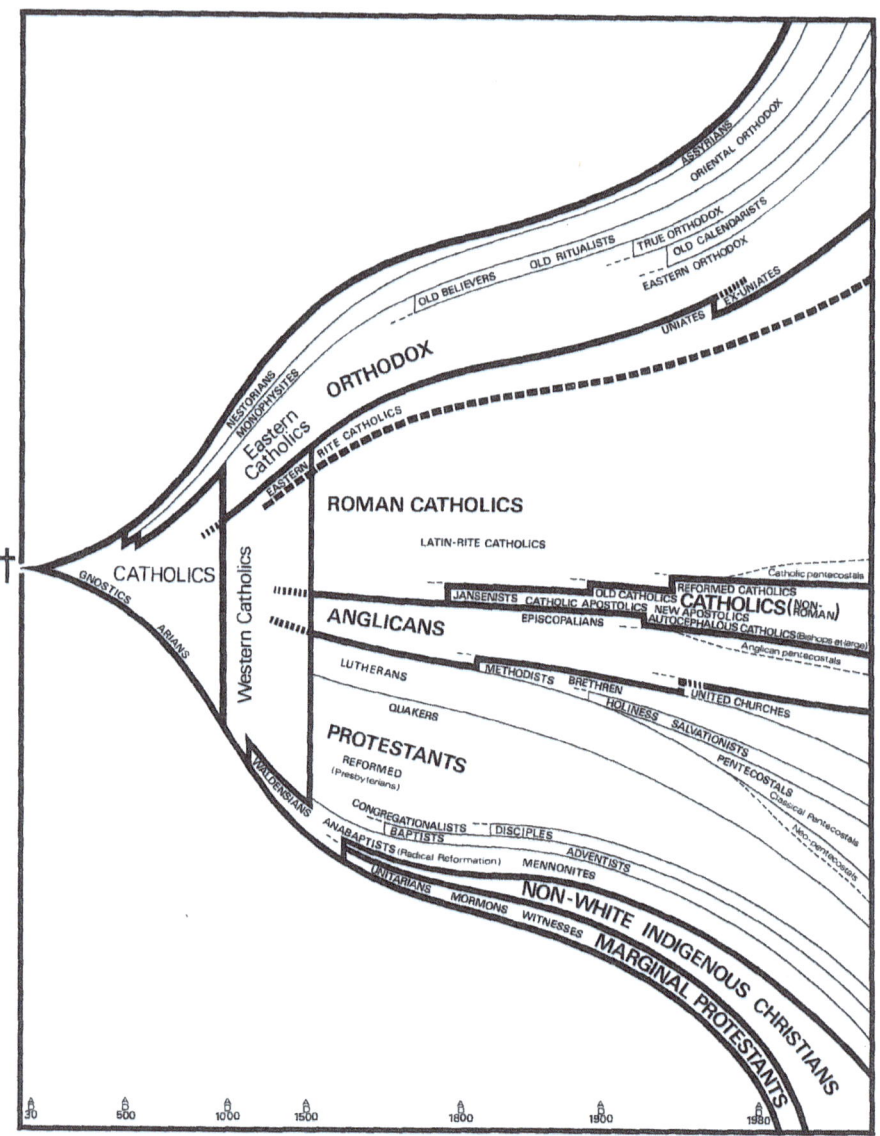

Source: David B. Barrett, ed. *World Christian Encyclopedia* (Nairobi: Oxford University Press, 1982), 35.

Christian organizations announced projects in anticipation of 2000. Examples included:

- Decade of Universal Evangelization inaugurated by Pope John Paul II, with the goal of uniting all Christians and churches worldwide and increasing Christians' share of the global population to 50%.
- Round the World Prayer Event, organized by the World Methodist Council of Great Britain, to inaugurate evangelism in the 1990s.
- Churches Uniting in Global Mission, formed as a coalition of pastors by Robert Schuller, an American televangelist and host of the popular Hour of Power television program.
- Church Growth International Seminars began in Seoul, South Korea, by megachurch pastor Yonggi Cho, with a specific plan to lead 10 million Japanese to Christ by the year 2000.
- Joshua Project 2000, a plan to establish a church planting movement among every people group over 10,000 in population within every country by December 31, 2000.

Barrett and Johnson's *Our Globe and How to Reach It* was part of this worldwide push to the year 2000, which described the rise, status, and future of the global evangelization movement as a kind of manual for the Decade of Evangelization. Figure 7 on world religions was important for this global evangelistic push and reminiscent of the graphics produced by 19th-century missionaries. Christians had to know the status of other world religions for effective outreach among them and spur fellow Christians to evangelistic action.

Figure 8 illustrates part of the third pillar of Barrett and Johnson's research: Christian activities. World evangelization was multi-faceted and included a wide range of topics, including Bible translation and distribution. Having the scriptures available in one's mother tongue had been an important feature of Protestant missions since Pietist missionaries left Germany for India with a Bible and a printing press in 1706. For missionary researchers in the 1990s, knowing the extent of Bible translation and distribution was critical for understanding the potential growth of Christianity among a people group. Figure 8 illustrates Barrett's understanding of this dynamic in a global diagram of access to complete Bibles, New Testaments, and selections.

*2000s*

The companion volume to the second edition of the *World Christian Encyclopedia* was *World Christian Trends, AD 30–AD 2200: Interpreting the Annual Christian Megacensus* (William Carey Library, 2001). In a sense, this book represented the culmination of Barrett's intellectual prowess and interests. It included

14 Portraits of Global Christianity

*Figure 6. World evangelization maps, 1900 and 1980*

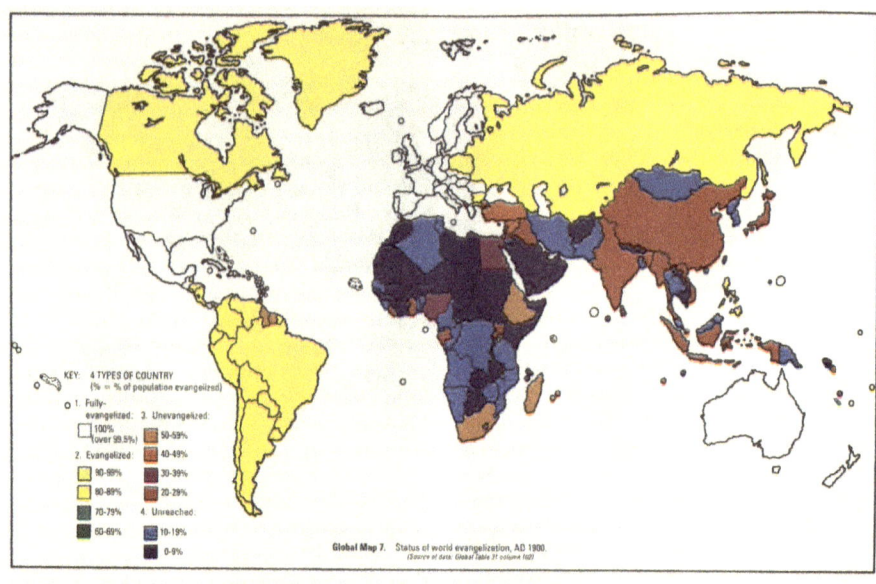

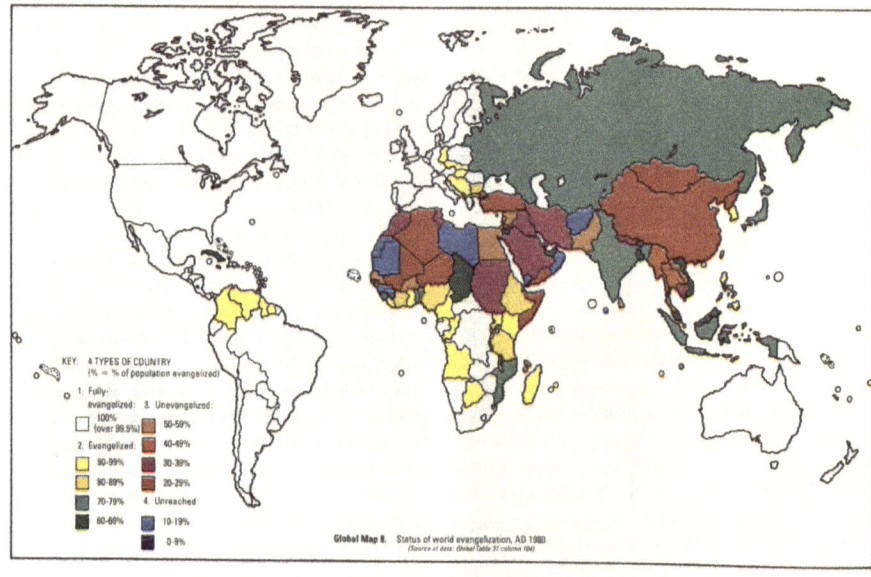

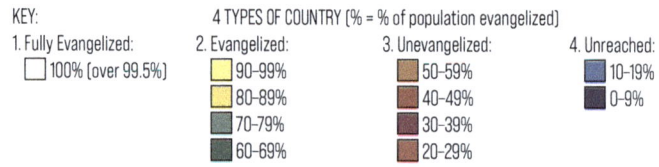

Source: David B. Barrett, ed. *World Christian Encyclopedia* (Nairobi: Oxford University Press, 1982), 868.

nearly everything he considered important to satisfy his scholarly attention related to Christianity and world religions, as well as every missiological tool for proper resourcing and outreach. Its 100-page chronology of Christianity contained 7,000 events in Christian history from the time of Christ to the year 2000; it included detailed quantitative, biblical, and historical information on evangelization, martyrdom, missions, global plans, Christian finance, and the future. From a design perspective, it featured 74 global diagrams on oversized pages as well as full-color global maps. It was a behemoth. It contained massive amounts of information on each of the core pillars: ecumenical Christianity, world religions, and Christian activities.

The global diagram in figure 9 illustrates the relationship of Christianity's major traditions (at that time, Catholics, Orthodox, Protestants, Anglicans, Marginals, and Independents) with Evangelicals, Pentecostals/Charismatics, mainstream Christians, non-Christians, and others; in short, it illustrated the unity and diversity of global Christianity. *World Christian Trends* would be the last publication from Barrett and Johnson with such complicated, often difficult to interpret, global diagrams.

Figure 10 contains the next iteration of a world religion graph, but with the addition of change over time. This graph is important because it illustrates the relative stagnant position of Christianity over time compared to overall population growth. It also shows Christianity in the context of the world's second-largest religion, Islam.

Figure 11 illustrates the third pillar, Christian activities, via missionary deployment. This detailed graph includes estimates for the number of missionaries worldwide and where they are deployed—unevangelized countries (World A), evangelized, non-Christian countries (World B), and majority Christian countries (World C). The six principles add another element to the graph: insight into the *potential* of missionary sending, not only the reality. For example, principle six represented actual missionary deployment at that time, resulting in the vast majority of missionaries serving in World C countries (those already Christian). However, if principle five had been adopted— deploying missionaries to all the unevangelized places in the world—there would be almost no missionaries at all in World C, and all resources would be invested in Worlds A and B, the places of greatest need.

*2010s*

Johnson moved the World Evangelization Research Center to Gordon-Conwell Theological Seminary (South Hamilton, Massachusetts) in 2003 and renamed it the Center for the Study of Global Christianity. He launched the *World Christian Database* (Brill) in 2003, and the *World Religion Database* (Brill)

16   Portraits of Global Christianity

*Figure 7. Religion pie graph, 1990*

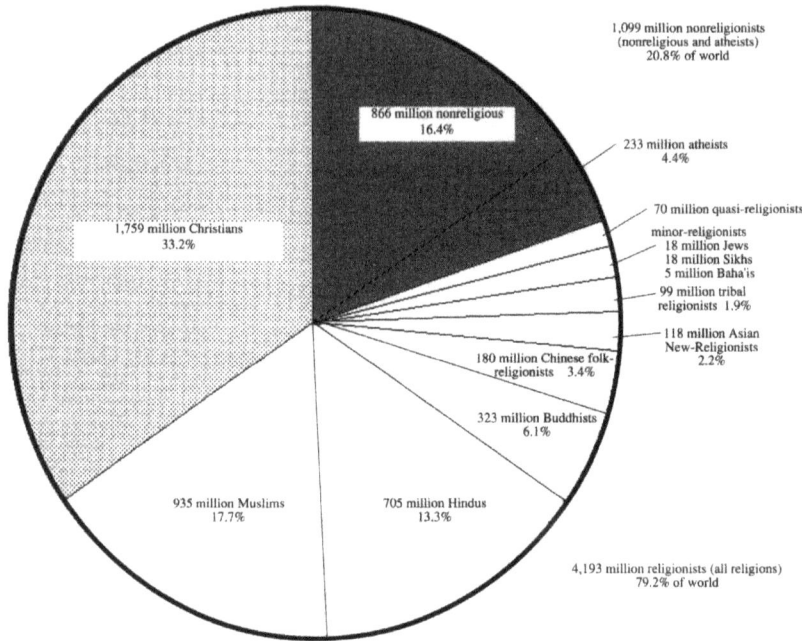

Source: David B. Barrett and Todd M. Johnson, *Our Globe and How to Reach it: Seeing the World Evangelized by AD 2000 & Beyond: A Manual for the Decade of Evangelization, 1990–2000* (Birmingham, AL: New Hope, 1990), 24.

*Figure 8. Bible translation and language diagram, 1990*

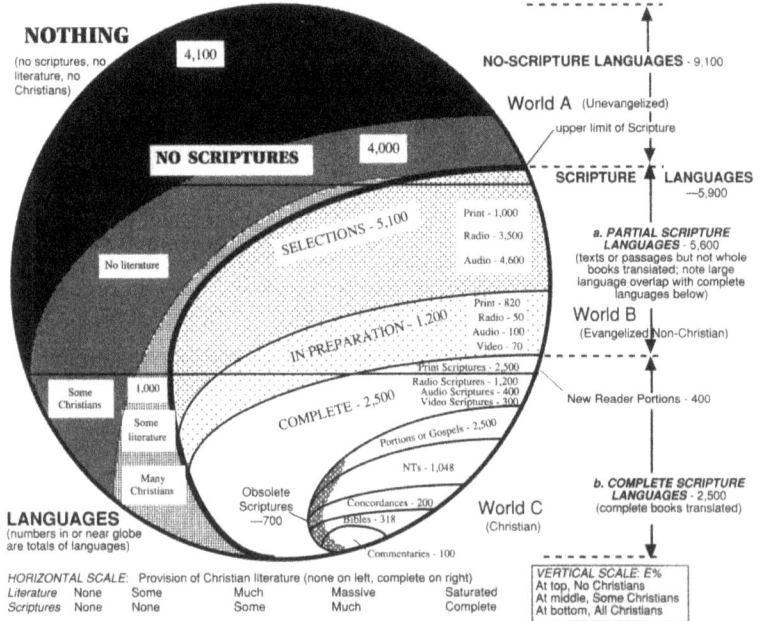

Source: David B. Barrett and Todd M. Johnson, *Our Globe and How to Reach it: Seeing the World Evangelized by AD 2000 & Beyond: A Manual for the Decade of Evangelization, 1990–2000* (Birmingham, AL: New Hope, 1990), 28.

in 2007, representing Barrett's decades-long desire to make quantitative data on religion available in computerized form. The *Atlas of Global Christianity*, co-edited by Johnson and Kenneth R. Ross, represented an entirely new era in design (see Ross's reflection in Part II of this book for more on the *Atlas*). Johnson surrounded himself with younger researchers, designers, and influences, and paid close attention to how quantitative data was communicated in economics, politics, and other fields. As a result, compared to the designs of previous decades, those that emerged in the *Atlas* were streamlined, simplified, less complex, and full of color. For the *Atlas*, color schemes were developed for each of the world's religions, for the six continents, and for Christian major traditions and movements. The *Atlas* also included a CD with a Presentation Assistant, allowing users to download any element from the book for use in presentations and publications. Figure 12 combined data on religions over time (1910 and 2010), religions by continent (Africa, Asia, Europe, Latin America, Northern America, and Oceania), and a quick-reference approach by color (blue for Christians, green for Muslims, etc.). The religious makeup of the world's largest cities is displayed in figure 13, which represents a new take on a classic quantitative table. Instead of presenting adherents by percentage in another column of numbers, it is presented visually in an imbedded bar graph to quickly see the religious and non-religious makeup of each city.

In 2013, the Center for the Study of Global Christianity released a free report online, *Christianity in its Global Context, 1970–2020: Society, Religion, and Mission*. This report was an update of many datapoints presented in the *Atlas of Global Christianity* and the *World Christian Database* to the year 2020 (projections), but in an easily accessible PDF for free download at the CSGC's website (www.globalchristianity.org). It continued the new design path of the *Atlas* in presenting data in a more streamlined, colorful way, and followed the CSGC's three pillars related to ecumenical Christianity, world religions, and Christian activities. Figure 14, for example, built upon the *Atlas*'s religion by continent rectangles, but instead of presenting the data in 1% squares, it presented each religion's proportion of the total population in 1970 and 2020.

Figure 15 presented a unique feature of the CSGC's data, pioneered by Johnson: religionists who know a Christian. This concept measures the number of non-Christians who personally know a Christian by applying a formula to each ethnolinguistic people group in the world. One of the most-cited statistics from the CSGC is that 86% of all Buddhists, Hindus, and Muslims have relatively little contact with Christians (see, for example, the reflection from Benjamin Thomas in this volume). The concept of personal contact is an extension of the decades-long research of global evangelization, pioneered by Barrett in the 1960s.

*Figure 9. The boundaries of Christianity, 2001*

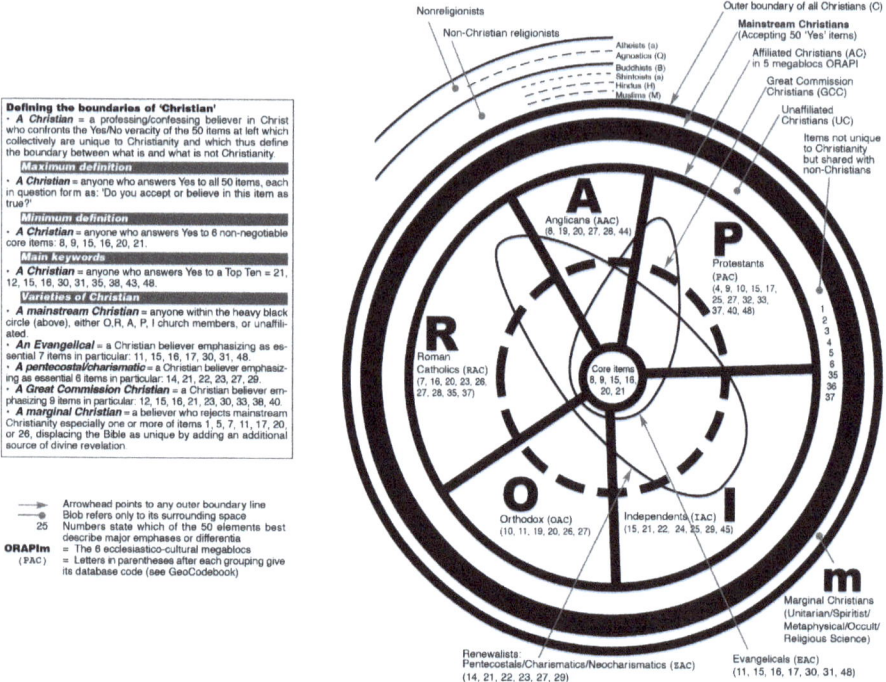

Source: David B. Barrett, Todd M. Johnson, Christopher R. Guidry, and Peter F. Crossing, *World Christian Trends, AD 30–AD 2200: Interpreting the Annual Christian Megacensus* (Pasadena, CA: William Carey Library, 2001), 15.

*Figure 10. Expansion of religions, 1900–2200 (2001)*

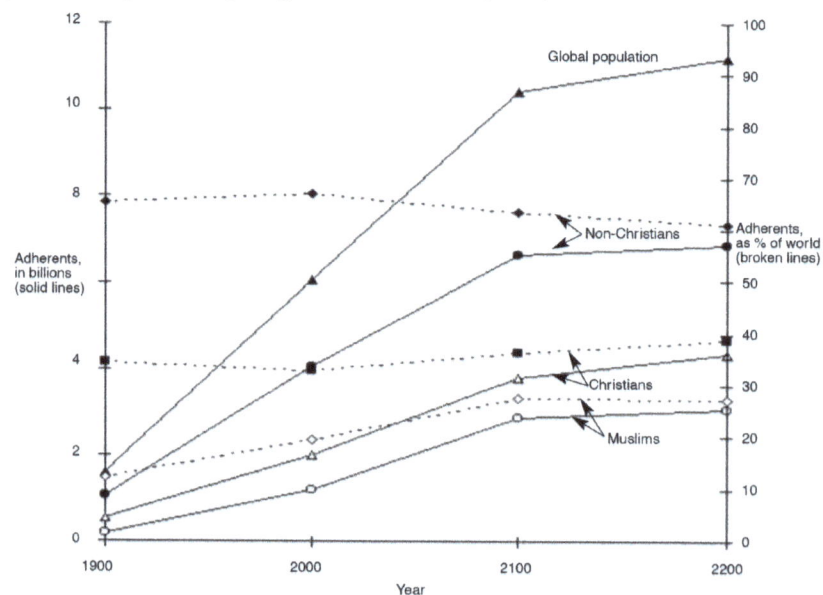

Source: David B. Barrett, Todd M. Johnson, Christopher R. Guidry, and Peter F. Crossing, *World Christian Trends, AD 30–AD 2200: Interpreting the Annual Christian Megacensus* (Pasadena, CA: William Carey Library, 2001), 73.

*2020s*

The current decade is marked by a major publication, the third edition of the *World Christian Encyclopedia* (Edinburgh University Press, 2019) by Johnson and Gina Zurlo, as well as the 10-volume series from Edinburgh University Press, the Edinburgh Companions to Global Christianity (2017–2025; see again Ross's reflection in this volume for the development of the Companions series). From a design perspective, the third *Encyclopedia* hearkened to the first *Encyclopedia*, a single volume with far fewer diagrams than the second edition. It featured a 32-page full color global overview to provide readers that quick-reference opportunity first pioneered by the *Atlas*, despite the 1,000 oversized pages of the *Encyclopedia* filled with large tables of data and narrative text. Figure 16 was the first element in that global overview, designed after the viral World as 100 People infographic found all over the Internet in 2015. This "global diagram" brought together the core of the CSGC's work: it showed what proportion of World Christianity was of each tradition (the ecumenical spirit), alongside numerous social, political, health, and gender indicators to contextually situate Christianity. This was the first analysis of, for example, Christian access to safe water, secondary education, and literacy, as well as the presence of HIV/AIDS among Christians, and what proportion of Christians live in countries with high governmental corruption. The blog post associated with this graphic, published in 2020, went viral via Twitter and Facebook. Social media has introduced new paths for design compared to the maps and charts of 20 years ago. No longer confined to expensive reference works, these elements are now easily shared and available to a much broader audience. Social media also demands accessibility, not complexity, and for most users, the simpler, the better.

The Edinburgh Companions to Global Christianity series is in a similar style to the *Atlas* and *Encyclopedia*, partly because of a continuation of the design team—cartographer Bryan Nicholson, designers Justin Long and Brad Coon, and desktop publisher Christopher Guidry. The advancements in mapping technology have been substantial since Barrett's initial hand drawn maps in the 1950s. Figure 17, for example, shows a beautiful map of Christianity by country in North Africa and West Asia, the second volume of the Companions series. Each volume contains a map of Christianity by country in the region, shaded by Christians' share of the population.

Likewise, in the third volume on East and Southeast Asia, figure 18 illustrates the diversity of religion in Southeast Asia, with provinces shaded according to seven world religions. The colorful religion by province maps have been among the most popular since the first version in the *Atlas of Global Christianity*. These maps really shine because of their attention to detail, colorful design, and ease of interpretation.

*Figure 11. Missionary deployment depicted under six organizing principles, 2001*

| Table A. Foreign missionary deployment enumerated in Worlds A, B, C, under six organizing principles. | | | | | | | |
|---|---|---|---|---|---|---|---|
| Locations | Basis | Principle 1 Christians | Principle 2 Evangelized | Principle 3 Population | Principle 4 Non-Christians | Principle 5 Unevangelized | Principle 6 No agreed basis |
| Persons in: | | | | | | | |
| World A peoples | | 17,873,000 | 420,117,000 | 1,106,766,000 | 1,088,893,000 | 686,649,000 | – |
| World B peoples | | 305,905,000 | 2,109,390,000 | 3,048,682,000 | 2,742,777,000 | 939,292,000 | – |
| World C peoples | | 1,675,773,000 | 1,896,038,000 | 1,899,601,000 | 223,828,000 | 3,563,000 | – |
| GLOBAL TOTAL | | 1,999,551,000 | 4,425,545,000 | 6,055,049,000 | 4,055,498,000 | 1,629,504,000 | – |
| | | Christians | Evangelized | Population | Non-Christians | Unevangelized | No agreed basis |
| Percentages in: | | | | | | | |
| World A peoples | | 1% | 9% | 18% | 27% | 42% | 4% |
| World B peoples | | 15% | 48% | 50% | 68% | 58% | 16% |
| World C peoples | | 84% | 43% | 31% | 6% | 0% | 80% |
| GLOBAL TOTAL | | 100% | 100% | 100% | 100% | 100% | 100% |
| | | Mission force | Mission force | Mission force | Mission force | Mission force | Actual Mission force |
| Missionaries (using above %s) in: | | | | | | | |
| World A peoples | | 4,000 | 40,000 | 77,000 | 113,000 | 177,000 | 18,000 |
| World B peoples | | 64,000 | 200,000 | 211,000 | 284,000 | 242,000 | 68,000 |
| World C peoples | | 352,000 | 180,000 | 132,000 | 23,000 | 1,000 | 335,000 |
| GLOBAL TOTAL | | 420,000 | 420,000 | 420,000 | 420,000 | 420,000 | 420,000 |

Source: David B. Barrett, Todd M. Johnson, Christopher R. Guidry, and Peter F. Crossing, *World Christian Trends, AD 30–AD 2200: Interpreting the Annual Christian Megacensus* (Pasadena, CA: William Carey Library, 2001), 80.

## Conclusion

The presentation of quantitative data from the Barrett/Johnson/Zurlo tradition has dramatically changed from Barrett's first global diagram in 1953 to the graphics in the early 2020s. These changes have been driven by several factors, perhaps chief among them technological advancement. As a trained scientist, Barrett knew the importance of technology and its advantages to make new discoveries about the world. As a result, the CSGC's research legacy has always paid close attention to the latest in computing, database engineering, and design. The ability to replicate a single graph over 200 times (one for each country) with a script has transformed the capacity to mass produce graphics for publications. Social media is now the place to present information for the broadest possible audience and these platforms motivate researchers to present their findings as clearly and succinctly as possible. Partnership in design and data visualization is also critical; it cannot be underestimated how important it is for quantitative researchers to surround themselves with creative types who think in colors, shapes, and patterns. Together, the team can make the data more accessible—and most interesting, indeed.

*Figure 12. Religions by continent, 1910 and 2010*

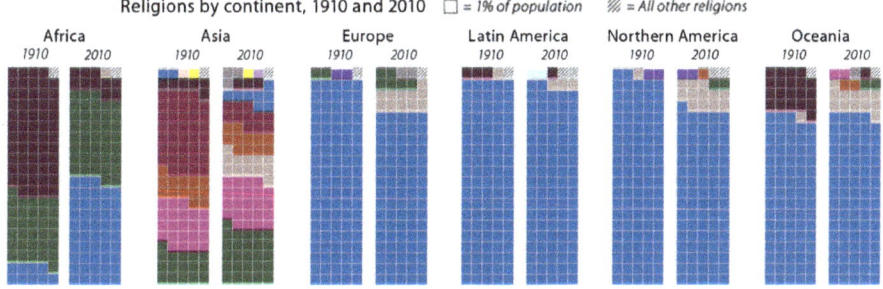

Source: Todd M. Johnson and Kenneth R. Ross, eds., *Atlas of Global Christianity, 1910–2010* (Edinburgh: Edinburgh University Press, 2009), 7.

*Figure 13. 100 largest urban areas by total population, 2010*

| | Urban area | Country | Population | Largest | % | Adherents by percentage |
|---|---|---|---|---|---|---|
| 1 | TOKYO | Japan | 35,467,000 | Buddhists | 56.0 | |
| 2 | MEXICO CITY | Mexico | 20,688,000 | Christians | 95.3 | |
| 3 | Mumbai | India | 20,036,000 | Hindus | 69.0 | |
| 4 | New York-Newark | USA | 20,009,000 | Christians | 65.0 | |
| 5 | São Paulo | Brazil | 19,582,000 | Christians | 88.5 | |
| 6 | Delhi | India | 16,983,000 | Hindus | 78.0 | |
| 7 | Shanghai | China | 15,790,000 | Chinese folk | 30.0 | |
| 8 | Kolkata | India | 15,548,000 | Hindus | 69.0 | |
| 9 | JAKARTA | Indonesia | 15,206,000 | Muslims | 65.0 | |
| 10 | DHAKA | Bangladesh | 14,625,000 | Muslims | 90.0 | |
| 11 | Lagos | Nigeria | 13,717,000 | Christians | 71.2 | |
| 12 | Karachi | Pakistan | 13,252,000 | Muslims | 93.0 | |
| 13 | BUENOS AIRES | Argentina | 13,067,000 | Christians | 91.4 | |
| 14 | Los Angeles | USA | 12,738,000 | Christians | 80.0 | |
| 15 | Rio de Janeiro | Brazil | 12,170,000 | Christians | 90.0 | |
| 16 | CAIRO | Egypt | 12,041,000 | Muslims | 87.0 | |
| 17 | MANILA | Philippines | 11,799,000 | Christians | 93.8 | |
| 18 | BEIJING | China | 11,741,000 | Agnostics | 36.0 | |
| 19 | Osaka-Kobe | Japan | 11,305,000 | Buddhists | 55.0 | |
| 20 | MOSCOW | Russia | 10,967,000 | Christians | 84.0 | |
| 21 | Istanbul | Turkey | 10,546,000 | Muslims | 95.0 | |
| 22 | PARIS | France | 9,856,000 | Christians | 61.1 | |
| 23 | SEOUL | South Korea | 9,554,000 | Christians | 45.7 | |
| 24 | Guangzhou | China | 9,447,000 | Agnostics | 36.0 | |
| 25 | Chicago | USA | 9,186,000 | Christians | 78.0 | |
| | | | | | | 0%    50%    100% |

Source: Todd M. Johnson and Kenneth R. Ross, eds., *Atlas of Global Christianity, 1910–2010* (Edinburgh: Edinburgh University Press, 2009), 238.

*Figure 14. Religious adherents, 1970 and 2020*

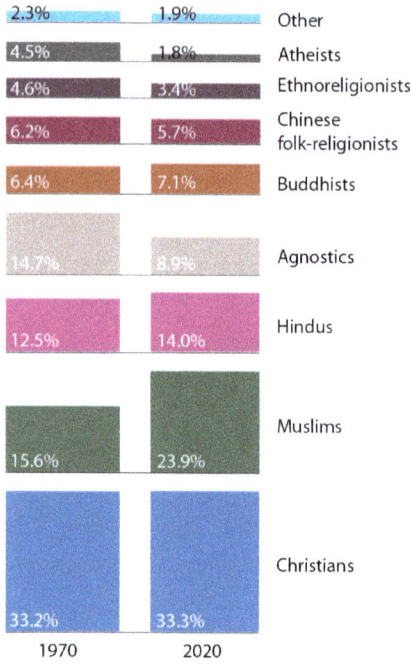

Source: Center for the Study of Global Christianity, *Christianity in its Global Context, 1970–2020: Society, Religion, and Mission.* June 2013, 6.

*Figure 15. Religionists who know a Christian, 2010*

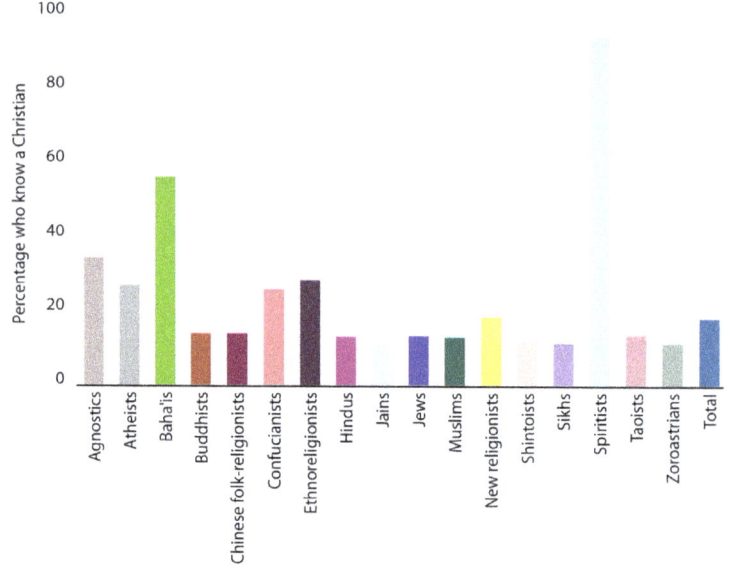

Source: Center for the Study of Global Christianity, *Christianity in its Global Context, 1970–2020: Society, Religion,* and *Mission.* June 2013, 8.

Trends in Global Christianity Through Design 23

*Figure 16. The world as 100 Christians, 2020*

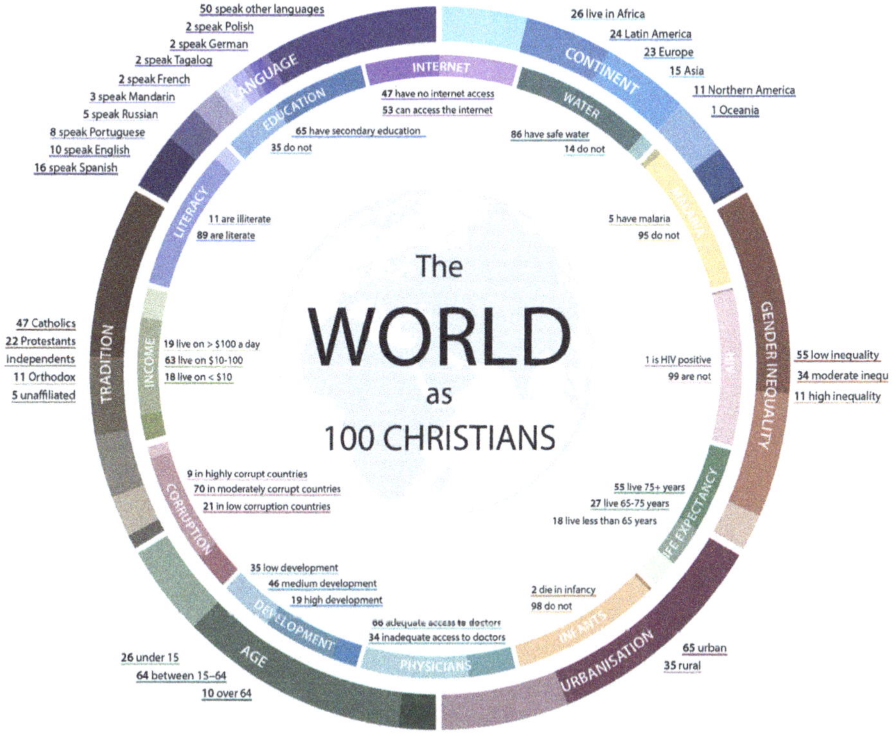

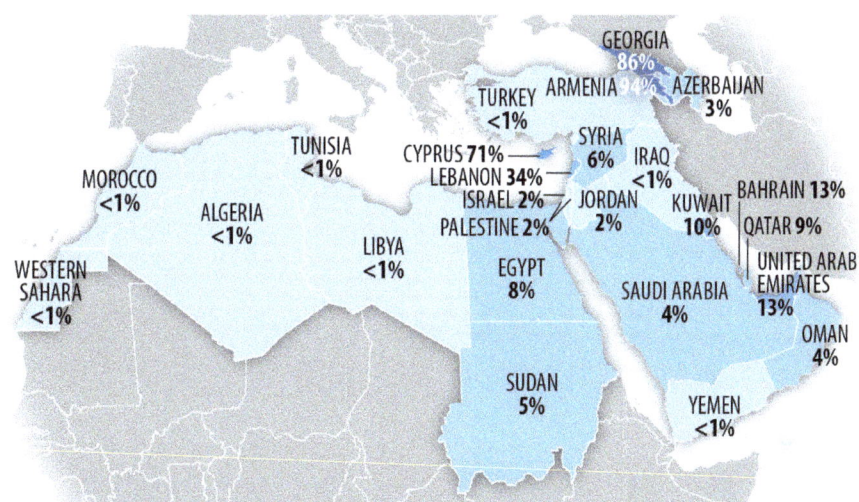

Source: Todd M. Johnson and Gina A. Zurlo, *World Christian Encyclopedia*, 3rd ed. (Edinburgh: Edinburgh University Press, 2019), 3.

*Figure 17. Christians by country, North Africa and West Asia, 2020*

Source: Gina A. Zurlo, "Christianity in North Africa and West Asia," in *Christianity in North Africa and West Asia*, ed. Kenneth R. Ross, Mariz Tadros, and Todd M. Johnson (Edinburgh: Edinburgh University Press, 2018), 4.

*Figure 18. Majority religion by province, East and Southeast Asia, 2020*

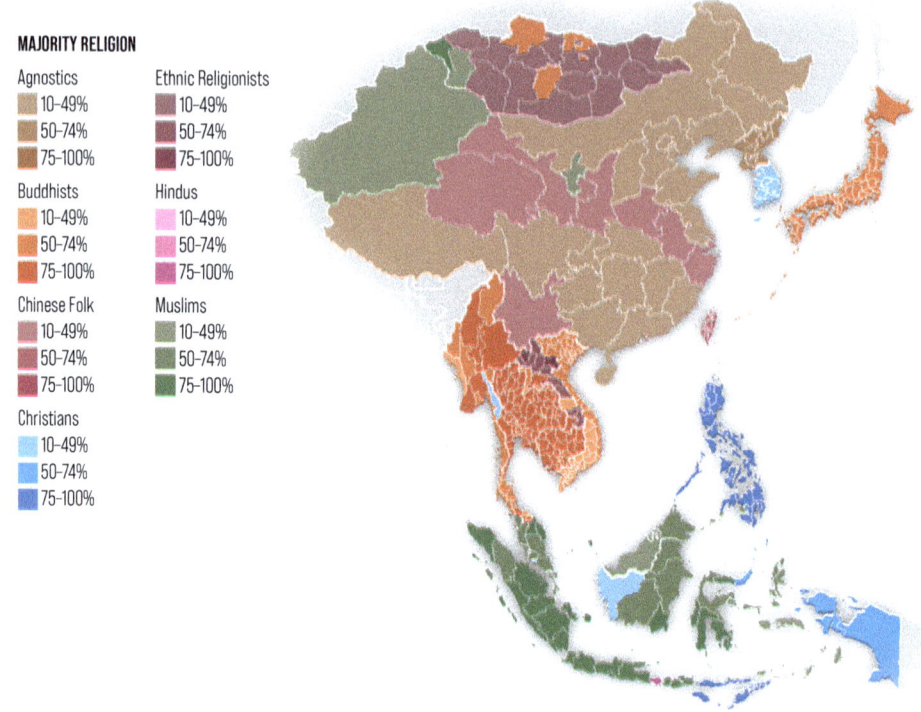

Source: Gina A. Zurlo, "Christianity in East and Southeast Asia," in *Christianity in East and Southeast Asia*, ed. Kenneth R. Ross, Francis D. Alvarez, and Todd M. Johnson (Edinburgh: Edinburgh University Press, 2020), 3.

## Works Cited

Barrett, David B. *Schism and Renewal in Africa: An Analysis of Six Thousand Contemporary Religious Movements.* Nairobi: Oxford University Press, 1968.
Barrett, David B., ed. *World Christian Encyclopedia.* Nairobi: Oxford University Press, 1982.
Barrett, David B., Mary Linda Hronek, George K. Mambo, John S. Mbiti, Malcolm J. McVeigh. "Frontier Situations for Evangelism in Africa, 1972, a Survey Report." In *The Gospel and Frontier Peoples: A Report of a Consultation December 1972*, edited by R. Pierce Beaver, 233–310. South Pasadena, CA: William Carey Library, 1973.
Barrett, David B., and Todd M. Johnson. *Our Globe and How to Reach it: Seeing the World Evangelized by AD 2000 & Beyond: A Manual for the Decade of Evangelization, 1990-2000.* Birmingham, AL: New Hope, 1990.
Barrett, David B., Todd M. Johnson, Christopher R. Guidry, and Peter F. Crossing. *World Christian Trends, AD 30–AD 2200: Interpreting the Annual Christian Megacensus.* Pasadena, CA: William Carey Library, 2001.
Botting, Michael H. *Fanning the Flame: The Story of Ridley Hall Cambridge. Volume 3: 1951-2001.* Cambridge: Hassall & Lucking Ltd, 2006.
Bullock, F.W.B. *The History of Ridley Hall Cambridge. Volume 1: To the end of AD 1907.* Cambridge: Cambridge University Press, 1941.
Center for the Study of Global Christianity. *Christianity in its Global Context, 1970–2020: Society, Religion, and Mission.* June 2013.
David B. Barrett Papers 1957–1985, Center for the Study of Global Christianity, Gordon-Conwell Theological Seminary (South Hamilton, MA, USA).
Johnson, Todd M., and Kenneth R. Ross, eds. *Atlas of Global Christianity, 1910–2010.* Edinburgh: Edinburgh University Press, 2009.
Johnson, Todd M., and Brian J. Grim. *The World's Religions in Figures: An Introduction to International Religious Demography.* Malden, MA: Wiley-Blackwell, 2013.
Johnson, Todd M., and Gina A. Zurlo. *World Christian Encyclopedia*, 3rd ed. Edinburgh: Edinburgh University Press, 2019.
Zurlo, Gina A. "Christianity in East and Southeast Asia." In *Christianity in East and Southeast Asia*, edited by Kenneth R. Ross, Francis D. Alvarez, and Todd M. Johnson, 3–14. Edinburgh: Edinburgh University Press, 2020.
Zurlo, Gina A. "Christianity in North Africa and West Asia." In *Christianity in North Africa and West Asia*, edited by Kenneth R. Ross, Mariz Tadros, and Todd M. Johnson, 3–14. Edinburgh: Edinburgh University Press, 2018.
Zurlo, Gina A. *From Nairobi to the World: David B. Barrett and the Re-imagining of World Christianity.* Leiden/Boston: Brill, 2023.

# Chapter 2: 1993: A Seminal Year

*Patrick Johnstone*

It is not easy to summarize what has been nearly half a century of intimate relationships between the *World Christian Encyclopedia* (housed at the Center for the Study of Global Christianity) and *Operation World*, and then to briefly examine the impact and interactions between these two volumes in their multiple editions on world evangelization over this period.

I first came to know Todd Johnson when I spent three months with the *WCE* team in Richmond, Virginia. Todd was still in his "apprenticing" period. I cannot remember how Todd became linked with the *WCE*, but by then he had been with the team for about four years. So, what I share has an emphasis on the intense discussions between us all—especially between David Barrett and myself. Todd was fully involved in these discussions, so I feel sure he had much to do in the application and implementation of these discussions.

While serving the Lord in Africa, Barrett in Kenya and I in southern Africa, both of us were initiators in the birth of the two major global surveys of Christianity. The surveys resulted in books born in Africa: The first edition of *Operation World* was printed in 1964–1966, and the first *Encyclopedia* in 1982. I first visited David in Kenya in 1977, and from then on came years of an intimate relationship and peer interaction that had an enormous impact on both our publications.

This co-operation brought together two very different informant networks and two very different readerships. The *Encyclopedia* was written with academia in mind, resulting in superb, detailed data in volumes few in the Christian world would ever handle, but were nevertheless constantly quoted. Meanwhile, with no claim to please academia—but not without a bent toward academic excellence!—*Operation World* was written to mobilize ordinary Christians to prayer and outreach to a lost world. We needed each other—I have two massive ring files of 25 years of letters between David and myself as we sought to interpret and explain the statistics and events convulsing the world we wanted to impact with the Evangel!

Todd came into the picture as we were finalizing the information for *Operation World* 5th edition, which was published in 1992 along with the highly successful children's version *You Can Change the World* written by my dear wife, Jill. The latter was published posthumously—she died of cancer a week after finishing the text. In my bereavement, and after the publication of the two books, I offered to use my sabbatical to join the *WCE* team in Richmond in the fall of 1993. I spent three valuable months with the team, which included Todd.

He most generously lent me one of his automobiles for the duration of my stay, enabling me to travel in and out of Richmond to the International Mission Board headquarters of the Southern Baptists where the *WCE* team was hosted. So, my first interaction with Todd was because of an act of extreme generosity!

I appreciated what I saw of Todd's Christian diplomatic skills. He was so intimately linked to two towering figures of the Christian world in the late 20th century—David Barrett and Ralph Winter, who was also Todd's father-in-law. Although individually unique and very different, both were tenacious in strongly holding and promoting visions and ideas that could either catalyze or offend. Yet from all I could observe, Todd was able to maintain good working relationships with both. He was also able to winsomely communicate the insights of *WCE* research on public platforms, classrooms, and in personal interactions.

Over those three months, our frequent team brainstorming sessions yielded remarkable results, illustrating well the multiple levels of global impact of our two ministries, of which Todd played an integral part. Over the years that followed, Todd had much to do with processing these fruitful discussions. While he does not figure as prominently in the items below, Todd nevertheless contributed to the foundation that was to set a course for many aspects of his future ministry.

**Evangelism and Evangelicalism**

David and I began our conversation on Evangelicals and measuring evangelization at our first meeting in 1977, the results of which were published in the 1982 *Encyclopedia*. I had developed a methodology for counting Evangelicals for *Operation World* 1978. This involved assessing the likely percentage of Evangelicals among affiliates of each denomination based on its theology. David had enthusiastically adopted this for use in the *Encyclopedia*. However, by 1993, David was re-thinking this and we discussed for hours about a re-definition of Evangelicals. From this emerged David's 2001 figures for Evangelicals which included only denominations with direct links to the Reformation and a much wider "small-e" evangelicals or so-called Great Commission Christians—based solely on their positive embracing of the Great Commission over theology. This is one point where we ended up in disagreement and explains the differing figures between *Operation World* 2001 and *WCE* 2001. Both assessments have validity, but the *WCE* 2001 figures did not really fit the perspective of major global Evangelical movements such as Lausanne and the World Evangelical Alliance. Todd and his team dropped the concept of "small-e" evangelicals and Great Commission Christians after publication of the *Atlas of Global Christianity* (2009).

## Denominations Database

For *Operation World* 1986 I was grateful that we could incorporate so much of the data for denominations in *WCE* 1982 as a starting point for our own database, which was expanded to include information every five years with sources. We used nearly all the categories and definitions in the *WCE* database with just a few adjustments and re-classifications. What we compiled, then fed back into the statistics used for the 2001 *Encyclopedia*, relied heavily on our *Operation World* 1993. Though David often said that the *WCE* database was "our" database, we were able to clarify the many areas of overlap. With the desire to converge and overlap as far as our sources and principles allowed, we provided fair comparisons of our data and a considerable degree of affirmation for our separate research teams.

We discussed also about including data on Charismatics to acknowledge the extraordinary impact of this movement across the world. It was interesting that our two different methodologies yielded results that were close to each other and within our margins of error! This cooperation between Todd and Gina Zurlo and the *Operation World* editors/authors, Jason Mandryk and Molly Wall, continues to this day.

## The Ethnolinguistic Peoples Database

David started his remarkable work on the peoples of Africa in the 1970s. This then expanded to the whole world, but the full results were only published nearly three decades later in the 2001 *WCE*. I had the privilege of accessing and studying, and then contributing to the database in the month I worked with David in Nairobi in 1979 using the original old Wang computer. I made the basic decision that we would not develop our own database but contribute extensively to the *WCE* listing. The whole Evangelical world was desperate for information on people groups from 1972 onward, and especially after Ralph Winter challenged the church to do something about the "hidden peoples" at the Lausanne conference of 1974. Thereafter, Evangelical missions began focusing on reaching and discipling peoples rather than focusing on just the political nations. In Richmond in 1993, after working extensively on editing and improving this database, I became very familiar with its remarkable content. We had much discussion on this database at the time.

*Nomads*

In one discussion, I mentioned to David and Todd that we could use the database to list all the nomadic and partially nomadic peoples in the world.

Though I assured him we could, David responded that this was impossible. However, within a few minutes I had achieved this on the database and then presented a print-out of this list to David. Much of David's computer-related work was delegated to others, and I think he had not fully grasped the huge range of possible applications of the collected data! Todd was able to transition to the digital age with the help and support of Peter Crossing, who still works with the team as data analyst of the *World Christian Database* and *World Religion Database*.

After taking this list back to my team in the United Kingdom, David Phillips was a great support to me in being a sifter of vital info of *Operation World* and accelerated the writing of the text as a result. I dropped the list on his desk. He became so enthused about it that he then undertook the research to write a book on the world's nomads. For nomads and those in Christian ministry, the book, *Peoples on the Move*, became the standard reference.

*The Joshua Project*

The Lausanne Movement (LM) held a second Conference on World Evangelization in Manila in 1989. In many ways this conference was an organizational disaster, but good things emerged from it. Thomas Wang, then Director of the LM, envisioned a great effort in the final decade of the 20th century. Out of this emerged a new, and dynamic movement, AD2000 and Beyond, with a slogan—"A church for every people by the year 2000." Together with John Robb of World Vision, I was asked to lead the track for unreached peoples. How were we to achieve such a goal when we did not have a workable list of the peoples and an indication of those which needed church planting? I provided a partial list of all the peoples of the world numbering over 10,000, together with some data to Luis Bush, Director from the Joshua Project database. This became the central focus of all that developed over the decade. It led to the formation of the Joshua Project and its brilliant use of the Internet to make information freely available for those with the vision to reach the unreached. It has become one of the most accessible and useful tools for world evangelization in recent years. The full list of ethno-linguistic peoples was published in the 2001 *WCE*.

As we compiled global information for the 2001 *Operation World* and for my book *The Future of the Global Church* (2011), the astonishing developments during the 1990s came into focus. It was probably the decade of the greatest ingathering of people into the church and the most extensive effort of evangelizing the unevangelized of the world that has ever been seen! Only eternity will reveal the astonishing impact of the 30 years of research in producing the full list of unreached peoples published in the *WCE* 2001.

The pioneering work of the *WCE* team with regard to the peoples database was the basic source for all other ethnolinguistic people lists, and we owe a great debt for this remarkable ministry.

*Missions Strategy*

One of the great achievements of David and his team was the development of a new categorization of the languages of the world, which has become known as the Dalby-Barrett system. The great research on languages and Scripture translation has been a focus of Wycliffe Bible Translators for many years, and many of us relied heavily on periodic editions of the famous *Ethnologue*, which has become the standard reference on languages for some time. In it, a three-letter code was applied to every language, a coding system that has become internationally accepted. While the letters selected frequently relate to one of the names of a particular language, they do not give any hint as to linkages with related languages. For example, while the text for each entry gives a language tree relatedness, it is only in text form. On the other hand, the Dalby-Barrett classification does provide an excellent coding that permits this. It shows a degree of cognancy between languages with each successive letter or digit indicating an ever-closer relationship. This enables a listing of clusters of languages, and hence peoples as well.

David Garrison of the International Mission Board (IMB) of the Southern Baptist Convention first explored this as a means of grouping all peoples and languages by major blocs—such as the Arab World, Tibeto-Burmans, etc. I took this further during my time in Richmond and was able to assign every people in the database to a cluster of peoples, of which there were about 250 distinct clusters, and then to a major affinity bloc, of which there were 15. This method helps people see how the myriad array of people groups can be ordered in a taxonomy. In addition, the peoples database contains listings for peoples by home area, that is, where they overlap political boundaries and migrant communities within the country to which they have migrated. In a globalizing world, and we must think globally for the Kurds, Somalis, Ukrainians, and others who migrate or flee war. Such a categorization allowed for global strategies to reach them with the gospel. I subsequently spoke to many mission leaders and suggested that in many cases we need to move from a nation-based field system to a people-based one. Many missions have taken this up, including my own agency. The Southern Baptist IMB actually restructured completely as a result. All this was made possible by this marvelous database tool.

*The 100% Rule*

One of our treasured and constantly affirmed statistical disciplines is what both of our teams call, "the 100% rule." It is the rule that the total for every component of a selected set of statistics or populations *must* add up to 100%. If it does not, we have either made a mistake in our assumptions or data, or there is a valid reason for the missing or extra data which must be accounted for. We carefully followed David and Todd's methodology in this for all our databases and publications. This allowed us to handle such aspects of double counting, secret believers, nominality in religions, etc.

During one of our brainstorming sessions, I made the suggestion that we could do the same with people groups and their religious adherences. While the text for each people listed in the database included assessments about religious affiliation, such information was not included in a set of separate data fields. Though David expostulated that this would be impossible, I explained how this could be done. Nevertheless, when the 2001 *Encyclopedia* was published I was delighted to see that the team had succeeded! In close association with the Joshua Project team, I helped to make the same derivations for their development. Taking this to another level, we applied the same for the six main streams of organized Christianity—Catholic, Orthodox, Anglican, Protestant, Independent/Indigenous, and Marginals. We even were able to do this with apportioning percentages for Evangelicals.

**A Final Word**

I have followed at a distance Todd's more mature ministry years after he took over from David. I am impressed with the developments in his ministry after the move to Gordon-Conwell Theological Seminary. My own contacts over the last decades have been more limited since I handed over my leadership of Operation World. In conclusion, I want to express my gratitude to God and to David, Todd, and his team for the years of working together in global Christian research. I also want to give praise to God for how the global church contributed toward making disciples of all nations and peoples.

# Chapter 3: Partnership in Quantitative Research on World Christianity

*Jason Mandryk and Molly Wall*

The last 65 years have provided a context like no other for researchers of World Christianity. An unprecedented amount of data is now available at an accelerated pace of analysis, reporting, and visualization, all occurring alongside a remarkable shift in the demographics of the global body of Christ. These changes make our work counting Christians worldwide utterly fascinating and as necessary as ever. A major factor that makes our work more rewarding is the collegial relationship between the Center for the Study of Global Christianity (CSGC) and Operation World (OW), and between their researchers, Todd Johnson, Gina Zurlo, Peter Crossing, and ourselves, Jason Mandryk and Molly Wall of Operation World. This relationship has made our work so much more enjoyable than it otherwise might have been, if we had to navigate these decades of change alone. This reflection summarizes several shifts that have occurred in quantifying Christianity since the pioneering work of David Barrett and Patrick Johnstone, founders of the CSGC and OW respectively. In doing so, we'd like to emphasize the importance of partnership and friendship in research, in Christian life, and in mission.

**Making Our Way to Timbuktu**

We started hearing about Timbuktu, Mali as the statistical center of gravity of global Christianity following a 2004 study conducted by Todd Johnson, the first person to locate the point on the map with an equal number of Christians to the north, south, east, and west. The study geographically illustrated that the increasing majority of Christians were located in the global South and in the East.[1] It was a clever way to help Christians re-examine long-held assumptions about Christianity. The global church looks different, lives differently, and speaks different languages than what most of us imagine on a Sunday morning.

*Shifting in Data and Methods*

Quantitative research on the family of God dates at least to the book of Numbers, and includes other prominent chronicling of God's people. The table of nations in Genesis 10 could be regarded not just as a significant structural component in the arc of Genesis—indeed, for all of scripture—but also as the

---

1 Todd M. Johnson and Sun Young Chung, "Tracking Global Christianity's Statistical Centre of Gravity, AD 33–AD 2100," *International Review of Mission* 93, no. 369 (2004): 166–181.

first ethnographic survey in recorded history. A long legacy of responsible data collection has helped Christians understand themselves and the world. British Baptist missionary William Carey's *Enquiry* is often considered the literary foundation of the modern Western missionary movement, and it contains the first attempt at enumerating the different religious populations of the world.[2] The methods developed by David Barrett and Patrick Johnstone for studying global Christianity established a new degree of sophistication in such work. The massive collection and analysis of data on religion and Christian denominations in every nation gave ecclesiastical, missionary, and intercessory movements access to data at a new order of magnitude.

As the church grows in size, expression, and complexity, existing research methodologies often become inadequate. Todd has grappled with many such challenges in his decades working in the demography of religion. New denominations keep mushrooming—especially in countries where tracking their presence is more difficult. Existing denominations continue to splinter, and on occasion, merge. Doubly-affiliated Pentecostals, charismatics within ancient Christian traditions, nominal Evangelicals, and Muslim and Hindu followers of Jesus all are par for the course in today's reality.

The charismatic "Third Wave" and the emergence of a globalized Evangelicalism revealed both the scale and the spread of these trans-denominational movements. The shift within the church from denominational silos to inter-denominational ministry networks has transcended long-held ecclesiastical distinctives. As the global church finds a way forward through these increasingly complex realities, a spirit of innovation and of collaboration among researchers becomes not just an asset, but a necessity.

Barrett and Johnstone developed their ministries and methodologies in an era where "the West" was home to the bulk of the world's Christians. Todd has served in a world past the tipping point, with the majority of Christians now located in Africa, Asia, and Latin America. In the century where Christianity's center of gravity shifted south from Europe to Africa, and in the decades where it began shifting back eastward, Todd's adjustments and additions to the methods of the CSGC have done more than simply kept pace with such changes. Whether tracking a statistical center of gravity, providing an estimate for the percentage of non-Christians who personally know a Christian, or attempting to provide a statistical framework for martyrdom and church embezzlement, Todd's work has started conversations the church didn't realize it needed to have.

---

2  William Carey, *An Enquiry into the Obligations of Christians to Use Means For the Conversion of the Heathens in Which the State of the Different Nations of the World, the Success of Former Undertakings, and the Practicability of Further Undertakings, are Considered* (Leicester: Ann Ireland, 1792).

*Shifts in the Field of Study*

Seismic shifts have taken place in this past generation not only within Christianity, but across the entire religious spectrum. Since the 1980s, much of the world has experienced a re-emergence of religious fervor. This contrasts with the prevailing secularization that governs a large number of mostly Western nations, where present or former state churches are in decline. These developments are made more complex by large-scale migration and increased communication technologies that have contributed to more religious diversity throughout the world. Perhaps due to such changes, social scientists seem to be remembering that religion plays a powerful role in the lives of most people and most societies. Qualitative studies may receive more attention than quantitative research on religion but the discipline of religious demography has truly grown in recent years. Todd's work on the seminal textbook for religious demography was only possible due to his decades of labor as a keen researcher of global Christianity and other world religions.[3] The digital platforms developed from his work—the *World Christian Database* (Brill) and *World Religion Database* (Brill)—are utilized by scholars and missionaries alike.

Quite apart from the opportunity a new field of academic study offers an eager researcher, responsibly acquired quantitative data on world religions is of greater value than ever. On the one hand, such data offer a bulwark against the secular dismissal of religion generally, and Christianity specifically. On the other hand, the data provide a fact-based antidote to the "evang*elastic*" exaggerations of some enthusiasts in the realm of Christian proselytism. Quantitative research in religion provides a neutral ground where the understanding of different faiths can deepen, prejudices can be eroded, and friendships across faiths can emerge. Fact-based research and reporting also contrasts with the recent notoriety of highly circulated videos with misleading or inaccurate claims of population growth, caricatures of religious belief systems, and the demonization of migrants and refugees. Appreciation of the nuances of religious demographics goes a long way to remediating the impact of both fearmongering and radicalization, regardless of which religion is in the crosshairs.

Finally, the demography of religion, when combined with other disciplines, helps us understand the distinctives of communities that a fast-changing world has forced into desperation. Whether from violence, environmental changes, or economic realities, people are on the move more than ever before. Understanding these people more deeply—where they are, how many they are, and what they believe—will equip us to better demonstrate kindness and

---
3   Todd M. Johnson and Brian J. Grim, *The World's Religions in Figures: An Introduction to International Religious Demography* (Chichester, UK: John Wiley & Sons, 2013).

compassion to those in need. The CSGC's work estimating access to the gospel will direct Christ's followers to those most overlooked in their efforts to make disciples of the nations.

*Shifting to an Information Age*

David Barrett and Patrick Johnstone both began as missionaries in the mid-20th century (in Kenya and southern Africa, respectively) with ministries that depended heavily upon information supplied by other missionaries to produce quantitative resources on Christianity in Africa and beyond. The scope of the work has expanded greatly since then, but the range of sources even more so. National church alliances, indigenous researchers, and well-connected mission and prayer movements have all contributed to significant improvements in data availability. Recent growth in the study of religion has prompted the development of new high-quality information sources. As we have frequently observed in the OW office, the first few editions of *Operation World* faced a constant struggle to find reliable information, but the last couple of editions have been a constant struggle to filter the deluge of information down to what is most valuable.

Beyond the expanded volume of material with which we work, the platforms we use have also changed; the transition to the digital age has been completely transformational. We no longer consume information primarily through books, articles, and other print materials, but via screens. We are in an era of instant global communication, online databases, and sophisticated data visualization (infographics, visual slide presentations, videos, blogs, and much more). In many ways, changes in research and information technology that have occurred in the 65 years of Todd's life that this publication celebrates have been more profound than the changes in the previous 165 years between the publication of William Carey's *Enquiry* and Todd's birth. The first edition of *OW* in 1964 included hand-drawn maps in hand-cranked copies on a Gestetner machine from the 19th century! This is in stark comparison to modern data visualization. Consider examples such as the COVID-19 dashboards from Johns Hopkins University and the World Health Organization, or the ingenious videos of statistician Hans Rosling, to see how far data visualization has progressed.

*Partnership Along the Way*

The CSGC and OW have, since their inception, occupied space at the juxtaposition of mission, research, global Christianity, and prayer. Both Patrick and David were pioneers in uniting these streams of the global Christian movement, in particular among Evangelicals, and initially worked independently until Patrick visited David in Nairobi in 1977. The two converged their research after that point, a move that was highly strategic, long overdue, and set the stage for partnership in research for decades to come.

The confluence of David and Patrick's work occurred just as the Majority World church regained prominence, and as new global data sets became more readily accessible, whether from secular sources such as the United Nations or from Christian sources such as the *Ethnologue*. Together with a resurgence of interest in the study of religion, these developments launched the work of the CSGC into an even greater position of influence within ecumenical Christian circles, academia, and beyond. This can be seen in the extent of citations and breadth of interviews and consultation that Todd and now Gina Zurlo provide to some of the world's leading journalism outlets, governmental bodies, and international agencies, such as the *New York Times* and the BBC. Nevertheless, Todd's roots keep him embedded in the Evangelical and missionary communities the CSGC has long served, where he has found an amplified voice and increasingly influential platform.

While traveling alongside the CSGC in quantitative research across these decades, Operation World has likewise blossomed as a mobilization tool with the globalization of both the missionary-sending movement and the prayer movement. This can be seen in OW's many language translations and widespread digital accessibility via the web and its mobile app. OW's voice has been amplified via events such as Urbana, Lausanne's Younger Leaders Gatherings, and by enthusiastic promotion by platform speakers such as Operation Mobilization founder and OW champion, George Verwer. While OW does serve the wider church and in rare instances reaches beyond, its primary constituency has remained situated within the Evangelical community. The spheres of influence of the CSGC and OW have diverged at points, as we each have walked through open doors of opportunity to serve the kingdom. But the spirit of collaboration thankfully, and necessarily, has remained.

Data sharing was a core aspect of Patrick and David's partnership and continues to strengthen confidence in our respective methods as we undertake similar research projects and yield consistently similar findings. Our projects have often leapfrogged each other across the years, each building upon the earlier findings of the other. This iterative process inevitably results in improvements in the quality of the data, in the range of sources unearthed, and in our respective data-led understandings of how the world is changing. The sharing of data sets has continued to the present, with select data from the 7th edition of *Operation World* referenced in the CSGC's research database, used to inform the 3rd edition of the *World Christian Encyclopedia* (Edinburgh

University Press, 2019), and their final data from the *Encyclopedia* in the OW database as a reference source for OW's forthcoming 8th edition. Todd is gracious, generous, and open-handed with the data, while always respecting his publishing agreements.

Many Christian groups find value in a combination of our respective datasets. The *World Christian Database* (*WCD*) presently has more current figures for the number and percentage of Christians by country, while the OW Evangelical figures tend to align more with the numbers expected by some groups based on their theological understanding of Evangelicalism. We have therefore mutually supplied data to groups such as the Lausanne Movement, the World Evangelical Alliance, the International Fellowship of Evangelical Students (IFES), and countless prayer initiatives, mission mobilization events, and classroom lectures. In fact, perhaps our most widely used presentation slide (or at least the one with the most "wow factor") places OW Christian data alongside *WCD* unevangelized data on a map, highlighting visually one of their most-quoted stats—that "86% of the world's Muslims, Hindus, and Buddhists do not personally know a Christian."[4] The CSGC's unique data set, and the generosity in letting it be used, has long combined powerfully with OW's platform for mobilizing. Many thousands of people have been first challenged by the data and then urged to respond with prayer and action.

Perhaps the most special collaborations between the CSGC and OW have come in opportunities to co-labor, co-author, and co-present. Among the most memorable was Jason and Todd's collaboration on the selection committee for the 2010 Lausanne III Congress in Cape Town, South Africa. The flowering of a truly globalized Christianity and the recession into history of a Western-centric Christian faith has been led by demographic realities, but one of the factors holding it back has been the disproportionate influence of finances and the well-oiled machinery of publishing, media, marketing, and communications from a very small handful of nations. Together with a diverse group of Christian leaders, Todd and Jason worked out a selection algorithm that helped to ensure maximum representation at the Congress. Not just nationalities, but generations, genders, traditions, ethnicities, and spheres of ministry involvement were factors in determining the limited number of candidates for participation.

The examples of partnership described here do not merely represent collaboration designed to improve our products, enlarge our coffers, or exploit one another's resources. It is our conviction that this sort of partnership in the

---

4   Todd M. Johnson, "Personal Contact," Gordon Conwell Theological Seminary. April 1, 2020. https://www.gordonconwell.edu/blog/personal-contact/.

gospel is also an expression of Christian unity, and as such can be a testimony to the church and to the world.

**Siblings in Our Global Family**

Scripture is filled with narratives of sibling rivalries, often fraught with tension, conflict, and outright murder! We are grateful that our own sibling dynamics between the CSGC and OW are much more wholesome. The origins of our own ministries—as attested by Patrick Johnstone's reflection in this volume—explain our similar lineage and shared organizational DNA. But our sense of kinship extends beyond common roots and shared ministry emphases. Our curious little cohort of researchers is a small one indeed, and this modestly sized tribe feels like a family. Better still, our shared vision for the global church, for world mission, and for global prayer means that we feel like a fairly well-functioning family. As Patrick described, the people behind the databases walked through not just changes in data acquisition and research methods, but also through the joys and challenges of life and ministry. David and Todd welcomed Patrick to the USA in the months following the death of Patrick's first wife, Jill, in 1993. They provided a valuable season of collaboration as well as a place to grieve. The decades since have brought significant changes to life circumstances for both teams—moves, ministry challenges, relationship ups and downs, births, Patrick's retirement from OW (2006), and eventually David's death (2011). Like any family relationships that span decades and generations, there are seasons of increased interaction and seasons of drifting apart, times where everyone is getting along well, and times of not seeing eye to eye.

*Sibling Rivalry*

The CSGC and OW share a great deal in common in terms of our history and research methods, but there are differences between us, especially regarding our constituencies. Since its founding in 1965, the CSGC has been located at a regional church body, a mission organization, as a stand-alone research center, and most recently with an accredited seminary, but the readership for most of its published resources work within academia. OW is part of a mission organization, formerly located at a mission headquarters and currently at a missionary training college with the majority of its audience to be found among church-going Evangelical Christians. Both audiences benefit from reliable quantitative research in the domains of religion, Christianity, evangelism, and mission. Despite the overlap, in the late 1990s Patrick and David chose to go separate ways regarding research methodology and data philosophies. This had not been anticipated, but given the different contexts in which they worked and their resulting areas of focus, it was not a surprise.

Todd's efforts to reconnect and establish a positive relationship between OW and the CSGC were pivotal to achieving the collegiality we now enjoy. Since 2005, OW has increasingly leaned into the global prayer and mission mobilization movements, while the CSGC has excelled in its academic milieu. While much of our data work is complementary and collaborative, we produce two different sets of data for Evangelicals, and to many outside our organizations, this creates an apparent tension—a debate over who is right and who is wrong. We are quite happy, however, to affirm both interpretations of this seemingly ever-changing sector of global Christianity. We affirm each other's work, since we each use a different definition of Evangelical to arrive at our figures.[5] There is room for differences, and multiple voices are needed to describe and measure Christianity around the world. No single measure, or even set of measures, could capture all that is worth researching in our field. The study of global Christianity will only deepen as our teams and research networks expand to include more Christians from around the world.

*Following in an Older Brother's Footsteps*

Another significant difference between Todd's time with the CSGC and ours with OW has profoundly benefitted us: Todd is a decade ahead of us on the journey. He took over the reins from David years ahead of Patrick handing over OW's leadership to Jason. In many ways, the relationship with Todd has been one akin to an older brother supporting, encouraging, and advising younger siblings who walk a few paces behind on a similar path. Todd is not so many years ahead that we miss gratifying connecting points or learning opportunities, and we are close enough in age to share generational traits and tastes. Watching him navigate stages of life and of ministry has provided a role model in global research, ministry, and discipleship.

With wisdom and maturity, Todd has grown the CSGC's leadership from a single founder to an experienced leadership team. He has taken a small, fledgling project from the basement of a condemned church to an academic research center at a leading seminary serving a global student population. He has had to make critical decisions, and discern the Lord's leading, at several key points along the way.

Over the years, we have regularly called on Todd for input and advice. He has never once been unwilling to fit a call into his very busy schedule, nor to

---

5   See Gina A. Zurlo, "The Demographics of Global Evangelicalism." In *Evangelicals Around the World: A Global Handbook for the 21st Century*, ed. Brian Stiller and Karen Stiller (Nashville: Thomas Nelson, 2015), 34–47.

take the time needed to listen, think, and pray with us as we face challenges and decisions around leading a Christian research team. He is not unfamiliar with running a small ministry gifted—and burdened—with outsized impact and influence. Todd shares openly from his experiences, what he's learned along the way, and what he wishes he knew then that we can benefit from now. In the areas where our situations differ, he willingly serves as a sounding board. His counsel is invaluable—no one else could understand the very specific niche we occupy, while appreciating the idiosyncratic ministerial and institutional factors we experience.

In the season when our mission sold the property that had housed Operation World for 36 years, Todd agreed to serve OW in a more formal capacity as part of an advisory group, helping us discern a way forward to a new location. He made himself available beyond group meetings to talk independently with us, and his support, encouragement, prayers, and determination to help OW continue on a good path were present in times when it was most needed. Perhaps some in his position might have counseled us to let OW wind down, Todd did exactly the opposite—he worked to make sure we could continue into the future.

*Our Clan of Researchers*

Todd and the team at the CSGC are able to uniquely offer insight, experience, and, dare we say, sympathy to those of us who labor at Operation World. We share the challenges of conveying the amazing diversity and breadth of the body of Christ, the scale and complexity of the unfinished task of the Great Commission, the need for robust research (rather than hearsay or sensationalism) to arrive at our convictions and conclusions, and the relationship between considered reflection and mobilization for action. Beyond that, we find Todd a great model of the need to pair graciousness with conviction in responding to the push-and-pull of the many, and often competing, agendas and priorities in the diverse expressions of the church.

This sibling dynamic extends beyond just our two teams. For over a decade, the CSGC and OW have been part of the GRC—the Global Researchers' Conversation—a small, familial group of key knowledge workers connected to the Great Commission. The GRC meets online every month to discuss and pray for our respective ministries as well as personal and family updates. The value of shared organizational knowledge and experience is eclipsed by the relational connection, mutual encouragement, and prayer that continues month after month and year after year. These connections are extremely consequential—the ministries represented in the GRC represent a tiny number of people with astonishingly low budgets given how important these groups are to how Christians understand and engage with the global church and the missionary endeavor.

*The Whole Family*

The *World Christian Encyclopedia* was at the forefront of establishing the fact that African, Asian, and Latin American Christianity had already become the "bigger brother" in the global church, a threshold that had been passed decades ago. Todd was likewise ahead of the curve in esteeming and honoring sisters and brothers from the global South accordingly. His publications, but also his actions, have been instrumental in normalizing the reality of the global church and of the West's shifting role from colonial dominator to equals as servants of one another.

When it comes time to write, speak, present, or build a team, Todd often purposefully chooses well-qualified women, people of color, and researchers from the Majority World. He has long made deliberate choices to co-author, co-present, and even cede the stage where most would continue taking opportunities for themselves. He can easily see what many seem blind to: that we succeed most when we look beyond the go-to candidates and lift up people at the margins—people without whose input we will suffer in the long run. In the realms of both academia and Christian ministry, choices like these run counter to the incessant demands for center stage that our attention economy claims are a veritable necessity. Molly has benefitted from this way of thinking, having been invited by Todd to serve alongside him in his former Senior Associate role with the Lausanne Movement. This included co-presenting as well as an invitation to stand in for him at a leadership gathering. At another large Lausanne leadership event, Todd ceded his plenary spot to his colleague, Gina Zurlo. Furthermore, given the opportunity to invite three fellow leaders to the gathering, Todd intentionally invited three younger female researchers to join him. Such actions do not go without notice, and they provide a model others feel emboldened to follow.

Our true family—the entire body of Christ—most clearly reflects the kingdom of God when the first are last and the last are first. Todd's intentional strategy of inclusion and promotion of all family members may come to mark his contribution to global Christianity as much as any published work. Where some other groups have crafted eloquent statements about the value of all members of the body of Christ, Todd has proved the rhetoric with action.

## An Atlas of Encounters

The statistical center of gravity for quantitative researchers of World Christianity has yet to be tracked, but the geographical overlaps between the CSGC and OW teams are worth a mention.

*Africa*

Both the *World Christian Encyclopedia* and *Operation World* have roots in Africa, during an era of profound transitions for the continent. Both David Barrett and Patrick Johnstone were Englishmen, serving as missionaries (arriving in 1957 and 1962, respectively), with educational backgrounds in the hard sciences. As their work grew and projects became known, each moved his ministry to the West to dock with a large mission organization.

*Minnesota & Manitoba*

The successors to David and Patrick also have similar roots. Todd's background growing up in Minnesota is echoed by Jason's childhood in neighboring Manitoba. Tales of blizzards, roof-high snowdrifts, and cross-country ski adventures have bounced back and forth between us. The remoteness of those empty spaces at the center of the continent seems to have provided impetus for many, Todd and Jason included, to travel widely and engage with the world in the context of Christian service. The strength of Pietistic traditions is another common thread, whether Scandinavian Pietism in the Lutheran and Covenant traditions of Minnesota or Radical Pietism in the Anabaptist traditions of Manitoba. Each engaged in missionary activity from a relatively early age that led, eventually, to each pursuing a lifelong commitment to research in World Christianity. The next leaders are two women, both from the USA—a vital development in representing and engaging more than half of the church—an area of study Gina has recently pursued.[6] Perhaps next up for both entities will be greater representation of Majority World Christians at the heart of both research teams.

*Massachusetts*

Jason first got to know Todd in person during a visit to Gordon-Conwell Theological Seminary in the CSGC's early days at that location. Shared interests and passions came to light very quickly, as did Todd's sharing nature—illustrated by the armload of books with which Jason returned to the United Kingdom. This visit also highlighted Todd's sense of humor. As Jason and Todd

---

6  Gina A. Zurlo, *Women in World Christianity: Building and Sustaining a Global Movement* (Malden, MA: Wiley-Blackwell, 2023).

were crossing a busy Boston street, Todd suggested—in jest—that perhaps they should cross separately, as it would be a grave disservice to research in World Christianity if they were both to get hit by the same runaway bus!

Molly first interacted with Todd while serving with the US Center for World Mission (now Frontier Ventures), an organization founded by Todd's in-laws, Ralph and Roberta Winter. Finding herself serving in a small role with the International Society for Frontier Missiology, she was aided by his ability to provide a potted history and valuable pointers. But like Jason, it was on a visit to Boston at Todd's kind invitation where she was introduced to their research center, to Gina and others on the team—and of course to his favorite lobster roll at a local spot. This visit came just as Molly had assumed leadership of Operation World when Jason stepped out for a season, and Todd confidently asserted that it was vital that OW continue, stepping in as an encourager, a champion, and an advisor.

*The Ends of the Earth*

It is a virtual inevitability that people involved in researching the global church and mission either already possess or eventually develop an enthusiastic appreciation for diverse expressions of culture—art, music, dance, textiles, food, and the like. Most of the occasions where Todd and either Molly or Jason (or both) have been able to spend time together in person have involved the shared enjoyment of a new or favorite cuisine from another part of the world, a music concert, art exhibition, or discussion of our latest book or film finds. Our shared passion for the diversity of the body of Christ and the awesome variety and brilliance found in human cultural expressions leads us to seek out such occasions when face to face fellowship is possible. With frequent participation in global Evangelical gatherings, we've had the privilege to meet from Cyprus to Thailand, South Africa to Germany, Brazil to Malaysia, and of course our London home!

**The World Christian…**

Encyclopedia. Database. Trends. Virtually all who know Todd know of these resources. But "World Christian," quite beyond serving as adjectives for these publications, is an excellent description of Todd himself. He is a true friend of the global church. The work of the CSGC has not only advanced learning about global Christianity, but more specifically the study of Christianity in the Majority World. Todd's own sabbaticals in Thailand can be counted as such, but even more so, the Silk Road course he developed has brought Christians from the West to learn about the history of their faith in places where the church thrived centuries before European Christians had traveled to the Americas. Todd's presentations demonstrate that "the global church" is not merely some abstract derivation of quantitative research, represented by statistical tables. His lectures are peppered with art and images that visually express Christianity worldwide, as well as personal stories of his countless interactions with real people, his spiritual kindred from every region who make up the global church.

*Called to Discipleship*

There always appears to be more work than there is time or capacity at both the CSGC and OW. We watch from a distance with something approaching awe at what the CSGC can coordinate and produce. Todd's prodigious output seems to be partnered with time for family, involvement in church fellowship, and the pursuit of personal interests as well as spiritual growth and health. The CSGC's place in the life of American—and global—Christianity could easily be swayed by ambition for increased influence in the church and to inform policy in several areas. The increase of attention from acclaimed news outlets for quotes, interviews, and consulting would have awakened such ambition for many. Instead, Todd has spoken from theological and spiritual conviction, and from honest conclusions led by the data. His internal compass appears fixed to a true north of a more simple, missional, family-orientated lifestyle. He travels less than he could, and practices hospitality and service more than most in his position would. It has been a greater encouragement to us than we have ever stated to watch Todd walk the walk not only as a Christian leader, but as a Christian disciple.

*Called to Mission*

Like Patrick and David before him, as with Molly and Jason in OW's leadership, Todd comes into the quantitative study of World Christianity with his own missionary background, having served for years with a mission organization. There is an aspect to one's journey in Christian discipleship and personal development that can only be experienced through cross-cultural living, language learning, and service to the body of Christ in places other than where we call home. It transforms one's perspective and priorities. Missionary service teaches humility in ways that few other experiences can. Living alongside the thriving, growing churches of the Majority World provides a particular schooling in prayer, faith, and sometimes suffering, that cannot be replicated by the top academic and training programs elsewhere.

One characteristic (of many) that both of us admire in Patrick is his lifelong commitment to discipling others, and to finding those outside their own culture to intentionally offer welcome, practical help, and friendship. He does this wherever he lives, whatever his role—and is even now in his 80s learning Farsi to better disciple new Iranian believers in his city. We see something similar in Todd, in his long-term friendships with leaders of other faiths, his care for the spiritual vitality of his team, and his choice to remain engaged with mission networks, organizations, and long-time colleagues. We are inspired by both men's commitment to live out a missional lifestyle regardless of role or location, alongside their lives of research.

*Called to Prayer*

On each occasion where we have been physically in the same place—occurrences that have been too few of late due to the COVID-19 pandemic—we recall sitting down to pray for one another's ministries and teams. The natural and organic inclusion of prayer into every significant interaction likewise characterizes Patrick's leadership, as well as Todd's. Readers may know that OW is a ministry whose primary function is to use research to inform and mobilize prayer. It therefore feels more than appropriate to close with a prayer for Todd, drawing from the prayers of scripture:[7]

> *Lord God, maker of heaven and earth,*
> *We thank you for your servant, Todd, and for all you have placed in him for his enjoyment, for your pleasure, and for the blessing of your church. We thank you for the grace you have given him to faithfully steward those gifts day by day, year by year.*
> *We are grateful to you for the faithful service in the gospel he has rendered until now. We are grateful to you for crossing our paths with Todd's, and we ask that his love may abound more and more, with knowledge and all discernment, so that he may approve what is excellent, and so be pure and blameless for the day of Christ, filled with the fruit of righteousness that comes through Jesus Christ, to the glory and praise of God.*
> *We ask you to bless Todd by letting him see much fruit from the decades of planting and watering that he has done. We praise you for establishing the work and legacy of the Center and ask that it, too, might bear even more fruit.*
> *We give thanks for 65 years of the gift of life, and we ask for many more—years full of joy with family and friends, years filled with*

---

7   Adapted in parts from the prayers found in Romans 15:16, Philippians 1:9–11, and Ephesians 3:14–21 in the English Standard Version Anglicized.

*opportunities to bless others, years of continued learning and growth. Equip him for every task and challenge that lies ahead.*

*Father, from whom every family in heaven and on earth is named, we ask that according to the riches of your glory you may grant Todd and all who surround him to be strengthened with power through your Spirit in their inner being, so that Christ may dwell in their hearts through faith—that, being rooted and grounded in love, they may have strength to comprehend with all the saints what is the breadth and length and height and depth of Christ's love, and to know this love that surpasses knowledge, that they may be filled with all your fullness.*

*You are able to do far more abundantly than all that we ask or think, according to your power at work within us. To you be glory in the church and in Christ Jesus throughout all generations, for ever and ever. Amen.*

**Works Cited**

Carey, William. *An Enquiry into the Obligations of Christians to Use Means For the Conversion of the Heathens in Which the State of the Different Nations of the World, the Success of Former Undertakings, and the Practicability of Further Undertakings, are Considered.* Leicester, UK: Ann Ireland, 1792.

Johnson, Todd M. "Personal Contact." April 1, 2020. https://www.gordonconwell.edu/blog/personal-contact/.

Johnson, Todd M., and Brian J. Grim. *The World's Religions in Figures: An Introduction to International Religious Demography.* Chichester, UK: John Wiley & Sons, 2013.

Johnson, Todd M., and Sun Young Chung. "Tracking Global Christianity's Statistical Centre of Gravity, AD 33–AD 2100." *International Review of Mission* 93, no. 369 (2004): 166–181.

Zurlo, Gina A. "The Demographics of Global Evangelicalism." In *Evangelicals Around the World: A Global Handbook for the 21st Century*, edited by Brian Stiller and Karen Stiller, 34–47. Nashville: Thomas Nelson, 2015.

Zurlo, Gina A. *Women in World Christianity: Building and Sustaining a Global Movement.* Malden, MA: Wiley-Blackwell, 2023.

# Part II

# Lived Global Christianity

Nalini Jayasuriya (1927–2014), *Banquet*, courtesy of the Overseas Ministries Study Center at Princeton Theological Seminary, Princeton, New Jersey, USA.

# Chapter 4: Invitation to the Kitchen, Not Just to the Table
## Todd M. Johnson's Motif of Global Christianity

*Uchenna D. Anyanwu*

It is now a widely accepted fact that Christianity as a faith tradition is "thoroughly global."[1] It is global in the sense that followers of Jesus the Messiah are found in all the countries of the world today—a scenario that was certainly not the case a century ago. Asserting that Christianity is a global faith does not, however, imply that there are followers of Jesus within all the ethnolinguistic peoples of the globe. Many people groups do not yet have at least 2% of their population following the way of the Messiah, and several of these groups have no known follower of Jesus living in close proximity to them to bear witness of Jesus's life, love, and *logos*. The task of creating awareness and mobilizing Jesus's followers globally to engage these unengaged and unreached peoples continue to preoccupy the strategies of mission leaders and organizations. Counting the remaining unreached and unengaged people groups, and identifying their geographical locations, are some tools that mission leaders and mission-focused agencies employ to inform their strategic ventures.

Quantifying trends in global Christianity has been the calling and vocation of Dr. Todd M. Johnson, under whose oversight I served as a research assistant at the Center for the Study of Global Christianity (CSGC), which he directed for many years and currently co-directs with Dr. Gina Zurlo. While reflecting on Todd Johnson's motif that drives his global Christian vision, the overarching image that came to mind is the illustration of the table, which I have heard him give many times either during a conference presentation, a lecture, or while speaking to mission leaders.

In 2017, Todd was invited to an Evangelical conference in Wittenberg, Germany, marking half a millennium since the Protestant Reformation. He was there to present his research findings showing that in 2017, 40% of Protestants worldwide were Africans. Yet, among the 100 conference participants, only six or seven were African. Todd was sitting next to a leader from Ghana, when someone from the podium said, "Africans are welcome at the table in this Evangelical movement" (my paraphrase). Upon hearing that, the Ghanaian leader leaned over to Todd and quietly recounted a proverb that says, "It is good for you to invite me to the table, but it is far better if you invite me into the

---

1 Philip Jenkins, *The Next Christendom: The Coming of Global Christianity* (Oxford: Oxford University Press, 2002), xi.

kitchen."[2] In what follows, I employ an African philosophical understanding underlying such a proverb to depict how it has informed Todd's motif of global Christianity. It is one that can be described as an invitation to the kitchen of global Christianity, not just to its table.

**Invitation to the Table Versus Invitation to the Kitchen**

Proverbs are generally pregnant with meanings, which if not explained, may be misconstrued. African proverbs are not exempt from this general rule. African proverbs are sayings that possess embedded philosophical meanings and are not to be understood literally. Why would a Ghanaian say it is better to be invited to the kitchen and not just to the table? Two important philosophical dimensions to bear in mind: first, collaboration or partnership, and second, trust.

An invitation to the table implies that the invited guests are given the honor to dine at the table without participation in the labor of preparing the meal. It denies the invited the privilege of collaboration and contribution. Invitation merely to the table implies that the guests are not seen as partners. An invitation to the kitchen implies an invitation to collaboration and contribution. In the kitchen, the invited do not claim ownership of the kitchen but feel honored that a place has been given to them to participate in the preparation of the meal. That is the aspect of collaboration and contribution.

The second aspect in being invited to the kitchen is trust. The invited in the kitchen sees the process of the preparation and all that go into the meal. While conducting ethnographic fieldwork in northeastern Nigeria, I sought to understand how Christians in the region can build peace in the context of acute violence perpetrated by Islamist Muslims. A participant responded to the discussion on hospitality and inviting Muslims to meals saying:

> The truth is that some of our Muslim friends, when you give them food they, throw it away, they don't eat. They would receive it with gratitude, but behind you they throw it away, because they do not trust what it is, especially, when it is chicken, because they believe you are the one that slaughtered the

---

[2] Compare this with the statement that V.S. Azariah (first Anglican Bishop of South India) made at the World Missionary Conference held in Edinburgh, in 1910, where there was not a single African invited. Azariah challenged Western Christians saying: "Too often you promise us thrones in heaven, but will not offer us chairs in your drawing rooms, ...You have given your goods to feed the poor. You have given your bodies to be burned. We also ask for love. Give us FRIENDS!" Brian Stanley, *The World Missionary Conference, Edinburgh 1910* (Grand Rapids, MI: Eerdmans, 2009), 125; Allen L. Yeh, *Polycentric Missiology: 21st-Century Mission from Everyone to Everywhere* (Downers Grove, IL: IVP Academic, 2016), 110.

chicken, and to them it is an abomination to eat anything slaughtered by a Christian. (Focus Group #1:467–471)[3]

The participant gave an example of how such barriers can be overcome through intentional and creative demonstration of love to Muslims. He described his own mother's creativity to overcome the barrier where, in her bid to demonstrate hospitality deliberately and creatively, she invited a well-respected Muslim to her home when she organized a community dinner for Muslims. She invited "someone that she was fully aware that this man would not keep quiet, so he will tell his friends that this woman called him to come and slaughter a goat for them… When she called them for dinner, they ate the dinner because the man told them that he was the one who slaughtered the goat … " (Focus Group #1:472–478).[4]

A strong bridge of trust is constructed when the invited are allowed into the kitchen to participate in the preparation of the meal. The invited are dispelled of fears and they can trust that the contents of the table conform to their religious dietary and ritual demands. In the context of some African ethno-religionists, the meaning is taken further to imply that what is being offered is not confectioned with anything harmful to those invited into the kitchen and involved in meal preparation. Invitation to the kitchen, therefore, carries with it the philosophical underpinning not only of collaboration and contribution, but also trust.

Todd Johnson underscores that the Ghanaian proverb helped him to articulate the shift in global Christianity from the global North to the global South, of which he and his research colleagues at the Center for the Study of Global Christianity have been studying for many years. It is a shift in leadership that, rather than implying that the global North is disappearing from the kitchen of global Christianity, means that brothers and sisters in Christ from the global North are re-learning what it means to see their fellow brothers and sisters from the global South as equals—in the same kitchen. Being together in the kitchen of global Christianity provides the space to ensure that everyone has an equal voice. Todd will tell you that, for him, that is a pathway to genuine partnership and true collaboration. He also believes that there are "encouraging signs of that happening and actually that one interesting thing is [that there is

---

3   The is an excerpt from one of the focus group interviews I conducted in Nigeria in 2018, cited in my book titled, *Pathways to Peacebuilding: Staurocentric Theology in Nigeria's Context of Acute Violence* (Eugene, OR: Pickwick Publications, 2022), 179. See also Uchenna D. Anyanwu, "Staurocentric Pathways to Peacebuilding: Peacebuilding-Contextual Theology in Nigeria's Context of Acute Violence." PhD Dissertation, Fuller Theological Seminary, School of Intercultural Studies, 2020. Focus Group #1:467–471 refers to Focus Group Number 1: lines 467 to 471 of the transcribed text.

4   Anyanwu, "Staurocentric Pathways," 208.

an on-going trend of] increasing diversity in the United States and this is really the place you would expect there to be good collaboration because we already have people from all over the world in virtually every neighborhood."[5] As Todd reflected further on the Ghanaian proverb, he mused, "Why are Christians from the Global South simply invited to a table in the Global North when they should be found with everyone else in the kitchen? What would it mean to have Africans as decision-making hosts instead of being relegated as perennial guests? And why, in light of Revelation 7:9, are Black, indigenous, and people of color always invited to a White table?"[6]

**In the Kitchen of Global Christianity**

I consider my walk with Jesus and my involvement in global missions as a product of an awakening that swept through Nigerian universities and colleges following the end of the Biafra-Nigerian War (1967–1970). The ministries of the Nigerian Fellowship of Evangelical Students (NIFES), the Fellowship of Christian Students (FCS), and the Scripture Union (SU) in Nigeria produced eminent Nigerian Christian leaders, many of whom were discipled by Pa Sidney Elton—a British missionary whom the Lord used to raise many Christian leaders in the country.[7] While studying at the College of Technology Owerri (now The Federal Polytechnic, Nekede) and at Ahmadu Bello University, Zaria, my faith in Christ was shaped by the Evangelical and Pentecostal ministries of these campus ministries. It was at Ahmadu Bello University, Zaria, that I had the initial inkling toward cross-cultural service in regions beyond where Christ has not yet been named (Romans 15:20). Providentially, after my undergraduate studies and the one-year mandatory National Youth Service Corps (NYSC), the Holy Spirit led me to Calvary Ministries (CAPRO) School of Missions where I was exposed to the massive need of people groups who had yet to hear of Jesus's first Advent, let alone his second coming.[8] At CAPRO School of Missions, I made a commitment to volunteer in cross-cultural service and then came on board CAPRO after the training. Sensing the call to go North, my spouse, Dolapo, and I were sent to Senegal to first learn French in preparation for ministry in North Africa.

---

5   David Jacob, "EP34—Missionaries in an Age of Global Christianity with Dr. Todd Johnson," The Missionary Mobilization Podcast, 2021, accessed April 18, 2022, https://bit.ly/3dIC18r.
6   Todd M. Johnson, "All Peoples in God's Kitchen," May 12, 2021, https://www.gordonconwell.edu/blog/all-peoples-in-gods-kitchen/.
7   See Ayodeji Abodunde, *Messenger: Sydney Elton and the Making of Pentecostalism in Nigeria* (Lagos: Pierce Watershed, 2016).
8   Festus Ndukwe, ed. *From Africa to the World: The CAPRO Story: The Birth and Growth of a Mission* (Lagos: CAPRO Media, 2019).

In Dakar, Senegal, I had a first-hand encounter with global Christianity, among workers from Brazil, Canada, France, Germany, Switzerland, the United Kingdom, the United States, and some Asian countries. As is normal for many, I experienced culture shock interacting with these workers from different parts of the globe—with their differing perspectives of lifestyle and doing Christian ministry—for the first time. Shock happened with a French missionary serving with a Western mission-sending organization. As the leader of his organization's team in Senegal, he identified our CAPRO team's effectiveness in connecting with the Senegalese and the impact of our workers in Senegal. He sought to control our team, portraying our work as an outcome of theirs. I personally had no problems at all working with Westerners, but skirmishes arose when I challenged the controlling spirit the man sought to cast upon our CAPRO team. He did not, in my estimation, see us as collaborators in the work. There was a clear display of superiority from this French man over African indigenous workers. Using Todd's reference to the Ghanaian proverb, the French man did not welcome us sub-Saharan Africans into the kitchen of global Christian mission. We were seen as inferior, deemed ignorant in bearing witness and proclaiming our testimony of Jesus's works in our lives.

Another brush in the house of global Christianity happened when my family and I moved to North Africa where we lived and served a little shy of a decade. My spouse and I, along with couples from three continents, were part of a multi-national team in which we were the only Black Africans. It was great working together, learning to love Muslims and inviting them to see Jesus through our lives. Insofar as the kitchen of global Christianity is concerned, some Christians from the global North presume that, as the affluent and educated, they are the senders in missions. And moreover, that those from the global South (Africa, Asia, and Latin America), as the poor and less educated, are the ones in need of their resources and support. Those with this view are like that fellow who stood on the podium at the Wittenberg Conference of 2017 and said, "Africans are welcome at the table in this Evangelical movement." My experience in North Africa buttresses this point further. After some years in the North African city where we were serving, an American missionary confessed he had always thought that "we White Christians were superior to you Black Africans, but having observed you over these years, I have come to conclude I was mistaken." It took this American worker some years to see my spouse and me as collaborators in the kitchen of global Christian missions.

There was another dimension of which I had not previously been taught, and of which my interaction with Todd Johnson years later brought into focus—the dimension of global migration. In North Africa, droves of sub-Saharan Africans traverse one of our planet's driest, hottest, and windiest deserts, the Sahara

Desert, to arrive at the northernmost Mediterranean coastal towns and cities of North Africa. These coastal towns and cities from Alexandria to Tangier serve as transition points for thousands of young sub-Saharan Africans fleeing the harsh unpromising life in their countries of origin to seek entry into Europe by crossing not only the Sahara Desert but also the Mediterranean Sea. Those who survive crossing the Sahara reckon the Mediterranean as no obstacle to walking the streets of Europe where they hope to find green economic pastures and safe havens away from oppression and the lack of opportunities in their home countries. Scores die in the Sahara Desert and yet more in the Mediterranean, yet many are undeterred from the journey. Alongside this gruesome migration, I observed that the sub-Saharan "adventurers" (as they are often referred to in North Africa) took their faith along with them. In their transition camps in North Africa, they establish communities of worship, particularly those who profess faith in Christ. They appoint pastors among themselves, some of whom I got to know personally. They preached God's word and had their own theology of immigration that supported their daring adventure to enter Europe.

However, not all sub-Saharan Africans in North Africa were "adventurers," there are numerous professionals who migrate for education and work opportunities. Many sub-Saharan Africans travel to study in North African universities, particularly in Algeria, Morocco, and Tunisia. In 2003, when the African Development Bank was moved to Tunis due to political conflict in Côte d'Ivoire, a number of sub-Saharan African professionals and employees of the bank found their niche in Tunisia for over a decade until the bank relocated back to Côte d'Ivoire in 2014. Followers of Jesus among those studying or working in North Africa establish their own worship communities in the cities where they reside, study, and work. I did not understand that my encounters with the different faces of immigrants represented a genre of global Christianity until I got to know Todd Johnson.

With a deeper understanding of dynamics within global Christianity, I began to read retrospectively into my past encounters through new lenses. Indeed, it was through my interaction with Todd, that I mused to myself: Had I met this man years before moving to Senegal or North Africa, had I interacted with him and received his perspectives on global Christianity through "counting," perhaps I would have made some different contributions during the years I spent in the field. He recognized my prior experience in cross-cultural ministry and then gave me a nudge to earn a Doctor of Philosophy (PhD) degree. For him, the question Western Christians must ask regarding their brothers and sisters from the global South should not be, "What can the church do for indigenous peoples?" but instead, "What must the church learn from indigenous peoples?"—a question that Todd will tell you reflects the heart of Jesus Christ.[9] His polycentric approach to global Christianity enables him to see his non-Western brothers and sisters as people who must be invited not just to the table (and house of global Christianity and theology), but also to the kitchen where the missiology and theology of global Christianity are being initiated. Todd has invited me to that kitchen in a number of ways, but he had a hunch that I may not be as welcomed by some without certain academic credentials.

Todd values the voices and stories of people from a global perspective, especially those from the global South. He invites voices from the global South to contribute to volumes he and his co-researchers at the CSGC produce, such as the 10-volume Edinburgh Companions to Global Christianity series. Contributors to each volume include a range of ethnicities, countries of origins, Christian traditions, and are equally split between men and women. It is in this optic, I believe, that he sensed that whatever stories I could bring to the missiological kitchen, will require me earning a doctoral degree to be able to tell them in the kitchen of missiological conversations. He believed that going through the rigors of doctoral studies will sharpen my research and scholarly writing skills so that others in the kitchen who do not have his polycentric vision will probably (not assuredly) be at ease to permit me come into the kitchen.

**Encountering Globalization and Global Christianity**

I took a class with Todd during the fall semester of 2014, Trends in Global Christianity, and among the required reading was the volume: Bob Goudzwaard, Mark Vander Vennen, and David Van Heemst. *Hope in Troubled Times: A New Vision for Confronting Global Crises*. Three among the learning outcomes in the syllabus were that we, the students, were to

- Comprehend the expansion of the world Christian movement, especially in the past 100 years,
- analyze the role of globalization in the spreading of the gospel, and
- examine and assess the efforts of Christians to alleviate social problems.[10]

I encountered globalization and global Christianity through the academic rigor to which Todd subjected his students. My personal encounters with these subjects took different forms and are described here in two inter-related themes. The first

---

9 Todd M. Johnson, "A Path to All Peoples—Psalm 67," filmed April 12, 2022 at Gordon-Conwell Theological Seminary, 12:17–12:31, https://bit.ly/3dIC18r.
10 Todd M. Johnson, WM 684 Trends in Global Christianity Syllabus, Fall 2014, Gordon-Conwell Theological Seminary.

is what I refer to as the coming boomerang due to global exclusion, and second is the impact of people on the move (migration).[11]

*The Coming Boomerang Due to Global Exclusion*

I encountered the coming boomerang due to global exclusion while reading *Hope in Troubled Times*. Among the several paradoxes that the authors investigated is one they called "the paradox of rising global exclusion."[12] Whereas government leaders around the world endorsed the Millennium (now Sustainable) Development Goals, which included reducing world poverty, many poor countries continued to experience "persistent exclusion, an exclusion that leads to increased poverty." My argument in this respect is the possibility of a boomerang effect that such "persistent exclusion" may bring upon the wealthy nations. To some degree, that boomerang effect may already be manifesting itself in microcosmic dimensions.

Having lived and served in a West African Francophone country, I observed how one European wealthy super-power controls the economic and political affairs of many Francophone countries in Africa. The leaders of these African countries have their hands and heads tied to the iconic Champs Élysée in Paris, and, therefore, can hardly make policy decisions that will benefit and alleviate the sufferings and poverty of their people, because they must dance to the tunes of Paris. If they don't, the next most likely narrative will be the emergence of a rebel group (often the brainchild of the wealthy super-power) to oust the sitting authority in that given country. It has happened, for example, in Burkina Faso, Côte d'Ivoire, and Rwanda. As long as an African leader is dancing to the tunes dictated by the powerful superpowers with vested interest in his or her country, that leader may remain in power until death, even if the said leader rigs elections and maintains a long record of human-rights abuses. Think of Cameroon—a country where Paul Biya has ruled for over four decades because he does the bidding of a wealthy European super-power.

When any African leader objects to do the bidding of some powerful Western leaders, the latter sense the economic and foreign policy of their country threatened, and then they plot to oust the former. Such was the case in Côte d'Ivoire, Niger, Chad, and Central African Republic. Most wealthy super-powers in the West exploit the wealth of poor African countries, leaving them with little or

---

11   I use the term "boomerang" here to simply indicate an act originated by someone (often against another person or group of persons) that ultimately backfires to act on the originator of the act.
12   Bob Goudzwaard, Mark Vander Vennen, and David Van Heemst, *Hope in Troubled Times: A New Vision for Confronting Global Crises* (Grand Rapids, MI: Baker Academic, 2007), 149.

nothing to survive without paternalistic dependence.[13] Many young people from these countries, therefore, leave their home countries for Europe or other Western countries. By reason of linguistic affiliation, the immigrants prefer to migrate to the countries of their colonialists in search for greener economic pastures. Thus, immigrants from Francophone African countries make France or Belgium their destination, and those from Anglophone countries head to the United Kingdom, the United States, or Canada.

Migration produces a bittersweet experience. The sweet part is the blessing that diversity offers a society. Les Blues (the French national soccer team), for example, lifted the prestigious FIFA World Cup trophy in 2018. Venezuelan leader, Nicolas Maduro noted in regard to that triumph, "The French team looked like an African team, in fact it was Africa who won… France won thanks to African players or sons of Africans."[14] Similarly, *The Daily Show* host, Trevor Noah, on July 17, 2018, joked: "Africa won the World Cup." Of course, as would be expected such comments received rebuttals from notable French authorities, one of whom was the then French Ambassador to the United Nations and the United States, Gérard Araud. In his rebuttal letter to Mr. Noah, he wrote:

> I heard your words about an "African" victory. Nothing could be less true. As many of the players have already stated themselves, their parents may have come from another country, but the great majority of them, all but two out of 23 were born in France. They were educated in France. They learned to play soccer in France. They are French citizens. They're proud of their country, France. The rich and various backgrounds of these players are a reflection of France's diversity.[15]

Diversity can enrich a nation. On May 26, that same year (2018) barely two months prior to France winning the World Cup, a Malian illegal immigrant, Mamoudou Gassama, acted swiftly to scale the balconies of four floors to rescue an unsupervised four-year old child who was dangling on the balcony of an apartment complex in Paris. Despite being an illegal immigrant, Gassama's

---

13  A glaring example is the currency of 14 African countries that remains the CFA Franc—a currency originally tied to the French Franc, and now to the Euro. Twelve of these 14 countries are former French colonies. France resists attempts from these countries to establish their independent currencies not tied to France. Those countries are some of the poorest countries in the world and economists argue that it is an instrument of "monetary repression" and "economic slavery." See Martina Schwikowski, "Protests Mount Against Africa's 'Colonial' CFA Currency," DW.com, September 22, 2017, accessed May 13, 2022, https://bit.ly/3DYW8K6.
14  Ben McPartland, "'Africa Won the World Cup?': French Players (and Obama) Have Final Word," *The Local France* (blog), July 18, 2018, https://bit.ly/3Sf52rw.
15  Gérard Araud via Twitter, @franceintheUS, July 18, 2018.

bravery did not only earn him a sobriquet—"Spiderman"—but also French citizenship and a job with the French Fire Service. The French President, Emmanuel Macron, received him and thanked him for his bravery.[16] That again is part of the gains of diversity. To employ Todd's allusion: invite people of diverse backgrounds to the kitchen and not just to the table. His vision of invitation to the kitchen of global Christianity informs his position that "…diversity is good for our organizations. It's good for humanity because the Scriptures are so clear that we are to love our neighbor and welcome the stranger and it is good for the body of Christ because it honors the image of God in all of us."[17] I maintain, therefore, that the diversity which African immigrants creates in Western countries can, to a degree, be a blessing.

A possible boomerang effect can emerge due to "global exclusion." The authors of *Hope in Troubled Times* observe that, "The rich countries are playing with fire. Already now at their borders they experience intensified immigration pressure from the countries of the South. The United States struggles with its Mexican border; and Europe has developed into a kind of bastion, foiling the streams of people who try to reach the West in small boats or by swimming. The pursuit of guaranteed security by the privileged boomerangs and afflicts their own lives."[18] As the West continues to siphon to themselves the natural resources from the poor countries in the South, the young people from these poor countries are obliged to migrate to the West. And as their number continues to grow, I envisage that this migration trend might reach such a critical threshold that the rich countries will be unable to handle.

I draw from an observation I made upon visiting southern France in 2010. Many North African migrants (mostly Algerians, Moroccans, and Tunisians) who live in Montpellier and Marseille have between five and seven children per family, even though the French authorities taunt a figure of 2.01 children per woman as the average number of children per woman in France.[19] The question the French demographers apparently ignore is: "What segments of the French society are having these children?" The fact that ethnically White French people are having fewer children appears to escape their notice, whereas, on the other hand, immigrants from Africa are having many children. In Montpellier, I learned that North African immigrants have a saying: *J'attends mon septième enfant pour bâtir ma deuxième maison*—"I am expecting my seventh child in

---

16 Paul Pradier, "Quick-Thinking Migrant 'Spiderman' Who Saved a Child Becomes French Citizen," *ABC News*, September 13, 2018, https://abcn.ws/2Mo8Js4.
17 Johnson, "A Path to All Peoples."
18 Bob Goudzwaard, Mark Vander Vennen, and David Van Heemst, *Hope in Troubled Times: A New Vision for Confronting Global Crises* (Grand Rapids, MI: Baker Academic, 2007), 150.
19 "2.01: The Average Number of Children per Woman in France," last modified October 23, 2013, https://lc.ambafrance.org/2-01-the-average-number-of.

order to build my second house." One should not be surprised by such a saying for, in France, the more children you have, the more financial social assistance your family will receive, a real benefit for immigrant African communities. If the trend continues, how may this affect France a century from now? Intuitively, I estimate that the table may be turned upside down for ethnically White French people. I argue that the wealthy nations should not imagine that their control of all things will forever remain secured.

If wealthy Western countries are sincere, the reasonable and right thing to do is to invite the poor countries into their kitchens of wealth and empower poorer countries to develop so they can be positioned to provide good economic opportunities, employment, education, infrastructures, and security for their citizens, thus drastically reducing the migration trend. If the paradox of global exclusion continues, then we may expect in the coming century a boomerang effect upon the rich countries of the West.

*People on the Move: Nigeria Diaspora Churches in the West*

Toward the end of 2013, Todd gave me an assignment to research and prepare a presentation to the Gordon-Conwell Theological Seminary community a lunch forum titled, "People on the Move: Nigerian Diaspora Church Planting." In my preparation I encountered the work of World Christianity scholar Jehu Hanciles. In his volume, *Beyond Christendom*, he argued that patterns of South-North migration point to the West as a contemporary frontier of missionary engagement. He posits that "non-Western initiatives and movements are among the most powerful forces shaping the contemporary world order."[20] Hanciles encapsulates this argument with his fundamental thesis that "every Christian migrant is a potential missionary."[21] Thus, missionary activity and globalization, formerly viewed as a North-South movement, should henceforth be reconceived because of the impact these migrants are making in their destination Western lands.

There are positive aspects to the migration trends of Nigerian Christian immigrants in the West. In her contribution to the volume, *History, and Politics in Nigeria: Essays in Honor of Ogbu U. Kalu*, historian Edith Miguda points to the fact that "Nigerian pastors, evangelists and Christians have been

---

20  Jehu J. Hanciles, *Beyond Christendom: Globalization, African Migration, and the Transformation of the West* (Maryknoll, NY: Orbis, 2008), 37, 112, 277.
21  Hanciles, *Beyond Christendom*, 6, 296, 351, 378. At the time of this writing, Hanciles is taking an initiative to revisit his research that led to the publication of *Beyond Christendom*. In the new research he hopes to study new African immigrants and their descendants in the United States. Meanwhile, Hanciles' most recent volume on this subject amply demonstrates the role that immigrants play in the spread of Christianity and identifies it (migration) as a propelling force for change. See Jehu J. Hanciles, *Migration and the Making of Global Christianity* (Grand Rapids, MI: Eerdmans, 2021).

a significant part of the African drive to plant churches worldwide is in no doubt ... A visitor to some of the cities in Europe, America, Australia and indeed several other parts of the world, is likely to become quickly aware of the existence of these churches and fellowships."[22] A survey of literature on diaspora churches shows that Nigerian followers of Jesus establish churches wherever they are, and that they operate some of the fast-growing churches in those places. Examples include the Church of Nigeria North American Mission (CONNAM);[23] the Embassy of God, an Evangelical-Charismatic mega-church in Kyiv, Ukraine (even though affected by the 2022 Russian invasion of Ukraine); the Kingsway International Christian Centre in London and other cities in the United Kingdom; the Redeemed Christian Church of God in the United States, Europe, and throughout Asia; the Deeper Life Bible Church; and many other church plants of various Evangelical and Pentecostal Nigerian Christian immigrants. There are also cross-cultural church planting contributions of indigenous Nigerian mission-sending organizations that have raised leaders among formerly unreached people groups.

In a personal communication with missiologist Paul Borthwick, I posed the question: How is the movement of Nigerian Christians outside Nigeria impacting global missions? Borthwick's response was that the presence of the immigrant followers of Jesus in the West "brings the zeal and Pentecostal expectancy of the Nigerian church to North American and European communities that have little experience with true Christian faith, especially faith that looks more like the book of Acts than American/European world views that have been shaped by post-modern mindsets."[24] This assertion coheres with Hanciles' position. There are not only positive aspects to the migration trends of Nigerian Christian immigrants in the West, there are also negative dimensions.

Nigerians who travel to the West as missionaries often come with the same cultural insensitivity of the missionaries of the past. Borthwick, who teaches and trains leaders in many countries of the global South, illustrated this by pointing out the comment attributed to one leader whose country has received Nigerian missionaries: "Look out! The Nigerians are coming!" They try to import Nigerian-style Christianity and forms of evangelism to the West that may attract attention at first, but in the long run, demonstrate that the

---

22  Edith A. Miguda, "Encountering History: Christianity and Identity in Nigerian Diaspora Churches," in *Religion, History, and Politics in Nigeria: Essays in Honor of Ogbu U. Kalu*, ed. Chima J. Korieh and Ugo G. Nwokeji, 216–229 (Lanham, MD: University Press of America, 2005), 217.

23  CONNAM is the mission of the Church of Nigeria (Anglican Communion) in North America.

24  Personal email communication with Borthwick, who serves on the staff of Development Associates International, a training group dedicated to the character and ministry development of leaders in under-resourced areas. Borthwick teaches missions and serves as an Urbana/Missions Associate with Inter-Varsity Christian Fellowship.

missionaries are not very skilled at contextualization and understanding the culture they are trying to reach. Some come with the "wealth-and-health" and "name-it-and-claim-it" message that they proclaim, which leads to the long-term disillusionment of economically poor converts as it has done in Africa. And others come to "plant churches" but what they really do is to establish congregations for diaspora Nigerians and other Africans. The churches they plant may be wonderful, but they do little to venture into strategic outreach to the communities in which they are situated.

**Conclusion**

I am not the only one from the global South whom Todd has invited into the kitchen. He and his spouse, Tricia, live the same vision in their home through a demonstration of hospitality to international students. A vast majority of international students who study in the United States will bear witness to the fact that they may spend between four and six years studying in U.S. colleges and universities and never get invited into an American home. Tricia teaches English as a Second Language in the greater Boston area, where several highly regarded universities, colleges, and research institutes are situated. Tricia and Todd have hosted a number of international students in their home for meals, especially during the holidays. Typical American Evangelical Christians make their Thanksgiving dinner all about their own families, but the Johnsons regularly invite international students to their Thanksgiving meal, including my own family. At these festivities, the world is in their home, including in the kitchen. For some of these internationals from different parts of the world—Asia, Europe, and Latin America—Thanksgiving at the Johnsons was their first time in an American home.

The boundaries of Todd's calling, ministry, and scholarly work in the field of global Christianity does not end at the Center for the Study of Global Christianity, or at meetings and conferences where he delivers scholarly papers and makes presentations of his research findings, or in his classroom. Instead, he takes it home. Within the space that God has granted him and his family, he invites you not just to the table, but to the kitchen of global Christianity.

**Works Cited**

"2.01: The Average Number of Children per Woman in France." Last modified October 23, 2013, https://lc.ambafrance.org/2-01-the-average-number-of.
Abodunde, Ayodeji. *Messenger: Sydney Elton and the Making of Pentecostalism in Nigeria*. Lagos: Pierce Watershed, 2016.

Anyanwu, Uchenna D. *Pathways to Peacebuilding: Staurocentric Theology in Nigeria's Context of Acute Violence.* Eugene, OR: Pickwick Publications, 2022.

Anyanwu, Uchenna D. "Staurocentric Pathways to Peacebuilding: Peacebuilding-Contextual Theology in Nigeria's Context of Acute Violence." PhD Dissertation, Fuller Theological Seminary, School of Intercultural Studies, 2020.

Araud, Gérard, via Twitter, @franceintheUS, July 18, 2018, https://bit.ly/3Sv5q4N.

Goudzwaard, Bob, Mark Vander Vennen, and David Van Heemst. *Hope in Troubled Times: A New Vision for Confronting Global Crises.* Grand Rapids, MI: Baker Academic, 2007.

Hanciles, Jehu J. *Beyond Christendom: Globalization, African Migration, and the Transformation of the West.* Maryknoll, NY: Orbis, 2008.

Hanciles, Jehu J. *Migration and the Making of Global Christianity.* Grand Rapids, MI: Eerdmans, 2021.

Jacob, David. "EP34—Missionaries in an Age of Global Christianity with Dr. Todd Johnson." The Missionary Mobilization Podcast, 2021, accessed April 18, 2022, https://bit.ly/3dIC18r.

Jenkins, Philip. *The Next Christendom: The Coming of Global Christianity.* Oxford: Oxford University Press, 2002.

Johnson, Todd M. "A Path to All Peoples—Psalm 67," filmed April 12, 2022 at Gordon-Conwell Theological Seminary, https://bit.ly/3DYVVqi.

Johnson, Todd M. "All Peoples in God's Kitchen." May 12, 2021, https://www.gordonconwell.edu/blog/all-peoples-in-gods-kitchen/.

McPartland, Ben. "'Africa Won the World Cup?': French Players (and Obama) Have Final Word," *The Local France* (blog), July 18, 2018, https://bit.ly/3Sf52rw.

Miguda, Edith A. "Encountering History: Christianity and Identity in Nigerian Diaspora Churches." In *Religion, History, and Politics in Nigeria: Essays in Honor of Ogbu U. Kalu,* edited by Chima J. Korieh and Ugo G. Nwokeji, 216–29. Lanham, MD: University Press of America, 2005.

Ndukwe, Festus, ed. *From Africa to the World: The CAPRO Story: The Birth and Growth of a Mission.* Lagos: CAPRO Media, 2019.

Pradier, Paul. "Quick-Thinking Migrant 'Spiderman' Who Saved a Child Becomes French Citizen." *ABC News*, September 13, 2018, https://abcn.ws/2Mo8Js4.

Schwikowski, Martina. "Protests Mount Against Africa's 'Colonial' CFA Currency." DW.com, September 22, 2017, https://bit.ly/3DYW8K6.

Stanley, Brian. *The World Missionary Conference, Edinburgh 1910.* Grand Rapids, MI: Eerdmans, 2009.

Yeh, Allen L. *Polycentric Missiology: 21st-Century Mission from Everyone to Everywhere.* Downers Grove, IL: IVP Academic, 2016.

# Chapter 5: Reflections and Lessons from Massachusetts to Uganda

*Joseph Byamukama*

I first met Dr. Todd Johnson in my first semester at Gordon-Conwell Theological Seminary in September 2017. I cannot recall the exact circumstances that brought us together, but he and Dr. Gina Zurlo were teaching a class on Trends in Global Christianity at Boston University School of Theology that semester. He put out a word for any students interested in this class, a call that I and my brothers—Dan Challapalli from India and Tim Py from Spain—heeded. We often got into Todd's car on Monday evenings and headed for Boston, about an hour's drive from Gordon-Conwell without traffic (which is an almost assured reality in the evenings). I always enjoyed our car conversations, which were cordial, candid, and illuminating. Todd is such a good listener for a man with a treasure store of wisdom. One could mistake us being long-time friends having a good time together in the car. Whenever we arrived earlier in Boston and found street parking (he liked parking on Boston streets), Todd would often treat us to a meal, sometimes offering suggestions of certain Chinese delicacies, which never disappointed. Such were extended periods of talking and learning, but they also demonstrated Todd's humility in serving others.

One could see Todd's love for what he does. From our first meeting onward, I could sense how his commitment to the global nature of the Christian faith filled him with enthusiasm. He was genuinely interested in the various Christian traditions, and his class on global Christianity at Boston University School of Theology made no exception. During these classes, I was first introduced to the Orthodox Christian tradition. Most Ugandan Christians know nothing about the Orthodox faith, and, sadly, the majority don't care. I was one of those to whom "Orthodox" rung a distant tune. But in this class, Todd would invite different speakers, two of whom were Fr. Luke Veronis of the Greek Orthodox Metropolis of Boston, and Razak Siriani, formerly of the Syrian Orthodox Archdiocese of Aleppo-Syria. Those were eye-opening sessions for me as I began to appreciate how vast, varied, deep, and ancient is the Christian heritage. It was the first time that I listened to Orthodox Christians, and it was worth it. We chatted with Fr. Veronis about his short-term mission to Uganda and his experiences as a missionary to East Africa. Such interactions were enlightening for me, and it was through Todd that these conversations could be.

Todd maintains his global perspective as a hospitable man. When he and his wife, Tricia, hosted my wife and me, fully knowing we were Ugandans, they chose to treat us to Indian chapati bread and apple pie. We liked them. But Tricia did not stop there. She ensured that we found some Ugandan food in a nearby store to make us feel at home. Todd and Tricia have lived in spaces where they felt like strangers and knew a thing or two about being welcomed into a new world. If one looked around his sitting room, it was evident that Todd was well-traveled. While one could conversationally tell his genuine interest in other people's cultures, his house is a testimony to his global outlook and home of artifacts collected from his travels, from Turkey to Mongolia to Egypt. Todd's face lit up and his voice became warmer whenever he narrated the story associated with each relic. There was real meaning attached to each of his collected pieces, every object being a microcosm of the vast world he inhabits and the universal faith which he holds. Therefore, Todd occupies a global space even in his house, a testament to the capacity of his heart and vision for global missions. And Todd's global perspective is also proper for the institution he serves.

At first, I sought training at Gordon-Conwell because of its theological rigor and orthodoxy. But the seminary's diversity and the opportunity for my wife and me to experience the church of Christ outside our cultural confines was an added advantage. It is one thing to believe in the catholicity of our Christian faith but quite another to experience it. Gordon-Conwell was itself such a place of diversity where we met Christians from various denominational heritages, continents, and countries, and all gathered to be trained for their God-given ministry by a diverse faculty. That the seminary devotes a fully-funded scholarship toward training African pastors and scholars is proof of this. This scholarship made it possible for me to receive my much-needed theological training. There is a sense in which the school is itself a microcosm of the multiethnic body of Christ, and it is fitting that Todd works there. Our trio of persons (myself, Dan, and Tim) was itself representative of three continents—Africa, Asia, and Europe. We were naturally drawn to Todd not just for his lectures but also by his personality and work at the Center for the Study of Global Christianity (CSGC).

It is difficult to estimate the impact my encounters with Todd have had on my life, faith, and ministry since we do not often recall every building block God uses to shape our lives, but I can note a few. One, which I hinted at, is my increasing desire to learn from other rich heritages—especially that of the Greek Orthodox. Todd's class opened my eyes to the depth and diversity of our Christian story; this is not to say that I agree with everything in these heritages, nor that such traditions are monolithic in belief and expression. Yet, listening to Fr. Veronis and Siriani in my first semester at seminary helped me shed any caricatures I held toward these traditions while, at the same time, making me appreciate their contribution to the global Christian story. My other classes—such as Systematic Theology with Adonis Vidu and the Trinitarian and Christological Controversies with Don Fairbairn—helped me engage deeply with other Christian traditions. Nevertheless, the seeds were sown by Todd.

Todd's work also enabled me to appreciate data-driven missions. As their website reads, the CSGC, which Todd co-directs, "monitors worldwide demographic trends in Christianity." While the desire to use data to "educate, equip, and empower" is noble, the concept is still new and less appreciated within African Christianity and Ugandan churches. Other than census data, which is released every ten years in Uganda, there is not, to my knowledge, a Ugandan organization dedicated to providing data and statistics to assist Ugandan churches in mission and discipleship efforts. My encounter with the CSGC awakened my appreciation for data-driven discipleship and evangelism. Often, I would make my way to the Center's library and became fascinated to find material about Christianity from almost every corner of the world, including Uganda. The CSGC held materials on Uganda that I could not find elsewhere, not even in my favorite Ugandan Christian bookstores (though there are very few such stores). The dedication to studying the latest global Christian trends is unique to what Todd does and undoubtedly beneficial for scholars, students, and shepherds. My indebtedness to Todd lies in how his numbers and projections shape what we do at Veracity Fount, the organization I helped found in Uganda.

Veracity Fount seeks to conduct cutting-edge theological research that uses data and historical theology for discipleship in the context of Ugandan churches, which we aim to resource for their renewal. Veracity Fount started as an unregistered small-group discipleship ministry in 2013. With my theological training at GCTS and the onboarding of Derrick Ntambi and Mugenyi Allan as co-founders, we registered it in 2018 as a ministry to provide theological research, resources, and discipleship, with a forthcoming theological training component. As far as we know, we are the only organization dedicated to contextual and accessible theological research for the service of Ugandan churches. We want to research the demographics of Ugandan Christianity, asking questions such as how many Ugandans self-identify as Christians and to what beliefs do they subscribe? What do the numbers suggest regarding people's view of what it means to be Christian? Do we hold to biblical and orthodox Christianity? Such information becomes crucial for how Ugandan pastors can shepherd their people well. This task moves beyond data to discipleship, and such research must be accessible to the ordinary Christian or clergy rather than being reserved for academic library shelves. Such a study alerts leaders of local churches, theological institutions, and mission organizations to the existing ministry gaps and opportunities. We think that such data-driven efforts would ground Ugandan Christians in historic biblical Christianity, and such mission would mirror, in part, Todd's work but on a smaller and more contextual scale.

In discussing data considering historical theology, we would seek to keep the global nature of the Christian faith—its catholicity—at the heart of what we do and believe, especially in our quest to incarnate the gospel within our Ugandan context. My interactions with Todd have been crucial for this philosophy of ministry. Most Ugandan Christians seldom have a global and historical view of the Christian faith, which is why Orthodox Christianity seems so strange. Unfortunately, not many Ugandans know of Athanasius, Augustine, Cyril, or Cyprian. No wonder many, especially pan-African anti-theists, think Christianity in Africa is a colonial religion. Few Christians know the weapons in the armory of ancient African Christianity on the continent. It is not uncommon for many Ugandan Christians to ignore God's work in history and the rest of the world. Such can be the extreme consequences of "personal faith" or "my personal relationship with Jesus." Veracity Fount hopes to introduce our people to Christian catholicity in geographical and historical terms (space and time) and doctrine. To be one body—Christ's body—is to participate in a bigger story than ourselves, both in scope and time.

The CSGC also helped me appreciate our place in global Christianity, specifically as African thinkers. Todd's research opened my eyes to the Christian trends, especially Africa's place in the present and future Christian conversations. According to the CSGC, 2018 marked Africa's first year with the most Christians of any continent. Many have mentioned how the center of gravity of global Christianity has already shifted to the global South, and more Africans must understand the times we live in, like the sons of Issachar, "men who had understanding of the times, to know what Israel ought to do" (1 Chronicles 12:32). There is a sense in which God is positioning churches in Africa to lead the present and future global missional efforts, not just numerically but also strategically and theologically. Todd's work somewhat acts as a precursor, a prophetic prodding, and perhaps a warning concerning the task ahead for some of us in Africa, where Christianity is exponentially growing. As I trained at Gordon-Conwell, the future projections about Africa's place in Christianity sounded a warning bell for me. I realized the weight of responsibility my brothers and sisters in Africa must carry toward shaping Christian conversations not just in our village churches but also on the global stage. Such a daunting task must make every knee quake in a Moses-like resignation: "Lord, please send another."

The realization that Africa is quickly becoming the center of global Christianity prompted me to pursue a PhD. I recall conversations on our Boston trips with Todd and Dr. Zurlo about doctoral studies. Dr. Zurlo would warn of the torturous travails of the PhD student life. I suppose she didn't mean to scare us. If she did, she surely didn't succeed with me because the need for theologically trained leaders in Uganda triumphs over the material and mental cost of pursuing a doctorate. Churches in Africa are ill-equipped for their task in many aspects, and the most pressing problem is how most Ugandan pastors have no formal theological training—not even a certificate in theology. Indeed, the majority, especially rural Ugandan shepherds, do not have basic academic training and have not even read through the Bible once. Such shepherds cannot explain the core of the gospel or the biblical metanarrative. Thus, wrong teachings triumph, and discipleship efforts drag. The teachers need to be taught before they teach others, lest they remain blind leaders of the blind. We cannot afford not to train teachers of today and tomorrow. Hopefully, my doctoral studies will equip me to equip the many Ugandan pastors and leaders for their ministry work. But my conviction, in part, is goaded by Todd's work, which awakened me to the place Uganda and Africa occupy within global Christianity.

Meanwhile, my travel to the United States opened my eyes to American Christianity's embarrassment of riches compared to the poverty of Ugandan churches regarding resources. The need to equip churches in Africa for their task is overwhelming, but the West takes theological research for granted, knowing its significance. Access to sound theological resources is almost a given in many parts of America. If you don't live near a library, Amazon and eBay entice you with minimal shipping costs. Not so with where I live. Not only do we lack access to relevant and contextual theological research, but we also do not have easy access to existing research publications. Veracity Fount seeks to resource Ugandan churches towards their mission, and we join in existing labors to build Uganda's theological foundations. Part of our activities is providing a public theological library in Kampala, where pastors and laity can study, read, and research. Such places are rare but necessary if we are to strengthen the missional and discipleship efforts of the churches here. Through this, we hope to encourage reading, theological research, and study among Ugandan Christians and clergy and, in so doing, awaken them to the riches and catholicity of their Christian heritage. Building the library will take time and resources, but we are taking small and necessary steps. Hopefully, Ugandans can begin to own the Christian story as they receive encouragement from the African saints who lived centuries before us.

These initiatives are partially the consequences of Todd's influence on my life and ministry. I am genuinely grateful for my time with Todd as I continue to benefit from his efforts at the CSGC. Todd's prophetic work continues to awaken the global church to the need and opportunity to further the gospel in every context. It thus depends on us, his former students and current admirers, to do our part in building God's kingdom wherever the Lord has placed us. And when all is said and done, may we be found faithful in what we do, as we serve the universal kingdom that has no end.

# Chapter 6: Moments in Time
## Challenging the Fabric of Faith

*Jane Kyong Chun*

Dr. Todd Johnson changed the way I experienced my time at Gordon-Conwell Theological Seminary. He's the kind of person that will look at you, tell a dad joke, and talk about Kanye West all in the same conversation. If you catch him at a bad time, he can be a bit awkward—an endearing trait I have loved during my time working with him—but his sense of humor will have you howling in laughter. This only continues until 8pm, when he's asleep, since he's been working since at least 5am. He's what many would call a unicorn; we affectionately called him "The Toddfather," a good-natured nod to his uniqueness, and his importance in our lives. Todd's impact in my life has come in moments.

The first time I ever heard Todd speak was during orientation at seminary. The air was humid from the remnants of a lingering New England summer, making everything sticky in Gordon-Conwell's Alumni Hall. I remember grabbing food and going to our seats in assigned tables, where we were told to make painful small talk with others. My palms grew sweaty, and I kept going to wipe them with my napkin under the table just in case someone tried to shake my hand. After lunch and the introductions of staff members and a mini lecture about financial stewardship, I eyed the door, ready to book it back to my dorm room. Then, an honest-looking man seemingly no more than 50, walked over to the podium. He began to give an overview of something called "World Christianity." It was the first time I had heard the term, and it was the first time that I had truly seen Christianity through the lens of the world. For ten minutes, Todd spoke of a global Jesus. He showed everyone graph after graph of trends of a Christianity that pushed the boundaries of the Western world before shuffling quickly into his seat. After everything was done, he was out the door before I could go up to him and ask more.

After that lecture, I didn't see Todd again for two years, until his colleague Dr. Gina Zurlo gave a guest lecture in my Systematic Theology II class. After running up to her and breathlessly asking, "Can I work for you?," I found myself at the Center for the Study of Global Christianity for Mentored Ministry and then as a research assistant. This unassuming student worker job in Building D at the bottom of the hill proved to become the most important experience of my time in seminary. Every week, my perspective on Christianity was broken open and decentered.

Although Dr. Zurlo was my mentor, Todd continued to make himself available and offered counsel during this time of discovery (of global Christianity) and decentering (of White male Christianity). It's not every day when one of the main people to help you walk out of White male thought is, curiously, a White male, but that's emblematic of Todd.

During his installation sermon as an endowed faculty chair at Gordon-Conwell, he whipped up jokes about his time in Cambodia, with YWAM, riling up the congregation into uproarious laughter, just to break down about the one lone boy that stood up in the middle of his Bible study that, to him, felt inadequate in front of children whose lives have been ravaged by war. He could not hold back tears as he recalled the moment the young Cambodian boy stood up to ask him, "Who is this Jesus, that the wind and waves obey him?" I looked on in awe and respect as Todd introduced the orphan and refugee to many Americans at Gordon-Conwell that day.

In this way, through things big and small, Todd has always been the type of teacher to inform his students in a sobering way that the world does not, in fact, revolve around the American church. From teaching global Christianity to incorporating rap and pop culture into relevant coursework, Todd is an active listener who challenges his students and peers to think critically about pressing issues. His knowledge of global Christianity and his belief in the beauty of diversity directly inform his passion for racial and social justice at home.

In 2021, I was awarded a Pastoral Study Project Grant from the Louisville Institute and provided an opportunity to study Korean churches in New England. Naturally, as a young woman in her mid-to-late twenties just beginning to embark on social scientific research on religion, I panicked and reached out to my mentors, Dr. Zurlo and Dr. Johnson. He told me to never underestimate the power of prayer and talked about his spiritual formation. He said, "Jane, the opportunity that you have before you to get your feet wet is unique. It is an opportunity that doesn't come by often—so do it excellently, see how you feel about it, see it through, and then decide what you will do from there." It's been several years since we had this conversation, but his words continue to stick with me as I grow in my calling and career.

Any interaction with Todd is a potential opportunity to challenge the fabric of your faith and your convictions, not because he's judgmental, but because of his high calling of service of others and working in diverse spaces. Todd's person and work have changed the course of my life for the better. I owe so much of who I am to him, Gina Zurlo, and the Center for the Study of Global Christianity. I was not always glad to be at Gordon-Conwell, but for them alone, I am so glad I went—that is how valuable Todd Johnson truly is. I am proud to have been his student and research assistant; I am honored to let him know how influential he is in my life.

# Chapter 7: Dismantling the Ethnic Foods Aisle in Theological Libraries

*James Marion Darlack*

My vision for theological librarianship was profoundly changed under the influence of Todd M. Johnson—particularly while studying and traveling with him in the Global Christianity and Development track of Gordon-Conwell Theological Seminary's Doctor of Ministry program. I first met Todd when the Center for the Study of Global Christianity moved to the seminary's Hamilton Campus (where I served as a librarian). The seminary was blessed to receive a collection of books and archives unsurpassed in its relevance to the demographic study of global Christianity. This collection served as an excellent complement to the holdings in Goddard Library—a traditional Western theological library.

Todd is best known for his demographic description of the church, but I have learned from his passion for amplifying the often-squelched voices of the Majority World. This passion is on full display in his blog post on "Dismantling the Ethnic Foods Aisle in Christianity."[1] Referencing the history of the "Ethnic Foods Aisle" in American grocery stores, he highlighted how global theological voices are inadvertently marginalized in Western theological libraries. At the grocery, Western cuisine is on full display in nearly all of the store, while "ethnic foods" are relegated to a single aisle. Similarly, he states,

> "Theology" is in the main part of the library while "ethnic theology" is relegated to its own small section. Like the grocery store, the library considers White contributions to be without context, while assigning non-White contributions an "ethnic" adjective. In so doing, both the library and the grocery store don't match reality.

Of course, the "reality" to which Todd refers is the profound demographic change that has occurred in Christianity over the past century—where the vast majority of Christians now reside outside of North America and Europe. Todd goes on to ask:

> What can be done for grocery stores and theological libraries? Increasingly, many grocery stores are stocking food from ethnicities all around the world in every aisle, and consumers are delighting in discovering new and delicious flavors to supplement and complement old favorites. Why not take a similar approach for theology?

---

1 Todd M. Johnson, "Dismantling the Ethnic Foods Aisle in Christianity," September 8, 2021, https://www.gordonconwell.edu/blog/dismantling-ethnic-foods-aisle/. See Priya Krishna, "Why Do American Grocery Stores Still Have an Ethnic Aisle?," *New York Times*, August 10, 2021, https://www.nytimes.com/2021/08/10/dining/american-grocery-stores-ethnic-aisle.html.

So, indeed, what can be done? In answer to Todd's query, I have outlined a few thoughts on dismantling the ethnic foods aisle in theological libraries. These thoughts were formed in no small part through Todd's influence on my own thinking as a librarian and as a global Christian.

"Dismantling the ethnic foods aisle" in theological libraries is a task that goes beyond simply changing shelf locations or adding titles. The problematic location of non-Western theologies in the "ethnic aisle" of the library is often the result of quirks inherent to library taxonomies. Much has been written about the biases of the Dewey Decimal System and the Library of Congress Classification system—let alone the problematically named "Anglo-American Cataloging Rules."

Indeed, every aspect of the library stands to be re-thought in terms of the demographic shifts taking place in Christianity and the attendant appreciation for its diverse history.[2] This re-thinking needs to move beyond collecting "adjective-theologies" or "adjective-hermeneutics" (though it must include them). Rather, this re-visioning seeks to place what historian Andrew F. Walls calls "the cross-cultural progression of the church" at the center of all theological studies—recognizing that even "traditional" Western theologies of the *Minority* World are deeply rooted in the enculturation of the gospel into Northern Europe and are no less "contextualized" than any other "adjective-theology."[3] This is not to minimize the rich heritage of scholastic and Reformation theology, nor downgrade the contributions of Greco-Roman philosophy to the Creeds. Nor is it to abandon solid exegetical practices that give proper place to authorial intent. Rather, it is to acknowledge that the deep roots of *Minority* World theology (that is, Western theology) are firmly planted in their own context along with other trees in other soils. To serve the church of the 21st century and beyond, theological libraries need to move beyond the European hegemony on Christian scholarship and give voice to Majority World theologies.

So, how can this be achieved? In what way can theological libraries move beyond the traditional role of "repository" and take on the role of "amplifier"? Are there ways that traditional Western theological libraries can leverage the depths of their collections and the experiences of their librarians to benefit the global church?

Amplifying global voices in the library often requires concentrated efforts on collecting materials from small publishers, and this can be facilitated through networks of students and alumni worldwide. I know that obtaining relevant Majority World publications can be a perennial problem for understaffed (and

---

2  On this statement, see the seminal article by Lamin O. Sanneh, "Global Christianity and the Re-Education of the West," *The Christian Century* 112, no. 22 (July 19, 1995): 715–18.

3  Andrew F. Walls, *The Cross-Cultural Process in Christian History: Studies in the Transmission and Appropriation of Faith* (Maryknoll, NY: Orbis Books, 2002).

underfunded) libraries. Many small (but important!) theological publishers do not have a presence in the United States, and they lack the licensing necessary to sell their publications out-of-country. In cases like this, perhaps library staff could work with students from under-represented global contexts in identifying these publishers and working out acquisition agreements.

Incorporating these materials—especially non-English texts—into a collection is no easy task. An example from my own experience is telling: In 2015, Gordon-Conwell's Goddard Library received a large donation of several thousand theological and devotional works published in Mandarin in support of a Doctor of Ministry program for Chinese pastors. Such a donation would have languished in boxes were it not for the donor's provision of funds for hiring a theological librarian with knowledge of the subject area, language, and Christian publishing industry. We were blessed to hire one of our alumni with all the skills necessary, but unfortunately, librarians with proficiencies in both language and theology are hard to find. Given this need, perhaps Western theological librarians could intentionally recruit student employees with language proficiency and the ability to learn basic library skills. These students could be recruited to serve in Western libraries as "amplifiers" of global theology, or they could serve as librarians in their own global contexts.[4]

While we were able to collect and catalog valuable Mandarin materials, two specific circumstances made the collection less than useful in serving the target audience. First, the academic program for which the collection was purchased met only occasionally in the United States. Due to visa concerns participating students were on-site for only one meeting of their cohort. Thus, this print collection was essentially inaccessible, and the texts were simply not available electronically. This kind of situation could be remedied in part through the systematic digitization of texts circulated through controlled Digital Lending, where materials are digitized in-house and made available in a manner that considers copyright restrictions.[5]

The other issue minimizing the effectiveness of the collection is that most of these books were written by Western authors and translated *into* Mandarin. Thus, while they could still be a useful resource to those without proficiency in English, they did not reflect a contextualized Chinese theology. Rather they

---

4 In a recent Atla "Listening Session on Diversity, Equity, and Inclusion," multiple librarians expressed the need to recruit international students for the sake of the profession. Atla's International Theological Librarianship Education Task Force is currently producing a series of open access publications designed to introduce the skills of theological librarianship to those without formal training in librarianship (see *The Theological Librarian's Handbook*). https://bit.ly/3fj9LtC.

5 On "Controlled Digital Lending," see https://controlleddigitallending.org/ as well as Brandon Board and Karl Stutzman, "Controlled Digital Lending: An e-Book Solution When There Is No e-Book?," *Atla Summary of Proceedings* 74 (December 2020): 157–65; James Darlack, Drew Baker, and Thomas E. Phillips, "Controlled Digital Lending … On the Quick and Cheap," *Atla Summary of Proceedings* 75 (2021): 233–36.

are a prime example of the export of the "West to the rest." So, libraries need to consider how to help facilitate the *production* of contextualized theology by becoming centers of student-faculty-practitioner collaboration. Here, libraries can shine by providing the space and resources necessary for students to produce and publish contextual theology—or at the very least—theologies that approach topics through multi-hued lenses. Librarians can then assist in making these writings more visible through institutional repositories and open access publication.

Theological librarians can also serve as advocates for the use of contextual theologies in the classroom by helping professors build syllabi and reading lists with materials that reflect the global church. For instance, a reading course could require a student to compile, read, index, and abstract contextual theologies on a particular topic. That index and collection of abstracts could then be used for collection development or to build an online research guide. Another potential assignment would be akin to the 1,000 Women in Religion project sponsored by the American Academy of Religion, the Society of Biblical Literature, and Atla.[6] In that project, the goal is to add 1,000 biographical entries on women in religion to Wikipedia. Students in a particular class could be assigned various topics and individuals could use their research to edit and create articles highlighting Majority World perspectives.

A theological library is more than a collection of books and databases. It is more than the services provided by dedicated librarians. It is far more than brick and mortar. At its most ideal, a theological library is a tangible representation of the people of God throughout the ages and round the world. In its stacks are heard the whispers of the historic church from "every nation, tribe, people and language." The theological library provides space to study and contemplate the experience, theology, and worship of the body of Christ throughout time, but it also serves as an amplifier of the globally diverse contemporary church. A rich feast awaits the reader in the theological library, where every aisle displays the many-flavored theologies of the global church.

**Works Cited**

Board, Brandon, and Karl Stutzman. "Controlled Digital Lending: An e-Book Solution When There Is No e-Book?" *Atla Summary of Proceedings* 74 (December 2020): 157–65.

Darlack, James, Drew Baker, and Thomas E. Phillips. "Controlled Digital Lending … On the Quick and Cheap." Atla Summary of Proceedings 75 (2021): 233–36.

---

6 https://en.wikipedia.org/wiki/Wikipedia:WikiProject_Women_in_Religion

Johnson, Todd M. "Dismantling the Ethnic Foods Aisle in Christianity." September 8, 2021, https://www.gordonconwell.edu/blog/dismantling-ethnic-foods-aisle/.

Krishna, Priya. "Why Do American Grocery Stores Still Have an Ethnic Aisle?" *New York Times*, August 10, 2021, https://www.nytimes.com/2021/08/10/dining/american-grocery-stores-ethnic-aisle.html.

Sanneh, Lamin O. "Global Christianity and the Re-Education of the West." *The Christian Century* 112, no. 22 (July 19, 1995): 715–18.

Walls, Andrew F. *The Cross-Cultural Process in Christian History: Studies in the Transmission and Appropriation of Faith.* Maryknoll: Orbis Books, 2002.

# Chapter 8: Who *Are* These People?
## A Rediscovery from Ephesians 3 and 4

*Darrell Dorr*

From May 2008 to June 2009 I had the privilege of working with the international team that produced the *Atlas of Global Christianity* (Edinburgh University Press, 2009). Editors Todd Johnson and Kenneth Ross assembled this team and did a remarkable job of shepherding the *Atlas* to completion by the autumn of 2009, with the *Atlas* released to the public later that year. My own heart and mind were shaped by this 400-page collection of maps, tables, and essays.

Though it was already widely known that Christianity's center of gravity had shifted to the non-Western world, the *Atlas of Global Christianity* helped the public to better understand the contours and textures of that shift—region by region—over the 100 years since the seminal 1910 Edinburgh World Missionary Conference. And the *Atlas of Global Christianity* appeared on the scene just in time to inform the array of global mission consultations in 2010—in Tokyo, Edinburgh, Cape Town, Boston, and other cities—that commemorated Edinburgh 1910 and launched new forms of cooperation in world mission into the twenty-first century.

**Odd Curiosities or Treasured Family?**

In 2008–2009, as I rolled up my sleeves and began my work as an Associate Editor, I expected that I would gain new insights in the process of editing. But what I did not expect was how the *Atlas* would affect my *heart* as well as my *head*. This personal impact was due, in part, to the convergence of my work on the *Atlas* with a sermon series at my home church (thank you, Greg Waybright, then senior pastor of Lake Avenue Church), a sermon series on the first chapters of Ephesians, where the Apostle Paul elaborates the "grand plan of God" in which (emphases mine):

> His intent was that now, *through the church, the manifold wisdom of God* should be made known to the rulers and authorities in the heavenly realms … And I pray that you, being rooted and established in love, may have power, *together with all the saints,* to grasp how wide and long and high and deep is the love of Christ, and to know this love that surpasses knowledge—that you may be *filled to the measure of all the fullness of God* . . . until we all reach unity in the faith and in the knowledge of the Son of God and *become mature, attaining to the whole measure of the fullness of Christ.* (Ephesians 3:10; 3:17–19; 4:13, *NIV*)

These truths from Ephesians were rattling around in my mind and heart while I edited essays from scholars representing Orthodox, Catholic, Pentecostal, Anglican, West African, Southeast Asian, Central American, East European, and many other streams of Christianity. As I read and re-read about streams of Christian vitality that are very different from my stream of American Evangelical Protestant Christianity, I began to ask myself, "Who *are* these people? Am I—and are most of the readers of this *Atlas*—likely to look on these people as odd curiosities, almost like animals in a theological and sociological zoo? Or—as these great texts of Ephesians affirm—am I, and are we, prepared to view these very different people as treasured family through whom we can apprehend the manifold wisdom of God, with whom we can grasp the love of God, and with whom we can enter the 'fullness of Christ' for which we were created? Do I really believe these truths from Ephesians, and do my perspectives on the global Church—and my behaviors—reflect what I say I believe?"

**Great Maps and Tables, But Don't Miss the Essays!**

As expected, the maps, tables, and other graphics attracted lots of attention to the *Atlas*. But my ruminations on Ephesians 3–4 were deepened even more by the sterling collection of two-page essays interspersed amid the series of map spreads, for the essays brought additional depth and nuance to the Ephesians 3–4 tapestry. My favorite essays included:

- Moonjang Lee on the future of global Christianity
- Andrew Walls on Christianity across 20 centuries (a masterful overview)
- J.N.K. Mugambi on Christianity in Africa (this critique has bite!)
- Ogbu Kalu on Western Africa (full of color and verve)
- Mark Noll on Christianity in Northern America (a terrific synthesis)
- Lamin Sanneh on the multi-cultural tapestry of World Christianity
- Dana Robert on the 100-year patterns in missionary sending
- Jonathan Bonk on Christian finance (vignettes of sacrifice and stewardship)

**Repercussions for Frontier Mission**

Since I'm a member of a missionary order that focuses on frontier mission among least-reached peoples, I was especially grateful for those parts of the *Atlas* that shed light on the challenges of frontier mission. Most of this material can be found in Part IV (Peoples, languages, and cities) and Part V (Christian mission).

For example, there is much benefit in such tables as "Global peoples with the most Muslims" and "Global languages with the most Buddhists." Delineation of the religious demographics of major cities in each world region is fascinating and useful; I soaked in the tallies of cities to allow my mind and heart to be moved. I liked the missionary scatterplot diagrams that revealed, region by region, where missionaries were and weren't, and the representations of missionaries received by people group, revealing the great need for pioneers among peoples such as the Northern Luri of Iran, the Lampungese of Indonesia, the Bagri of India, the Daza of Chad, and the Zaghawa of Sudan.

The *Atlas* also included portrayals of the extent of personal contact between Christians and non-Christians, including the assertion, "Buddhists, Hindus and Muslims have relatively little contact with Christians. In each case, over 86% of these religionists globally do not personally know a Christian." I contrasted these pages with those explaining a "Responsiveness Index" for different countries and regions, with the index revealing that the world's least-evangelized sectors have shown the highest average responsiveness to Biblical witness. Go figure!

**An Embarrassment of Riches in 2010**

The *Atlas of Global Christianity* was part of an embarrassment of riches in 2010, the first installment in a series of great reference tools that came to include Patrick Johnstone's *The Future of the Worldwide Church* and Jason Mandryk's new edition of the much-loved *Operation World* handbook. Inevitably, the *Atlas* was compared to and contrasted with these other two books, even though the *Atlas* is a larger and more expensive tool, includes an electronic "presentation assistant," and was written for a wider audience than that of the Evangelical mission community. Indeed, I expect that some Evangelicals have approached the *Atlas* with ambivalence: admiration for its scope and breadth, yet unease at its insistence at pressing beyond the social bounds of Evangelicalism. Yet I was honored to be part of an editorial team that married Evangelical conviction to ecumenical perspective.

**Reprise:** *World Christian Encyclopedia, Third Edition*

Many of the *Atlas* memories—and the Ephesians 3–4 ruminations—came flooding back into my heart in 2018–2019, when once again I volunteered with a few other editors and specialists to help Todd Johnson and Gina Zurlo bring the third edition of the *World Christian Encyclopedia* to completion (Edinburgh University Press, 2019). As I wielded my editing pen, I was also reading for my own edification, and I was especially impressed by Brent Fulton's portrayal of how the Church in China has deeply internalized the biblical emphasis on suffering as a necessary (and privileged) participation in the life of Christ.

Wow, I thought: our Chinese sisters and brothers have much to teach middle-class Americans in this regard.

## Reinforcement from Andrew Walls and John Flett

Todd Johnson and I are part of the (Ralph and Roberta) Winter extended family, and we've been wonderfully enriched over the years by the fellowship and iron-sharpening-iron dynamics in this extended family. I'm indebted to another Ralph Winter son-in-law, Brad Gill, for recently sharpening my Ephesians 3–4 sensitivities further by pointing me to how John Flett has built on the work of Andrew Walls. In this book *Apostolicity*, Flett fuses two of Walls' writings: "The full stature of Christ is revealed only as a fresh cultural entity is incorporated into the church, which is his body."[1] This indicates the nature of the body's own maturity. The "full stature of Christ" (Eph 4:13) occurs only in this cultural encounter and exchange. "Only 'together,' not on their own, can we reach his full stature."[2] I'm so grateful that Walls and Flett have given more eloquent voices to insights I first stumbled into during 2008–2009, and which I've sought to articulate since then.

## Discoveries in Greater Seattle

Since October 2015, my wife and I have lived in a northern suburb of Seattle, and in these recent years I've recognized that Ephesians 3–4 insights have colored and filtered a variety of my experiences in this metro region. A great blessing!

For example, a little south of my home is St. Mary's, a large Coptic Orthodox Church that is a hub for the Coptic community in the metro region. Much of the Coptic tradition seems odd or jarring to me, but I'm so grateful that these brothers and sisters are part of my neighborhood, for they challenge and stretch and complement me, and I'm glad that the essays and maps of the 2010 *Atlas* alerted me that they, too, are part of my treasure. I still have much to learn!

And I'm so grateful for the predominantly Black churches in greater Seattle. (I'll give a particular shout-out to Mt. Zion Baptist Church.) Their sermons have a prophetic edge on racial justice, reminding me that there's a time and place for sharp, unequivocal language. Their music reappropriates the lament of the Psalms, reminding me that I can give voice to the full range of my emotions. And I'm grateful that my own church (predominantly White) is learning more

---

1 Andrew F. Walls, "Old Athens and New Jerusalem: Some Signposts for Christian Scholarship in the Early History of Mission Studies." *International Bulletin of Missionary Research* 21, no. 4 (1997): 148.

2 Andrew F. Walls, "The Ephesian Moment: At a Crossroads in Christian History," in *The Cross-Cultural Process in Christian History* (Maryknoll, NY: Orbis Books, 2004), 77.

and more (albeit slowly) from these Black brothers and sisters, with discoveries heightened by the nationwide discussions about race in the United States in 2020–2022.

Then there are the Koreans—thank God for the Koreans! About an hour east of my home is a YWAM base that is predominantly (though not exclusively) Korean-American, and this community has honed my appreciation for the zeal, faith, enterprise, generosity, and resilience of the Korean Church. I also love the glimpses I've received of the intergenerational discussions in the Korean-American church and of their desire to shape their young adults in Christ.

My family lived in the United Kingdom during most of the 1990s, and that's when I first gained an appreciation for the Anglican tradition (and especially its Evangelical wing). But I've found that in my current season of life, as I approach my 65th birthday, I'm drawn even more to the strengths of the Anglican Church and am pleased that I can occasionally tap into Anglican riches represented by churches in greater Seattle, many of whom are part of the Anglican Church in North America. As an InterVarsity student in the 1970s, I was drawn to the life of the sanctified mind, as modeled by John Stott and J.I. Packer. As a grandfather, I now am helped when I eclectically appropriate the rhythms and structures of Anglicanism.

**Evangelical Conviction with Ecumenical Perspective**

I earlier observed that, in 2008–2010 work on the *Atlas*, I was honored to be part of an editorial team that married Evangelical conviction to ecumenical perspective. Todd Johnson has epitomized that integration for many years; I've been delighted to be a Barnabas who can testify to the grace of God in and through him. I'm indebted to Todd for pulling me into a few of his initiatives, and for opening the door for me to appropriate Ephesians 3 and 4 in new ways.

**Works Cited**

Walls, Andrew F. "Old Athens and New Jerusalem: Some Signposts for Christian Scholarship in the Early History of Mission Studies." *International Bulletin of Missionary Research* 21 no.4 (1997): 146–53.

Walls, Andrew F. *The Cross-Cultural Process in Christian History*. Maryknoll, NY: Orbis Books, 2004.

# Chapter 9: Story as a Bridge to Understanding
## The Role of Narrative in Creating Global Empathy

*Sharon Ellis*

In season three of the science fiction television series, *Battlestar Galactica* (2004–2009), Lt. Tucker "Duck" Clellan—a character that the audience had spent the last season coming to know—blows himself up in a suicide bomb attack on the sentient robots occupying New Caprica and oppressing a human colony seeking to establish a new home. Suddenly, suicide bombings, a concept far removed from the vast majority of the show's audience, associated only with rare foreign news stories, became personal. The audience had witnessed the crucial events that brought Duck to accept this mission. They had experienced the dreadful suspense of hoping someone would stop him before it was too late. They felt the shock, disbelief, and horror as the man pushed the trigger. What he did was not mindless, it was done out of desperation—something the audience could understand because they had been pulled into the story and into the lives of the characters. They had developed empathy for someone who committed a horrendous act, empathy that could then be translated from the world of science fiction and find a place in reality.

Story, when done well, has the incredible ability to foster identification. It allows us to enter into the thoughts, hopes, dreams, and fears of another—even those who are vastly different from ourselves. Far too often we find ourselves idolizing our group identity, whether that be religious, ethnic, or political, subsequently causing those outside of our clans to be seen as opponents. They are the ones who are unlike us, who look different, sound different, or pray differently and so they become viewed as fearsome entities rather than living, breathing human beings. Many of us are also beginning to realize (while others have known for a long time) just how nationalistic our world is and is increasingly becoming, with populations pitted one against another both domestically and internationally. Founding myths and national stories all play a part in forming our perspective on the world. Unfortunately, these tales tend to be one-sided, convincing the listeners that only their perspective is the correct one.

Listening to a single story is dangerous. It is akin to blinders that prevent us from seeing the rest of reality. We need to recognize the multiplicity of stories that exist in this world—ours is not the only story, nor is it the most important. In his reflections on his experience volunteering with a peacebuilding ministry in the West Bank, Michael McRay remarks that there is in fact a danger to hearing the stories of those who are different from us. He writes, "Such stories are indeed dangerous because they threaten our preconceptions and routines of privilege. The more [we] make [ourselves] vulnerable to these 'from below' stories, the more some false part of [us] dies and some new, truer part springs to life."[1] The hearing of such stories and the opening of ourselves to stories from elsewhere in the world serves to propel us toward peacemaking and reconciliation rather than alienation and retaliation against the other.

Those who have had the privilege to sit under Dr. Todd Johnson's teaching, or simply converse with him, know that he is an avid advocate for listening to the stories of others. He is determined to upset the power imbalance in World Christianity and longs to see the church of Europe and North America learn from the church of the global South. He does this by telling a wide array of stories, by pointing out blind spots in our worldviews, by stocking the library of the Center for the Study of Global Christianity with books that speak of Christianity around the globe, and advocating for a reassessment of the way the church and theological education in the West perceives theology and academia coming from the global South—reinforcing the statement that all theology is contextual, regardless of where in the world it comes from. Todd presents the Christian faith as diverse, multicultural, and colorful, because that is in fact what it looks like. Moreover, it is a reality he continues to promote to those within religious and academic work around the world.

It was that same desire to help people reassess their perspectives on those who are different that drew me into photography and storytelling. Over the years I have been gifted with opportunities to hear the stories of people from around the world. I have witnessed the generosity and hospitality of individuals on the streets of far-flung cities as they allowed me to step into their world and capture a moment of their life through my lens. I have been welcomed into the homes of strangers and invited to partake in their lives, even if only for a few hours. I have heard the stories of men and women who have faced extreme hardship and yet continue to choose hope, joy, and kindness. It is an honor and privilege to be welcomed into such vulnerable spaces and I am very much aware that my subjects are placing their trust in me, trusting that I will tell their stories truthfully and that the way I portray them in photographs will be honoring.

When I set out into photography my desire was to capture glimpses of the world for an audience who had never seen it. I longed for people from my own country of origin, with their preconceived notions of what it means to be Buddhist or Muslim, to see people who held those faiths in a different

---

1 Michael T. McRay, *Letters from "Apartheid Street": A Christian Peacemaker in Occupied Palestine* (Eugene, OR: Cascade Books, 2013), 101.

light, recognizing their earnest searching for truth and desire to do what is right. I wanted people to look past the media images of places like war-torn Afghanistan and focus instead on the tenacity of a people who would not back down, how their laughter and dancing amid adversity was a form of resistance, and the emergence of a new generation of artisans being trained up in the ways of their forefathers—among them, women.

The goal was not so much in building up and supporting the bearers of these stories, but rather to help those in their ivory towers in the West to see the beauty, strength, and nobility that the rest of the world held. Consequently, there lies a danger of the people themselves being overlooked in such interactions. While many have welcomed me into their personal world, over the years I became conscious of the fact that both my White face and my camera can be threatening to some. Unfortunately, this was at times overlooked in such interactions.

In my early twenties I spent some time in Botswana photographing various communities I visited. I remember being painfully aware of the way Africa had so often been portrayed in much of Western media and photography. I was hesitant at first to ask people if I could take their photo, knowing that cameras had done damage in that region. To this day I still remember the strength, dignity, and hospitality of the men and women I photographed there, and the joy and laughter of the children. That time in Botswana served as the beginning of my own journey in asking: how does one honor people and ensure that they are not being used to push yet another White agenda? I have come to believe that the role of storytellers such as myself must be two-fold: helping educate the audience whose eyes we are trying to open, while also seeing and caring for those who stand before us and whose stories we are capturing.

I recall Todd emphasizing on several occasions that people can tell when they are a project. His conviction of valuing people as they are, not as a means to an end, was and continues to be a challenge to me in the work I do. How can I care for them and value them in the moment? One way is to learn about their faith, their practices and their beliefs, recognizing that there is no such thing as a homogenous group in which everyone in that particular group is identical. The stories I have been given the opportunity to tell come from across the globe, many from those who claim a different faith from my own—each story differing greatly. In my work I have discovered immense beauty in the lives of those who are different from myself, what they contribute, and how I can learn from them. Todd also imbedded this truth in his teachings: we can always learn from other faiths, even if we do not necessarily agree with them. In a world where the other is questioned, doubted, kept at arms-length, Todd encourages his students to learn from those who are different from us. The place of mutual respect, recognition, and valuing of those from other religious practices is crucial, not only in the work of academia, but also in being a follower of Jesus—a calling that requires humility and learning to see through the eyes of another so that we might better love in the name of Christ. Todd exhibits much humility in his recognition of the wealth of knowledge that can be learned from those who are different from himself. In a world brimming with aggression toward "the other," Todd takes Jesus's words, "Blessed are the peacemakers," to heart and seeks to be a part of that process, one story at a time.

**Works Cited**

McRay, Michael T. *Letters from "Apartheid Street": A Christian Peacemaker in Occupied Palestine.* Eugene, OR: Cascade Books, 2013.

# Chapter 10: A Missiological Hermitage
## Representing Jesus Across Cultures

*Jarrett Fontenot*

When I arrived at Gordon-Conwell Theological Seminary in 2007 to begin my Master of Divinity as an aspiring missionary, I was eager to connect with the missions-minded community on campus. Whether it was through classes with missions trainers and leaders or through cross-cultural excursions among the communities of the Greater Boston area, life on campus at Gordon-Conwell provided a myriad of opportunities for me to grow in my sensitivity to the nuances of cross-cultural ministry. Ironically, however, it took months of living immediately next door to the Center for the Study of Global Christianity (CSGC) before I realized the significance of the work going on behind its doors and its impact on the global missions movement.

Walking into the CSGC at Gordon-Conwell, where Todd has held an office for 20 years, was like walking into a missiological hermitage. Hidden away from the busyness of the rest of campus life, at the bottom of the hill, the CSGC was for me a sanctuary of sorts where I was encouraged to think critically about the church and how Christians can better represent Jesus across cultures. Whenever I walked through those doors, I knew that I was entering a unique community, where the staff and visiting scholars saw the world from a culturally-sensitive and missions-minded perspective, with Todd as the community's abbot.

When I began working at the CSGC, I remember finding Todd an intellectually imposing personality. Perhaps it was the stacks of books regularly engulfing his desk, always changing and seemingly ever-increasing. Perhaps it was Todd's reserved nature, which often left me wondering with what grand thought or nuanced concept he might be wrestling with. Regardless, I initially found Todd both intimidating and intriguing. For example, I remember one day asking Todd if he had read all the books in his office. In response, he recounted how, in the first year of his PhD work, he had read one book every day... 365 books in a year. I initially thought, "That's a joke." But then I reconsidered, thinking, "Todd doesn't make jokes, so it must be true." I have since learned that Todd does make jokes and that he read bits of 365 books that first year of PhD work, though probably not each book entirely! From that conversation, Todd encouraged me to read Mortimer Adler's *How to Read a Book*, in which Adler describes the complexities of reading different genres and how to read deliberately and with purpose. From Todd's recommendation, I learned to read more critically and to make better use of my time doing research. I'm happy to report that I am now free from the burden of feeling I have to read every book in its entirety to reap its benefits, though I admit I'm lucky to read a book a month.

During my three years at Gordon-Conwell, I worked at the CSGC for a number of semesters, both in a research capacity and in editing the *Atlas of Global Christianity* (Edinburgh University Press, 2009). Some of the work I most appreciated was counting denominations around the world. It was this hands-on statistical work that helped me see the complexities of divisions within the church in different parts of the world. Some divisions are intuitive, including those involving language or ethnicity. Other divisions are more surprising, including those that arise because of personality or power struggles. Each division within the church carries with it a story, and the work Todd has been about for decades has helped to tell those stories around the globe.

Perhaps what I appreciate most from my time working with Todd is his determination to describe the church, throughout time and around the world, as she is and not as we might want her to be. Admittedly, accounting for all the different Christian denominations and divisions around the world is a humbling experience. For me, it was impossible to do that kind of study and not mourn some of those divisions. I find so many of them tragic and unnecessary. But I never found Todd critical of the divisions within the church around the world. Rather, he was able to see beyond them to the beautiful tapestry that God has created and to how God uses the messiness in the church to accomplish his purposes. It always felt like Todd saw nothing but beauty in all the distinctives, complexity and diversity within the church around the world. Even today, I am indebted to Todd for that important perspective.

# Chapter 11: What Is the Posthuman Gospel?

*Michael Hahn*

> *I listened to you*
> *Too long. Within the churches*
> *You built me you genuflected*
> *To the machine.*
>
> *— from "Soliloquy" by R.S. Thomas*

Midway through another film in the Marvel Cinematic Universe, I encountered a strange but familiar malaise.

That's the best way I could describe watching mass terror from another super-villain destroying Manhattan. I had no misgivings of what I paid for: biblically-proportioned cataclysms, the destruction of cities by demigods and metahumans—all of it a costly fantasy: a conservative estimate places the hypothetical property damage of the first *The Avengers* film alone at $160 billion, not counting the casualties and the financial collapse of insurance agencies due to acts of terrorism. At least human attorneys will prosper in the Marvel universe.

But having endured years of the COVID-19 pandemic and a constant newsfeed of violence, the scenes of panic and the diminishing of human life hedged too close to reality. The on-screen fantasy touched on a real affect: I didn't need CGI magic to imagine mass despair. The happy endings just don't hit as they used to. The catharsis of its easy-fix Hollywood endings became a ritual of diminishing returns.

Of course, no matter what the box office says, society isn't turning *en masse* to Marvel films for redemption. However, in these past few years a collective hope has been more in demand than at-home COVID testing kits. Despite our experience of the pandemic, political divides, and racial tensions, the message of hope, especially in the church, seems to be uncommonly distributed. That is to say, divine redemption speaks differently, whether one is rich or poor, Democrat or Republican, White or a person of color. With Christian identity fractured along identity lines, pastors are resigning over ideological impasses within their own congregations, while others, in refusing to confront such issues, resort to palliative messages to preserve a thin veil of multiculturalism. In either case, gospel hope is limited to natural affinities—nice if you can afford it, while others quietly endure the dehumanizing affect of being unseen and devalued, silenced at the margins.

*You Belong Here* read the banners of the Christian college in sunny California, but my new role teaching diversity and inclusion on campus suggests a concept of belonging that is overshadowed by division. The past two years had sown enough of it: people of color livid over meager support following the murders of George Floyd and Breonna Taylor, while others—among students and faculty alike—continued their denial of systemic racism while criticizing the place of "diversity" at a Christian university (e.g. "Why preach diversity when we are united as Christians?"). With another year of austerity due to the pandemic, the return to in-person classes in 2021 was set to be an experiment in what it meant to embody hope—and belonging. After all, shouldn't a Christian institution be the vanguard? Doesn't the gospel of Jesus Christ, the good news that unites all people into common kinship, help us see past our differences?

"We are children of God," commented one student after my lesson on positionality. However, the feedback read as a critique. Using a *truth* to obscure another *truth*, it was a rebuttal to the message that we are refracted through our differences: that place, time, and culture all shape the way we view the world and each other. As a Christian, I still believe in the *imago Dei* the notion that we possess a divine relation that transcends our differences. However, as a Korean American, I own a heritage and an identity that has been made and treated as *different* by the culture around me—especially by an American Christian culture in which I had rarely seen someone who looked like me in church leadership. In sacred spaces, racial reconciliation, a topic central to unity in light of human oppression, was simply relegated to an after-service activity.

Ending the session, I leave students with a few questions to ponder about their worldview and empathy—the best I can do as a West-raised Korean American Christian cisgender male speaking to a diverse crowd on what it means to belong to each other. I acknowledge that I am speaking to a post-everything generation suspicious of ideological agendas and resistant to authoritarian voices assuming to speak for all humankind. In that sense, I am one of them. As a former seminarian, I have seen American Christianity buckle under the weight of its own presumptions and cultural hegemony. The messages preached from its pulpits, rarely aimed at systemic inequality, are often indifferent to our freefall into a hyper-individualistic culture. And with interpretations of scripture increasingly fragmented, who will speak for the hope of unity in the church?

One thing we've learned from the Marvel Cinematic Universe is that we love stories about superhumans. Stories that frame us as plebeians adrift on a sea of despair, prone to a multiverse of godlike foes and magical forces. We love to idolize our *transhumans*—human beings like Iron Man, Spiderman, and the Hulk—men who transcend human limits by the power of technology (e.g., Elon Musk, Jeff Bezos).

But we also love the antihero: despite projecting our dreams onto these superheroes, we still want them to convey a part of our own fears and failures—Tony Stark, narcissist; Peter Parker, immature; Bruce Banner, really angry. That is, though it takes fantasy to dream of the super-man, we need a reminder of the reality we're stuck with, after all: the tragically-irresponsible-man (e.g. Elon Musk, Jeff Bezos). Perhaps you cannot take the humanism out of superhumanism. Rosi Braidotti wants to do away with all of it.

In her book *The Posthuman*, Braidotti decries the legacy of Humanism, a philosophy that, while stressing an individual's dignity and capacity for self-realization, became a ploy for Western exceptionalism as it centered the human ideal through a Eurocentric, heteronormative male lens. However, she admits that being anti-humanism is not enough when one is pulled into competing orbits: "To be simply secular," she says, "would be complicitous with neo-colonial Western supremacist positions, while rejecting the Enlightenment legacy would be inherently contradictory for any critical project. The vicious circle is stifling."[1]

In other words, how do we reckon with our Humanistic enterprise in a way that resonates with our humanizing virtues? Braidotti takes the position of a post-humanist, applying a monistic worldview that brings humans in equal connection with nature, thus redeeming humankind's deteriorating relationship with the environment, let alone with the marginalized in its own species. She supports the notion of *zoe*—a term denoting life, but in her version, a life-force that reverberates between all things both human and non-human in an affirming, self-organizing manner.

Humans, having been exposed as morally neutral, must accept their ontological status as mere *things*.

So much for inheriting the earth.

Of course, Christians would contend with their own brand of Humanism. With proponents as early as Erasmus, Christian Humanism describes a view of human potential compatible with biblical teaching. Native human reason combined with its moral compass, would be made whole with divine redemption. Further validating humans' privilege as the pinnacle of God's creation, we are fit to realize our fullest potential, affirming Christ's purpose that we are to live more abundantly.

---

[1] Rosi Braidotti, *The Posthuman* (Cambridge: Polity Press, 2013), 36.

With versions of such thought ranging from a thinly-veiled rationalism to Christian exceptionalism, I was raised somewhere in-between, believing I can seamlessly bridge the academy and the church. Reason and individualism became my God-given, self-actualizing milieu. But with human-caused ecological disasters, structural inequality, failures of Christian institutions, and ideological impasses with the church, where does a Christian Humanism stand? While many resort to the purity of the "gospel" or a "biblical worldview" as antidotes to the culture wars, they can only go so far before realizing that such terms have always been primarily embodied by their own parochial viewfinders.

We are all children of God, indeed. But our sibling experiences are far too different—and thanks to the human enterprise, unequal—to take unity for granted.

And yet even Braidotti admits that she cannot escape the hopeful endeavor of Humanism and the hope of "a globalized, technologically mediated, ethnically and linguistically diverse society that is still in tune with basic principles of social justice, the respect for diversity, the principles of hospitality and conviviality." She writes, "I am aware but do not mind the residual Humanism of such aspirations, which I take at best as a productive contradiction."[2] In other words, as long as we are human, we cannot help but claim our right to be the conduits of hope.

Stumbling to the goal, the cost of our failures inflict some more than others.

Growing up Korean American, I wondered what it meant to be a "person of color." *Jesus loves the little children*, we sang in kindergarten. *All the children of the world / Red and Yellow, Black and White / They are precious in his sight / Jesus loves the little children of the world.* Though I hadn't met any kids who were Red (and where's the love for the Brown?), in a society where racism was framed between the polar opposites of Black and White, I assumed that Yellow, with all its pejorative connotations, was the Asian domain of racial belonging, even though my skin color was more olive, thank you very much.

I never knew how to negotiate my alterity in White spaces. Raised under the false flag of "model minority," my Asian identity was hardly spoken of outside of racial jokes and stereotypes—my assimilation paid in monthly installments of dignity. Still, to this day, I feel unsure being designated as BIPOC (Black, Indigenous, Persons of Color). In institutional BIPOC groups, I still secretly seek a few other Asian faces to make sure I belong, afraid to speak of my own experiences alongside those of Black and Indigenous persons, as if there were a hierarchy of oppression. And so, I bury my negative affect while learning how to be an ally.

---

2 Braidotti, *The Posthuman*, 183.

But the reminders of my otherness are still there, especially in the church. I am reminded of it when a pastor introduces me to another White pastor who then asks about me as if I weren't standing in the room, directly in front of him. I am reminded when another pastor dismisses notes for racial reconciliation from an Indian American church leader because her endeavor *isn't in line with the gospel*. These may not be examples of acute violence, the kind White people ask for when they demand that I explain racism, but some wounds inflict beyond sight. In her book, *Grave Attending*, Karen Bray speaks to this negative affect among Christians marginalized at church by coded messaging that puts blessedness out of reach. Bray writes, "Radical theologians of all bents have fallen short of analyzing how it is not just what the goal is—wealth, happiness, Whiteness, heterosexuality, able-bodiedness—but also the exclusive character of particular goals made into universals that cause a cruel limiting of options for our present flourishing."[3]

That is, as long as the church frames the life abundant through the privileged elite, its exiles will brood at the margins. Meanwhile, peace is preached from the pulpit and banners of Christian institutions will continue to proclaim: *You Belong Here.*

Humanism may lose its capital H, but perhaps, in contrast to Braidotti, it is too soon to abandon its goals. Just because the Eurocentric White male lost his privilege, doesn't mean that the human endeavor is lost on the rest of the world. We can only benefit from a multifaceted view of human potential—one in which the West is just another voice at the multicultural table. For instance, what happens when we cede the Western individual as the interpretive basis (*cogito ergo sum*) in favor of the community—the primary mode of identity in the global South? How can we stop the unequal effects of gentrification by relinquishing policymaking to the systemically oppressed? How can non-dualistic cultures with a more holistic view of nature and human potential help us pass on a healthier ecology to our children?

For Christians, the rise of scholarship in World Christianity, especially from adherents in the global South, has shed new light on a more holistic vision of the *imago Dei*. While the Enlightenment has influenced Christians to champion human dignity and civil rights, its unweeded legacy has also spawned a "gospel" that the West uses to sanction a neo-liberal (e.g., hyper-individualistic, consumeristic) vision of blessedness. Japanese theologian Kosuke Koyama writes that while "the cultural values of Asia and the Pacific have not been appreciated…judgment has been given in terms of the values found in the Western life-style for which Jesus Christ does not necessarily

---

3  Karen Bray, *Grave Attending* (New York: Fordham, 2020), 51.

stand."[4] Stripped of grace and sacrifice, the groundbreaking message of the kingdom of God continues to be modified, pawned as a tool for exclusion and religious imperialism.

Or, to paraphrase Dr. Todd M. Johnson of the Center of the Study of Global Christianity at Gordon-Conwell Theological Seminary, *The gospel is not a utility. It is good news.* Rather than acting on the words of Christ, instrumentalizing the gospel for one's own agenda ruins it.

With Christian salvation appropriated by an androcentric, Eurocentric cultural dominance, the Western church becomes blind to the spectrum of God's redemptive plan in the global church.

But for many Christians who have been unseen and undervalued as a result—having once seen the Technicolor of this prophetic vision, there is no going back.

In Peter's First Epistle, the Apostle writes to the "exiles" (*parepidenois*) in Asia Minor: mostly Gentile Christians needing encouragement in their faith. However, rather than denoting a physical displacement, the term is also used to refer to the experience of being an alien or part of a marginalized social class.[5] It is likely, having written the letter pre-diaspora, that Peter was addressing the Christians' exile in a metaphysical, spiritual sense.

In other words, in the normal course of the Christian life, one will feel the affect of unbelonging because of the greater, ultimate home to which believers are destined. If, as philosopher Karen Bray suggests, a Western gospel implies "a soteriological and theological impulse in neoliberalism that demands we be productive, efficient, happy, and flexible in order to be of worth and therefore get saved out of the wretched experience of having been marked as worthless,"[6] then the church can only learn from its affectual exiles on the true meaning of the *imago Dei*—and of a Christian joy that transcends a materially privileged circumstance.

The stubborn fear of anything less than material privilege in the Western church may preclude this needed shift. Still, I find shelter with the marginalized whose devotion to Christ gives me a resilient hope through the unending barrage of discrimination, violence, and oppression. Rather than a sign of scarcity, the feeling of unbelonging can gird a spiritual longing for eternal redemption, of which its temporal effect (and affect) is one of love and hospitality, healing and justice. It might not be called humanism, nor post-humanism, but it is a vision of humanity that has at its center, a risen Christ who, having dwelt

---

4 Kosuke Koyama, *Three Mile an Hour God* (Norwich: SCM Press, 1979), 9.
5 Stephen Ayodeji A. Fagbemi, "Living for Christ in a Hostile World: The Christian Identity and its Present Challenges in 1 Peter," *Transformation* 26, no. 1 (2009): 2.
6 Bray, *Grave Attending*, 11.

among, became our poor, our rejected, our exiled. Radically transcendent and immanent, it is a transcultural, trans-difference, embodied hope that, in these disorienting and oppressive times, dares to spark a unifying affect of joy.

**Works Cited**

Braidotti, Rosi. *The Posthuman*. Cambridge: Polity Press, 2013.
Bray, Karen. *Grave Attending*. New York: Fordham, 2020.
Fagbemi, Stephen Ayodeji A. "Living for Christ in a Hostile World: The Christian Identity and Its Present Challenges in 1 Peter." *Transformation* 26, no. 1 (2009): 1–14.
Koyama, Kosuke. *Three Mile an Hour God*. Norwich: SCM Press, 1979.

# Chapter 12: Many Books

*Richard L. Haney*

The Good Book tells us that "of making many books there is no end, and much study is a weariness to the flesh" (Ecclesiastes 12:12). I don't believe Todd Johnson has taken that proverbial wisdom to heart—at least, not yet. He has studied thousands of books and has made quite a few as well. His vocational world has focused on research, writing, and teaching, and such disciplines form the pillars of academia. Most academics might agree with the preacher of Ecclesiastes—especially at the end of term or at the completion of a publishing project—but the work of accumulating knowledge is ongoing. There always is another semester, another class to teach, more questions to ask, more topics to research, and more data to analyze. As we grow older, one day we realize there will come a time for less activity, for deceleration, for passing the baton. A time arises when we give way to younger colleagues and when we begin giving or disposing our books to family and the next generation. That time has not quite arrived for Todd or myself but "we can see it from here."

As I express appreciative thoughts about my friend and colleague, Todd M. Johnson, my mind turns quickly to the reading, writing, and collecting of books. Todd and I have spent many hours in bookshops perusing the shelves and helping each other learn about a new author or finding a classic title hidden in a dusty corner. Todd's professional undertaking in these explorations was to find titles for the Center for the Study of Global Christianity.[1] Such a center reasonably holds books about every country, about the world's religions and people groups plus works on anthropology, culture, languages, geography, and many more topics. And such a center would hold many reference books, too, dictionaries, atlases, encyclopedias, and so on. My own purposes in the bookstore were more personal; as a pastor and mission leader, I followed my curiosity in matters of theology, missiology, linguistics, and philosophy. Both of us also indulged our personal interests. For Todd, there was always another book to be collected on religious pilgrimage, world music, the Silk Road, or St. Francis of Assisi. For me, I was on the

---

1 The Center for the Study of Global Christianity (CSGC) is a research center at Gordon-Conwell Theological Seminary located in South Hamilton, Massachusetts. The CSGC's work has its origin in David Barrett's research in Nairobi, Kenya. After Nairobi, the work continued under the auspices of the Southern Baptist Foreign Mission Board (International Mission Board; IMB). Next, David and Todd operated independently as researchers for the World Evangelization Research Center (WERC) that belonged to the non-profit entity, Global Evangelization Movement. Both the work at the IMB and the independent WERC were conducted in Richmond, Virginia.

lookout to discover another poet, a new or old work on the Inklings (C.S. Lewis, et al.), and another set of essays on translation or hermeneutics.

*World Christian Encyclopedia, 1st Edition*

The first book that brought us together was probably David Barrett's monumental effort to research and write the *World Christian Encyclopedia* (Oxford University Press, 1982). I met David when my mission professor, J. Christy Wilson, accepted my invitation to come to Richmond, Virginia to speak at a church missions conference. It was 1987 or 1988 and Christy was teaching at my alma mater, Gordon-Conwell Theological Seminary in South Hamilton, Massachusetts. He said yes to my invitation on one condition: he would come for the weekend if I secured an appointment for him with David Barrett at the Southern Baptist Foreign (now International) Mission Board. I'm still a bit embarrassed to admit that at the time, I replied with, "Who is David Barrett?" I did atone somewhat for my ignorance by purchasing the *World Christian Encyclopedia* for $100. At that time, it was my most expensive book.

David, an Anglican missionary who served in Kenya, had traveled throughout Africa doing research on church growth in the 1960s and 1970s. Eventually, he would traverse most of the globe to count Christians, country by country and province by province; all that time he was researching trends related to demographics and Christian mission. He asked, "Where are the world's Christians located? And where are the places where Christian churches and missionary witness are absent?" David was motivated to see the Christian gospel made available to all peoples in all countries. He was the world's expert on the size and location of Christian populations worldwide and Christy naturally wanted to visit with him. I sat in on some of their conversation and hung on every word. This meeting initiated by Christy Wilson gave me boldness to ring David every time I traveled overseas. I visited him at the Mission Board and asked about Tanzania, Morocco, Croatia, or wherever I was heading to take a mission team. Without ever consulting a book or a computer, David would spin out facts and figures and sometimes a fascinating story, too. He gave me this good advice: "When you visit a town or a village, find the community's oldest Christian and ask to hear his or her story."

Soon afterward, I was reading a mission journal and noticed Todd Johnson's name linked to David Barrett. I figured he was a younger scholar working with or under David's tutelage. I tucked that away until I heard from someone that Todd actually lived in Richmond. I invited him to give a mission talk at Swift Creek Presbyterian Church where I served as pastor. Our first encounter showed us we had many interests in common and our friendship grew quickly after that first meeting. And the visits to bookshops followed in short order.

## History Books

In the 1990s, Todd was a teacher in the Perspectives on the World Christian Movement course that was taught throughout the United States and in many places worldwide.[2] This 15-week course is hosted by churches and coordinated by area volunteers who have completed the course. Various seminary and college professors often serve as the "professor of record" since a student could receive college or seminary credit for successfully taking these classes. The course was designed and co-written by mission professor Ralph D. Winter, one of the original professors of mission at Fuller Theological Seminary's School of World Mission in Pasadena, California. Ralph was also Todd's father-in-law, and Todd had a front row seat to see the Perspectives course developed and rolled out.

Lesson Six is Todd's favorite, "The Expansion of the Christian Movement." This lecture and accompanying readings cover the growth of the Christian church and its missionary expansion from about the year 100 to 1600. It is a daunting challenge to describe in less than two hours of lectures, how the Christian movement moved from Rome and the Mediterranean past the Reformation and into the Age of Discovery that propelled the Jesuit mission to Latin America and East Asia. It also is my favorite lesson to teach and I have benefited from hearing Todd teach it and also borrowing many of his slides. Todd taught me to avoid the dreaded use of PowerPoint presentations that display only text. I adopted his preferred method to use maps and images from great artworks to identify personages and illustrate eras and periods.

The founder of the Franciscans, Francis of Assisi, is one of Todd's favorite subjects for book collecting. As I read a few tomes on Francis, I learned that the images of Francis' life (d. 1226) had been captured by the painter Giotto di Bernardone in the late 1290s/early 1300s. Giotto's cycle of 28 frescoes adorn the walls in the St. Francis Basilica in Assisi, Italy. Images of these paintings artfully help the lecturer tell the inspiring story of Francis, the monk, the friend of Brother Sun and Sister Moon, the founder of the Franciscan Order, and the admirer of Lady Poverty. In 2019, I saw these images in person for the first time, and I was struck by how powerfully they conveyed scenes of Francis' remarkable life and ministry.

Todd's Perspectives class also taught me about the 16th-century Jesuit pioneer who gave himself to bringing the gospel to China, Matteo Ricci (1552–1610). Todd's favorite biography is Jonathan Spence's masterpiece, *The Memory Palace of Matteo Ricci* (Penguin Books, 1985). This book barely

---

2 Frontier Fellowship, the mission agency where I work, has raised funds over the years to translate *Perspectives* into Arabic, Spanish, and French.

beats out another with a superb title, *The Wise Man from the West* by Vincent Cronin (Ignatius Press, 2016). The "memory palace" is Ricci's astonishing technique he learned in Italy reading the works of the Latin scholar, Quintilian.[3] Ricci memorized Confucius' classic work, *The Analects*, and dazzled dinner party guests by reciting long paragraphs. Ricci died in 1610 and is buried in a Jesuit cemetery in Beijing. Because I had friends living in East Asia, I first read this Spence biography and then collected all of Spence's other works on Chinese history. I'm thankful that Todd introduced me to both Ricci and Spence.

Another work that impressed Todd and made it into his history talks also served as the inspiration for a PBS series: Maria Rosa Menocal, *The Ornament of the World: How Muslims, Jews and Christians Created a Culture of Tolerance in Medieval Spain* (Back Bay Books, 2009). Menocal's portrait of medieval Spain tells the story of a golden age when Muslims, Jews, and Christians collaborated to create a culture where science and the arts flourished, and the people lived in harmony. Cordoba, Spain was the center of this remarkable experiment in peaceful living. This work belongs to a larger collection of books Todd has collected that narrate intellectual history and appreciate episodes of "cultural exchange." Spain, and much of Europe, was linked to China and Japan by the Silk Road. Todd has collected numerous works on the Silk Road, and he has a sharp eye for art books showing the sculpture, painting, and tapestries that reveal how similar designs and patterns traveled East and West along its routes. A particular favorite is Richard C. Foltz, *Religions of the Silk Road: Overland Trade and Cultural Exchange from Antiquity to the Fifteenth Century* (Palgrave Macmillan, 1999). In 2007, I heard Todd share some of Foltz's insights with a group of attentive religious leaders in Kazakhstan. This was the first time these Kazakh pastors heard that Christians lived in their land before the rise of Islam. A more recent addition to this collection is Peter Frankopan's, *The Silk Roads: A New History of the World* (Vintage Books, 2015) that rightly points out that the Silk Road had a number of parallel routes all traversing similar territory. I'll never forget seeing a map of this region with several routes depicted displayed in the National Museum of Tajikistan in 2015.

Perspectives Lessons 7 and 8 also present mission history and feature various mission pioneers of the 19th and 20th centuries, though these lessons tell stories mostly about British and American men.[4] William Carey, Hudson Taylor, Adoniram Judson, David Livingstone, and others truly did pioneer gospel forays into parts of Africa and Asia, but I was fascinated when Todd introduced

---

3 See Quintilian V, *The Orator's Education*, Books 11–12 in the Loeb Classical Library series (2001), 63–72.

4 The Perspectives course includes a lengthy reader with essays by a host of authors. It is to the editors' credit that they are updating the material to include more subjects and more authors, especially more women and more voices from the global South.

me to "the trio" of women mission pioneers and writers, Mildred Cable (1878–1952) along with sisters Evangeline French (1869–1960) and Francesca French (1871–1960). I first saw several volumes by these intrepid ladies on Todd's book shelves. Patient perusing helped me turn up two titles in Wales in 2002, when I took a weekend off from my Oxford studies and traveled by train and bus to Hay-on-Wye, the beloved used book capital of the world. A stopover town along the scenic Wye River, Hay-on-Wye boasted more than 30 bookshops at the time of my visit. One of the treasures I found during my trip was Cable and F. French's *The Making of a Pioneer: Percy Mather of Central Asia* (Hodder & Stoughton, 1935). The other find was their book on spiritual formation, *Towards Spiritual Maturity: A Book for Those Who Seek It* (Hodder & Stoughton, 1939). In 2005, I found a copy of their history of the British and Foreign Bible Society, *Why Not the World?* (1952) in another famous bookstore, Loome Theological Booksellers in Stillwater, Minnesota. In 2011, I discovered another Cable and French title, *The Book Which Demands a Verdict* (SCM Press, 1946) while studying in Oxford. This little book recounts stories of Bible translation. I wonder if the more famous book by Josh MacDowell, *Evidence That Demands a Verdict* (Thomas Nelson, 1999) did some title-borrowing! Another title I found in Half-Price Books in Dallas, Texas, tells part of the stirring story of why three British female missionaries traveled in the Gobi Desert beginning in 1923; *Something Happened* (Hodder & Stoughton, 1933). Another part of that story is in the final book in my Cable and French corpus, *The Gobi Desert* (Hodder & Stoughton, 1944), discovered in a used bookstore in Culpeper, Virginia. It remains my favorite because of the many black and white photos of people and places in the Gobi region.

You cannot collect books and prints unless you know where to find them. I have referred to a number of curious and wonderful stores in the paragraph above. Bookshops used to abound but the number of quality used bookstores is diminishing due to the rise of digital books and the reach of Amazon. When I first visited Oxford in 2003, I counted more than 20 used bookshops, but today there might be six or seven if you include the charity shops. The reduced number of used and antiquarian bookstores is sad for a bibliophile but a few stellar places continue to serve the reading public. Some of the memorable places I visited with Todd include the Book Barn in Niantic, Connecticut, Baldwin Books in Philadelphia, The Strand in New York City, Rockville, Maryland's Second Story Books, Nice Price Books in Raleigh, Daedalus Books in Charlottesville, plus another Daedalus in Springfield, Maryland. When Todd moved to Gordon-Conwell Theological Seminary in Massachusetts my visits there often included a trip to Boston. Raven Books in nearby Cambridge specializes in slightly used academic books and we have found many useful works there.

On our way to Second Story Books in Rockville, we stopped at the Wheaton Public Library where they had a large selection of used books for sale. We discovered an almost complete set (54 volumes) of the *Great Books of the Western World* and I walked happily away with several boxes for less than a dollar a book![5] Todd vowed to find me a copy of the missing volume, number 31, Descartes and Spinoza. And of course, he did.

Todd introduced me to two other sets of books I have come to collect, read, and pass on to others. One is the *Penguin Lives* series that presents brief biographies of an interesting assortment of famous persons. My own set now includes biographies of Amadeus Mozart, Charles Darwin, Martin Luther, Winston Churchill, Dante, Charles Dickens, Joan of Arc, and Julia Child. The other series is Oxford University Press' *Very Short Introductions*. I have titles on Buddhism, The Silk Road, The Koran, The New Testament, Globalization, World Music, and Post-Colonialism, among others. Both sets offer books that are compact and readable for a plane ride.

*Books Today*

In 2001, Oxford University Press published the two-volume *World Christian Encyclopedia* (2nd edition) by David Barrett and Todd Johnson. They also wrote a third volume, *World Christian Trends*, that was published in the same year by the mission publishing house, William Carey Library. In 2009, Todd Johnson co-edited the *Atlas of Global Christianity, 1910–2010*, with the Scottish mission scholar, Kenneth R. Ross. In 2019, co-authors Todd M. Johnson and Gina A. Zurlo and their cast of global contributors produced the *World Christian Encyclopedia*, 3rd edition, named one of the 10 outstanding books of 2019 by the *International Bulletin of Mission Research*.

After David's monumental effort in researching and writing the first *World Christian Encyclopedia* (1982), Todd followed his mentor's example by continuing to publish such encyclopedias and always doing so in cooperation with other scholars. In their days of collaboration and research in Richmond, Virginia, David and Todd were the principals in a non-profit agency called Global Evangelization Movement (GEM, now World Christian Research). As a member of the board of GEM, I was privileged to get many glimpses at the ways David mentored his younger colleague and treated him as an esteemed colleague. Lessons from David influenced Todd to include other researchers, scholars, and students in all his projects. One example is how he has made way

---

5 The *Great Books of the Western World* is a series of books first published in the United States in 1952 by Encyclopædia Britannica Inc. The project began at the University of Chicago when president Robert Hutchins collaborated with Mortimer Adler to present the Western canon in a single set of 54 volumes. The series is now in its second edition and contains 60 volumes.

for his younger colleague, Dr. Gina Zurlo, to join him as co-director of the Center for the Study of Global Christianity housed at Gordon-Conwell. He does so because he values the work of others and because he wants to encourage and inspire younger scholars.

It makes sense to trust and involve other gifted and industrious workers to complete a project with excellent results. Yet, it takes humility and respect to hand assignments over to others and to trust them to do the requisite work. Todd embodies that humility about himself and that respect for others; for younger scholars, for students, for colleagues far away in the Majority World. I remember a time when Todd traveled to Salt Lake City, Utah to consult with leaders of the Church of Jesus Christ of Latter-day Saints. They were thrilled and pleasantly surprised that someone from the Evangelical Christian world would take time to listen to them and report on their own church statistics.

Researchers like David Barrett, Todd Johnson, Peter Crossing, Gina Zurlo, and others glean data from many sources and present the information as in narratives, tables, and charts accompanied by images. I believe that knowledge is for sharing and is necessary to become wise. Wisdom is expressed in how we live, determine priorities, make choices, treat other people, and serve our God. I have come to regard my friend and teaching colleague, Todd Johnson, as much more than one who does superb research to help audiences know about the details of religious demographics. His reading, writing, and life experience gleans ideas and lessons from wise persons who went before him. I am sure he would be quick to give credit not only to his parents and mentors, but to his wife Tricia and their three daughters for offering him life lessons along the way.

He was privileged to learn from missiology mentors like Ralph Winter and David Barrett. He once commented on another wise teacher: "Oh yes, Andrew Walls. He is one of the few meta-historians we have today." By meta-historian, Todd meant that Andrew had this rare grasp of the global expanse of history covering the entire world and across all time periods. Until his recent passing, Andrew was to Christian history what David was to mission demography.

Since I began this essay with a verse of Scripture, I'll conclude in the same fashion by another passage from Old Testament wisdom literature, Proverbs 24:3–6:

> [3] By wisdom a house is built,
> and by understanding it is established;
> [4] by knowledge the rooms are filled
> with all precious and pleasant riches.
> [5] Wise warriors are mightier than strong ones,
> and those who have knowledge than those who have strength;

> [6] for by wise guidance you can wage your war,
> and in abundance of counsellors there is victory.

Todd is a dedicated scholar whose trade is converting data into knowledge. But in his faith, temperament, lifestyle, and relationships, he displays a life of wisdom. He believes in and practices learning from an "abundance of counselors" and his own memory palace is "filled with rooms of precious and pleasant riches." May his tribe increase!

# Chapter 13: Global Hermeneutics and the Ethical Potency of Scholarship
## Reflections on the Character and Expertise of a Religious Demographer from an Aspiring Biblical Scholar

*David A. Hannan*

I first encountered Todd Johnson while taking a Perspectives on the World Christian Movement course in Huntington, West Virginia when I read his contribution to the course's textbook. Little did I know then that within four months I would be working for him and Dr. Gina Zurlo as a research assistant at the Center for the Study of Global Christianity (CSGC) at Gordon-Conwell Theological Seminary, a hope that had come to fruition more rapidly than I could have imagined. Yet, still, that within three years I would consider him among the most important personal influences in my life. Despite feeling compelled to pursue a field other than religious demography and global Christianity, Todd has instilled in me numerous professional, intellectual, and personal skills indispensable to my wholeness and flourishing as a human being and aspiring scholar of ancient Near Eastern religions and literature.

Like any educational experience, being trained in ancient Semitic languages and exegesis of the Hebrew Bible in an inter-denominational Evangelical institution has its benefits and drawbacks. The philological rigor of my education often led to near grammatical determinism, reinforcing the idea that the "true" meaning of a biblical text could be found by painstakingly investigating every lexical and syntactic idiosyncrasy of a biblical excerpt, often at the expense of thorough historical, hermeneutical, and cultural nuance and sensitivity. At best, this means that Gordon-Conwell students might feel more confident in parsing Hebrew verbs than students elsewhere, but, at worst, it means that socially and ethically regressive views can be all too easily propped up by this purportedly rigorous approach. In my courses, I often felt (with few notable exceptions) that ancient Near Eastern "cultures," when they were acknowledged at all, were often unconsciously treated as a monolithic cultural force of hostility towards "the people of God" when this is patently false (considering, e.g., Mesopotamian texts pre-dating the Hebrew Bible had long talked about the "care of the orphan and the widow"). The Hebrew Bible was itself considered to be a quasi-supra-cultural set of texts that served as the inevitable predecessor to Christianity, texts whose interpretive methods themselves were taught as though they were not a product of Western intellectualism. Non-Hebrew literature, iconography, and history were treated with severe selectivity to reinforce a particular interpretation of a text, but this was considered sufficient engagement with extra-biblical material to warrant the label "historical background" in lectures and term papers. I came to believe that this manner of speaking about "other" ancient Near Eastern cultures was not only incorrect but actually morally concerning not only because it often entailed engaging in intellectual dishonesty about the assumptions informing the interpretive processes being employed by and instilled unconsciously in future Christian leaders, but also because it reinforced a harmful way of thinking about non-Western cultures in our contemporary world. It supported what Todd might call "fortress Evangelicalism" and its view of "culture" that must be critiqued, resisted, and rejected—that there was an "us" and "them" in the Hebrew Bible just like there is an "us" and "them" for Christians who should focus on that "us" feeling secure.

While much of this may seem rather remote from Todd's work as an expert on global Christianity, religious demography, and missiology, none of the preceding reflections on my educational experiences and growing concern for the intellectual and ethical implications of the way that biblical scholars with confessional leanings might speak and write about "culture" would have been possible without doing research for and taking courses with someone as culturally aware and humble as Todd. The fact that I trace my own concern for these issues to someone working in another field is a testament to the profound impact that Todd can have on those who meet him, take a class with him, or work with him. Alongside Dr. Zurlo, Todd helped me slowly begin to see my own cultural blind spots that began with being able to identify the methods and questions engaged in my biblical studies courses as questions mostly asked by White male theologians; to acknowledge that these are not the same as the questions that, for example, Christians from Nagaland ask (nor should they); that the failure to acknowledge this is a dangerous form of cultural imperialism that does not properly dignify the worldviews of people who do and did not look like me or share my experiences. By extension, it was not hard to realize that mine were not the questions or intentions of an ancient Levantine scribe composing a Hebrew text.

My relationship with Todd filled numerous gaps that I didn't even know existed in my education and Christian formation through his character and creativity as a scholar. Todd possesses an incisive and subtle ability to instill the contextual nature of all thinking and knowing in his students and research assistants. Cultural consciousness—the capacity to situate one's own beliefs and the kinds of inquiries their worldview leads them to pursue from within a particular social, economic, regional, and ethnic location is a result of being around Todd and learning with him—learning *with* him is most accurate because he is highly collaborative and genuinely considers the insights and reflections of his research assistants. This consciousness of the cultural-situatedness of even (or sometimes especially) the work of theologians and religious scholars is not something that he inculcates in his students through dogmatism or cynicism nor is it borne of the desire simply to be reactionary or contrarian as an end in itself but to be honest, critical, *and* charitable about the world in which we live and the data with which we deal (whether the data is quantitate or qualitative, contemporary or historical).

This is clear in the methodology long employed by the CSGC that Todd helped to develop with Dr. David Barrett, which incorporates traditional quantitative religious demographic approaches to studying religious change with sensitivity to the geo-political, theological, economic, and historical complexity of Christianity as a lived, global religion in often highly disparate cultural, ethnic, and linguistic and social milieu in collaboration and relationship with Christian leaders and communities from those countries. It is not an abstract or impotent pluralism but rather an embodied pluralistic disposition toward ideas and people with a bold commitment to universal human dignity, and that is transparent, for example, about complex history of collusion between Christian mission and colonialism. It was precisely this kind of critical realism and honesty that I needed to develop to be able to begin to see the Hebrew Bible as a product of its own particular time and culture, and more importantly to begin to critique and reject many of my own experiences within predominantly White, American Evangelical communities.

During my time as a research assistant, I primarily worked for Todd and Dr. Zurlo on a project focusing on the historical religiosity of India across all its major religious groups. Early in the project, as we began to explore 20th century ethnographic profiles of Indian communities who, for example, participated in practices of both Hinduism and Islam, Todd insisted that for the purposes of our research, such communities were more religious, not less. Throughout the project, Todd kindly but adamantly insisted that we actively resist any tendency to project unconsciously a Protestant understanding of what it means to be more or less "religious" (often erroneously equated with subjective notions of "orthodoxy") onto the hundreds of communities we were encoding into our dataset.

At the same time that Todd was challenging me intellectually to become more culturally humble and aware, working with Todd presented opportunities to not only think differently, but to live differently. I once wore a button-down shirt with a black and sapphire zig-zag design to a project meeting. Because the shirt resembled the patterning of indigenous clothing from an African country, Todd, accustomed to encountering students and scholars from or who had traveled frequently outside of North America, kindly and enthusiastically asked me whose culture the shirt represented and how I had acquired it. Much to my chagrin, I could only say, "Um…American Eagle." Todd, perhaps, not desiring to make me feel worse, simply said, "Oh, alright!" smiled, and moved on with the meeting. I never wore the shirt again and recently recycled it—not because Todd embarrassed me (he didn't!) but because in the nicest way possible he had drawn attention to the possibility that wearing it as a White male was potentially participating in a dangerous form of cultural appropriation. This is one of many examples of how working with Todd can incrementally make one a more culturally sensitive human.

Todd also instilled in me that being a scholar with a personal religious affiliation does not mean writing only or even primarily confessional scholarship (another implicit assumption I had encountered and begun to internalize during my education). Excellence in one's research is to be pursued even when the immediate or ostensible outcome challenges long held personal or institutional, traditional, denominational, confessional beliefs. At the same time, scholarship is not simply an outlet for confirming one's own worldview, pursuing personal, intellectual or ideological vendettas, or the radical rejection of tradition on principle, nor is it solely about pursuing perennial intellectual novelties or esoteric curiosities. It is not *eruditio gratia eruditionis*—learning for the sake of learning. Scholarship that is purely hypothetical, overly abstracted or hyper-spiritualized is potentially self-indulgent at the least, and morally vacuous at the worst. Instead, Todd embodies both the contemporary and classical notion of erudition both in his own research and in his teaching and mentoring. In, perhaps, a more classical understanding of erudition, education and expertise means not primarily the acquisition of knowledge but, rather, the removal of ignorance. Unfortunately, one can gain a lot of information in a seminary course and achieve a relatively high grade without becoming less ignorant of the real world in which they live and how they are living in it—or how their religion shapes and engages that reality and that life. At a time in many American Protestant theological educational institutions where little time is dedicated to embodied ethical formation, activism, or pursuing more universal human flourishing, it is startling to hear lectures or conversations that can so readily move someone toward voting differently, recycling and composting more often, or changing their wardrobe to remove from it any potentially culturally appropriating items; that is the removal of ignorance that a holistic education ought to provide. Todd does not teach such principles, however, through highlighting himself as the source of wisdom or moral authority with pithy *sententia*, but through everything from the reusable sandwich wraps in which he brought he packed lunches to the CSGC to the proverbs and narratives he has acquired from a lifetime of cross-cultural listening whereby he also frequently elevates the voices of non-White, non-male, non-Western figures by quoting them and adhering to their wisdom so often. Here, one of his favorites is to cite Korean theologians who critique Euro-American, Anglophone theologians or biblical commentators whose expertise they consider oxymoronic, stating that one cannot master a subject (e.g., Christology) without being mastered by the subject (i.e., Jesus, through embodying self-sacrifice, humility, and more).

Todd has a powerfully, subtly subversive approach to undermining Western, Anglophonic, empiricist, ethnocentric, and subtly orientalist assumptions in the history and demography of Christianity (terms he may not even need to use to convey these ideas and translate them into intellectual and practical postures)—love. He knows that people are universally more attracted to someone who loves others and is passionate about their work than someone who is only critical or cynical. Todd lives the art of enjoying and loving people and ideas authentically and publicly, as a form of critique and correction. He spends equal amounts of time, for example, condemning Islamophobia among American Christians, as he does telling people how much he admires and looks up to Malala Yousafzai. As much as his brilliance sharpens his colleagues and mentees, that palpable enthusiasm and love is even more endearing, infectious, and transformative.

# Chapter 14: I Am Where I Am Today Because of Todd Johnson

*Bert Hickman*

Perhaps all his former students could—and do—say some variation on "I am where I am today because of Todd Johnson." In my case, it is quite true. I serve RUN Ministries as Director of Research, helping a vast family of house churches conduct and analyze research on the movements to Christ of which they are part.

My initial contact with RUN came while I was working with Todd as a research associate at the Center for the Study of Global Christianity (CSGC) at Gordon-Conwell Theological Seminary. Our colleague Justin Long contacted me about helping another organization (at the time I did not know whom) with a research project, which I was glad to do. That initial project led to requests to train trainers on research methodologies and, eventually, to an invitation to join them full time. From that simple request has come the opportunity to be part of an incredible work of God, which includes bringing awareness of this work to the global church by sharing some of our data with the CSGC.

I must confess, however, that I do not remember exactly when or where I first met Todd. It might have been hearing him speak, or it might have been talking to him about interning with him at the CSGC. I do remember, however, how happy I was that I met him. I had come to Gordon-Conwell as a "second-career" student, sure that I had been called there but uncertain of what might lie ahead. My background was in engineering and applied science, so seminary was quite a change. But in Todd and his work I discovered how research (and numbers!) could be used in the service of the church and her mission globally, and that reshaped the trajectory of my life.

As I was preparing to graduate, I asked Todd if I could continue to work with him at the CSGC. In his straightforward way, he said, "If you can find the money, you can work here." Though I was never the best of fundraisers, God did provide what I needed to live on, and I was able to continue working with Todd for 10 more years.

One of his characteristics as a leader is his desire to match people's work with their skills and abilities, including those that they do not realize they possess. Todd discovered in me an ability and love for editorial work that I did not know was there. Because of Todd's insight, I have been able to work with—and continue to work with—the CSGC as an associate editor of numerous published works. Beyond that, I have been able to assist others with books and projects and have been encouraged to do more with this skill. Calling forth this ability in me might be one of the greatest effects Todd had on me during my time with him.

Thanks to my relationship with Todd, I also had the privilege of traveling to several global gatherings of Christians, among them the Lausanne Congress in South Africa in 2010, the Pentecostal World Conference in Malaysia in 2013, and the World Evangelical Alliance Mission Commission meeting in Panama in 2016. Meeting fellow Christians from around the world and hearing their stories put names and faces to the concept of "global Christianity." One memory in particular stands out from the Lausanne Congress: participants from the global South were eager to participate in a survey administered by the Center for the Study of Global Christianity. They seemed genuinely grateful that people were interested in their experiences and perspectives, and it opened my eyes to how underappreciated these brothers and sisters could be on the global stage.

It is impossible to think of Todd—and Tricia, his wife—without thinking of their hospitality. This is perhaps one of their strongest personal values and commitments. From opening their home to students, to making sure that visitors at the CSGC feel welcome, to eating meals with guests, hospitality is an integral part of their lives. And that hospitality extends to the most intimate details. For example, Todd always took care to ensure that people of other faiths who might be visiting the CSGC or the campus had meals that accommodated their dietary restrictions. Their hospitality is a shining example of faith in action, one that I am challenged to emulate in my own life.

In thinking of his hospitality, I wondered if I could sum up Todd in a single word, and several came to mind: Humble. Unassuming. Gentle. Irenic. As I mulled over the various possibilities, 1 Corinthians 13 came to mind. Sometimes we are challenged to put our own names into the words of Scripture, to apply them directly to our lives. I dare say that we often feel we fall short of the picture the Bible presents of the reality of the Christian life. But in this particular case, I was struck by how wonderfully apt the words of the Apostle Paul are when applied to Todd:

> Todd is patient.
>
> Todd is kind.
>
> He does not envy.
>
> He does not boast.
>
> He is not proud.
>
> He does not dishonor others.

He is not self-seeking.

He is not easily angered.

He keeps no record of wrongs.

Todd does not delight in evil but rejoices with the truth.

He always protects, always trusts, always hopes, always perseveres.

In truth, Todd is good at doing what he does—and has affected both individuals and his field of work—because he is good at being who he is. To know who you are and to be who you are is a blessing for both yourself and for those whose lives you intersect. Thank you, Todd, for being who you are and for helping me and others discover more of who we are.

# Chapter 15: Lessons and Gifts of Interreligious Encounters

*Daryl R. Ireland*

"If there is a purpose for other religions, it is so their adherents can be converted to Christianity."

I had never said or even thought that explicitly—I never had to. It was just part of the strong missionary and conversionary impulses of my Evangelical faith community. I thought the Christians who were less zealous in making converts were theologically suspect. Lowering the boundaries between Christians and non-Christians was the kind of goal I expected to hear at the Boston University School of Theology, something I would have to endure as a PhD student at a mainline Protestant institution but an aim I would never need to endorse. It was a relief, therefore, when Todd Johnson offered a guest course at Boston University on global Christianity. For once, I could relax my defensive posture. I knew we were on common ground. He taught at Gordon-Conwell Theological Seminary, the premiere Evangelical institution of theological education in the northeast; he had studied at William Carey International University, which was dedicated to global missions, and he was the son-in-law of Ralph Winter, the American missiologist who galvanized Evangelicals' outreach by focusing their energies on unreached people groups. No one could have had more credibility with me than Todd Johnson.

I was eager and ready to digest everything he had to say, expecting his class to be something like comfort food for the Evangelical mind. However, I found it unexpectedly hard to swallow his admonition that we must embrace our place not only in the global Christian family, but also as members of the diverse human family. He insisted that there is no virtue in being a suspicious or manipulative sibling, and it never honors Christ to demean or undermine another. Friendships across faith boundaries are not a failure in missions—that is, a failure to convert. Friendship wasn't even the first step in or final point of missions. Generosity, curiosity, and kindness simply described the baseline obligation we had toward others. We should owe nothing to anyone, except our debt to love them.

In hindsight, none of this was radical or even necessarily at odds with my Evangelicalism. Yet, it challenged me in ways I had not anticipated. Was it the way Todd was so clearly at ease with the guests he brought to class, including the many people of other traditions and faiths? He obviously enjoyed their company, delighted in their insights, and spent time with them outside the classroom. They were not his projects, but his colleagues, neighbors, and friends. If he, as my projected paragon of Evangelical mission orthodoxy, could live so joyfully with his worldwide family, then surely I had permission to, as well.

That was a decisive moment in my life. It relieved me of some of the need to fix other people. It also deepened my understanding of the missionary and conversionary impulses I cherished. I had imagined them as being directed outward toward "unbelievers," but discovered they also moved inward toward me. I was the one changed in that class because Todd Johnson never turned the gospel off for his Christian students. He lived and spoke in such a way that every encounter with him was an opportunity to turn toward Life. What a magnificent lesson, and what a beautiful gift!

# Chapter 16: Capacious Faith

*S. Kyle Johnson*

Many joys fill the life of the Christian scholar. Much has been written about these. However, I'm not sure that enough time has been spent reflecting on the temptations. One of the most dangerous vices endemic to Christian scholarship is the fruit that fear can produce. Fear is itself, not a sin. It is, however, a gateway to defensive insularity. The Christian scholar must be on guard against a limited scope of vision, afraid to look beyond the safe confines of one's tradition, presuppositions, or cultural and demographic milieus. When one avoids anything that might trouble, challenge, or expand their faith—they fail to fulfill their vocation. Faith must be a real journey of *faith*, which presupposes confrontation with anxiety and liminality. In other words, to be faithful is to be open to the surprises of God. It is bravery in the face of the collapse of all that is safe and familiar. I believe this is part of what Paul Tillich meant when he said that the theologian (or the Christian scholar, broadly defined) is both "committed *and* alienated … inside and outside the theological circle."[1] She is always the centered explorer, the stalwart wanderer. Todd Johnson is, for me, a compelling example of these very qualities.

One of the most extraordinary powers of an effective role model is that they tap into a desire or intuition that one might already possess but does not know how to actualize. They clear a path for what it could mean to confidently inhabit a particular way of life, especially in spaces that do not always nurture those qualities. This sort of role model is a source of liberation. For me, Todd has provided this sort of leadership. He has modeled a brave, capacious faithfulness that has made it possible to unlock the sort of teacher, scholar, and Christian I aspire to be.

When I think of the ways my life has intersected with Todd Johnson, I reflect on the remarkable depths of my respect for him. I contemplate the many ways that his research and teaching have shaped my work. Underlying these technical dimensions, however, are the underlying qualities of character, the fruits of the Spirit, that serve as inspiration for my life as a whole.

## Memories of the Silk Road

In 2011 I had the privilege of an academic venture that Todd and Tricia led to Central Asia. Our primary objective was to study the history of religions along

---

1 Paul Tillich, *Systematic Theology: Three Volumes in One* (Chicago, IL: University of Chicago, 1967), Volume 1, 10.

the Silk Road, capping several months of research and preparation. My memories of this time are filled with images of the gorgeous blue mosaics of mosques and madrasas, silk tapestries, dissecting religious symbols on artifacts, and a touch of delirium from one too many nights spent in the desert. I remember the particular delight of seeing the place through Todd's eyes, as it was his first time making his journey. "Giddy" might be the right word.

The trip had an indelible impact on my outlook as a theologian. One of the many highlights was witnessing how Todd inhabits this capacious faithfulness I have described. He thoughtfully and pastorally guided us beyond the temptation to view the world and our faith from our American Evangelical vantage points. As we toured century-old mosques and museums, we explored the remarkably complex religious dynamics of the history of this region while discussing Christian engagement, competition, and at times integration with the many faiths that all met along the Silk Road. We reflected on the influence of Zoroastrianism on Judaism and Christianity and the exchanges and sharing of spiritualities (whether intentional or accidental) between Muslim, Buddhist, and Christian communities. To experience this place and its history is to confront a diversity of Christian expressions and modalities of mission as well as the complex interreligious identities that people have inhabited in this milieu. This sort of journey requires a dose of bravery and a willingness to hold one's presuppositions and preferences loosely. It requires a kind of faith that is not afraid of complexity, surprise, and a desire to transcend parochialities.

After our return, I wrote a paper as a capstone for the course. I am disgruntled to deduce that the paper exists somewhere on a backup drive that I cannot locate. But I do recall encountering the work of John C. England, a leading scholar on the history of Christianity in Asia. England provides an attractive picture (to be taken with a grain of salt on account of his slightly heavy dose of romanticism) of the egalitarian and world-facing spirituality of the churches of "the East." England argues that Christianity in Asia, particularly around the Silk Road, pioneered and exhibited a robust spirituality and ethic of service that persons of all stations could participate in. England writes, "the Church of the East was able to develop a piety that nourished the trader and traveler, the tribes-woman and princess, the nomad and farmer, the artisan, physician, teacher, and administrator."[2] As my research has shifted toward contemporary systematic theological concerns, particularly those related to spirituality, this history remains strong in the back of my mind. Evangelicals, whom I think similarly possess a charism for nurturing a faith that is egalitarian and holistic,

---

2 John C. England, *The Hidden History of Christianity in Asia: The Churches of the East Before the Year 1500* (Delhi: ISPCK; Hong Kong, CCA, 2002), 40.

and integrated with life, can draw inspiration for mission from these traditions essentially lost to Western Christianity.

England bemoans that theological education ignores Christianity's deep and rich history across Central, Eastern, and Southeastern Asia. This fact is true for theological education in both the West and the East, the latter dominated by institutions rooted in Western missiological and colonial enterprises. England writes: "Then too the study of this extensive story remains almost entirely absent from the offerings of our seminaries and universities, so that Christians in east and west alike are denied a large part of their own history."[3] Our time along the Silk Road, and in the days of research before and after, forced me to reckon more deeply with the fact that to be a Christian is to be a part of a story much larger than the one to which we are typically limited. It is a gift to be liberated from a singular narrative.

To learn about Christianity along the Silk Road is to encounter a faith shaped by a complex, global economy that is not unlike our contemporary global society. A text we read in preparation for this trip emphasized this fact: Richard Foltz's *Religions of the Silk Road*.[4] Foltz points out that the complex commerce and cosmopolitan constitution of the Silk Road at its height of activity represents a precursor to contemporary globalization. For this reason, the story of Christianity along the Silk Road is one of profound relevance. Recently, I encountered a theologian making the astonishing claim that Christianity has never, before the 20th/21st centuries, lived in a pluralistic milieu.[5] Many branches of Eastern Christian traditions, not the least of which those which existed along the Silk Road, are undoubtedly evidence to the contrary. Having encountered some of these traditions, I find confidence in knowing that I have ancestors and peers in the faith who have long histories of facing some of the questions and problems that strike some of us as entirely unprecedented.

This experience in Uzbekistan helped me grow in my conviction that it is neither prudent nor tenable to remain within one's theological silos. While my research interests eventually transitioned from the history of Eastern Christianities to systematic theology, the imperative to include the *whole* of the Christian tradition in my reflection remains paramount to my theological vision. Hoping to resist the dynamics of power that have privileged certain narratives over others, my research today prioritizes the voices of those who live

---

3 England, *Hidden History*, 163.
4 Richard Foltz, *Religions of the Silk Road: Premodern Patterns of Globalization* (London: Palgrave Macmillan, 2010).
5 Tim Hartman writes, "The context of pluralism is unprecedented in the history of the Christian church. Never before have Christians not known the dominant societal narrative." Tim Hartman, *Theology After Colonization: Bediako, Barth, and the Future of Theological Reflection* (South Bend, IN: University of Notre Dame Press, 2019), 25.

on the "undersides" (from the vantage point of Euro-American subjectivities), as the leading authorities for the people of God today. I strive to center diverse conversation partners, such as Latin American liberation theologians, African and Afro-Caribbean critics of Christian colonialism, queer theologies, global Pentecostalism, and Black religious thought. I hope my work in these areas lives up to the example that Todd has set of a capacious faith that opts for widening circles, learning at the margins, governed by a Christ-centered, missiological commitment to justice for all the peoples of the world.

After completing my Master of Divinity at Gordon-Conwell Theological Seminary, I sought a Master of Theology (ThM) from the School of Theology and Ministry at Boston College and then went on to begin my doctoral work in the Theology Department at Boston College. Transitioning from the world of Evangelical education to a Jesuit Catholic milieu required exercising the ecumenical spirit that Todd possesses in abundance. I recall occasionally attending the weekly student mass during my ThM degree. There were moments that could easily have been a source of discomfort—finding myself as one of the very few attendees to remain seated while others lined up to receive the Eucharist. Occasionally I would join the line to request a blessing, but typically I stayed put. Instead of feeling awkward conspicuousness, I remember mainly feeling joy. Although this could also be an occasion to mourn the divisions of Christianity, I experienced sheer delight at the opportunity to be in the presence of other Christians communing with Christ and one another. This is the spirit that Todd has helped nurture in me and countless others; joyful gratitude for all the many expressions of the people of God, and *all* the people God has made, near and far. More than any other quality, I hope my work as a theologian brims with this sort of joy.

**The World in the Classroom**

I am also grateful for how the work of Todd Johnson and the Center for the Study of Global Christianity (CSGC) has strengthened my work as a teacher. In my capacity as an instructor of Christian theology in a diverse Catholic university setting, a global perspective and the study of religious demography, in particular, provides an essential foundation for my teaching.

One of the most significant challenges to teaching theology in this setting is confronting the assumption that many of my (mainly White American or European) students have: Religion is irrelevant and increasingly so. This assumption reflects the general blind spots of Western secularity and Eurocentrism.

Therefore, one of my primary objectives in the classroom is to help students appreciate *that* religion remains a vital force around the globe. Research from the CSGC and other resources based on the CSGC's work are imperative classroom tools. Students are often surprised to learn about the Christian tradition's constantly evolving breadth and diversity. Many of my students are interested in various sorts of public and private international work and suddenly confront the need to understand the way Nigerian Pentecostalism shapes West African politics, how debates over different Catholic political theologies shape Latin America, or the experience of Syrian refugees coming from a variety of Eastern Christian traditions; not to mention the origins and contours of culture wars here in the United States. This global emphasis reaps very robust rewards. By the end of the semester, countless students testify to a remarkable shift in their outlook. I find that (despite some cynicism in my field) students are hungry to learn about religion and theology once they witness its global, world-shaping dimensions. My students quickly become conscious of the need to be conversant in the study of religion and theology to be well-rounded leaders able to appreciate the current situations of the globe.

In some of the more advanced classes I have taught, I try to press students to think critically about the boundaries between theology and religious studies as academic discourses. Specifically, I want to help students think about how religious ideas and power structures (i.e., Christian theological and colonial influences on the social sciences) inform so-called "secular" research. I have discovered that an introduction to the study of religious demography is beneficial for this task. While preparing a lesson in early 2022, I turned to an article that Todd Johnson and Gina Zurlo wrote in 2014, "Christian Martyrdom as a Pervasive Phenomenon."[6] This article helped stimulate my thinking about the difficulties of the religious demographer as they attempt to balance critical distance with authentic attention to the internal languages and divisions within a religious tradition. Specifically, this article delved into the academic debates about how to define martyrdom—whether there is some set of universal criteria or whether the definition must remain contingent upon the standards within a religious tradition, further troubled by the fact that different iterations of a tradition will have different standards and language. In the classroom, I synthesized some of the meta-issues raised by this research. We discussed the difficulties of determining who "counts" as a member of a particular religious tradition from the perspective of demography. Does it come down to self-identification? What if the leadership of a denomination would not recognize every self-identifier as an authentic member? What about a baptized Catholic who doesn't go to church? By tackling

---

6 Todd M. Johnson and Gina A. Zurlo, "Christian Martyrdom as a Pervasive Phenomenon," *Society* 51, no. 6 (2014): 679–685.

these questions students appreciate that the scholar, despite their neutrality, must delve into theology. The subsequent conversations I have with these students help them think more critically about the blurry lines between theology and religious studies and the difficulty of studying religion in ways that avoid bias, anachronism, and adverse power dynamics.

In a similar register, global Christianity (and engagement with other global faith traditions) provides a holistic foundation for the way I try to teach theology. Operating under the mission of the liberal arts tradition, I maintain the conviction that an education that remains in the silos of Eurocentrism (and the gendered, sexualized, and racialized subjectivities reified along with it) is a failure to live up to the mandate to form students into critical, well-rounded, empathetic, thinkers. In my classroom, specifically, to study theology is to learn about the theologies and religious traditions of the African diaspora, the history of dialogue and exchange between Christianity and Islam, or the witness of Archbishop Oscar Romero's martyrdom. In this regard, prioritizing a global perspective helps unleash the possibility and promise of the liberal arts, where students are indeed able to expand their thought, empathy, and comprehension to ever-new horizons. For those students who identify as persons of faith, it is also to fulfill the particular calling of *faith*-based liberal arts education, attending to the diverse work of God around the globe as a way of delighting in God's mission and creativity.

**My Hope**

It is Todd's capacious faithfulness that forms the unifying thread across his influence on my work and faith. I hope that something of these qualities will filter through in the way I inhabit my vocation as a scholar, theologian, and teacher. Above all I hope, in all my life, to imitate how Todd has modeled the boundless and borderless love of the One from Galilee.

**Works Cited**

England, John C. *The Hidden History of Christianity in Asia: The Churches of the East Before the Year 1500*. Delhi: ISPCK, 2002.

Foltz, Richard. *Religions of the Silk Road: Premodern Patterns of Globalization*. London: Palgrave Macmillan, 2010.

Hartman, Tim. *Theology After Colonization: Bediako, Barth, and the Future of Theological Reflection*. South Bend, IN: University of Notre Dame Press, 2019.

Johnson, Todd M., and Gina A. Zurlo. "Christian Martyrdom as a Pervasive Phenomenon." *Society* 51, no. 6 (2014): 679–685.

Tillich, Paul. *Systematic Theology: Three Volumes in One*. Chicago, IL: University of Chicago, 1967.

# Chapter 17: An Appreciation for Todd Johnson
## A Personal Reflection

*Grace Ji-Sun Kim*

There are only a few people in the world whom you meet once and then want to stay in touch with them, as they are genuinely kind, thoughtful, and interesting. One such person is Dr. Todd Johnson, and I have become a better person, scholar, and writer because I met him. I came to know Todd a few years ago when he and Kenneth Ross invited me to join them in co-editing *Christianity in North America*, volume 7 of the 10-volume Edinburgh Companions to Global Christianity. They had already edited the first 5 volumes of this series and had just completed volume 6.

The Edinburgh Companions series is an enormous and ambitious project that covers Christianity historically, regionally, and globally. When Todd first reached out, I became overwhelmed by the enormity of this project and believed that there was no way that I could join them in editing this important volume. I doubted whether I could even consider taking on this enormous task of co-editing such a large-scale volume; having co-edited several books in the past that turned out to be fantastic, the process was always challenging and stressful. Hence, I was very hesitant to take on this big responsibility as a co-editor. But, Todd assured me that he had assistants who could manage the more tedious tasks of an editor. After much hesitation and several emails with Todd and co-editor Ken Ross, I decided to join them in working on this important book. I never regretted my decision.

I went to Boston with anticipation and excitement to meet my two co-editors. This initial editorial meeting was at Todd's home and was full of laughs, good work, collegiality, and food. Todd and his wife, Tricia, went out of their way to make sure I was comfortable during my stay and ensured that I was well fed. We joined together in breaking bread and enjoyed our time together as co-editors and colleagues. Tricia cooked a delicious meal and offered cookies, tea, snacks, and dessert. Their practice of warm hospitality brought a lot of joy and warmth to my visit, paired with wonderful collegiality and a time to get to know Todd better both personally and professionally.

Visiting Boston also means eating lobster! I will never forget when Todd treated Ken and me to a fantastic lobster restaurant. I love seafood—to devour a bucket full of lobster was the craziest thing that three scholars can do and from that moment, I knew that we would have a great friendship. We ate to our hearts, content. It was truly an unforgettable dinner and a great conversation. Food fellowship should never be underestimated. Korean culture emphasizes the importance of sharing food, with the common greeting, "Have you eaten?" If your guest hasn't eaten and you have, it is still common to go out and eat together to make sure your friend is well fed. Eating and breaking bread is how we come together as community and as friends, something that Todd enjoys and certainly practices. Through food, Christians come together to learn from one another, enjoy one another, and share joy with each other.

**Decolonizing White Christianity**

As a Korean American theologian, I am usually skeptical of White American scholars and professors who are engaged in the study of World Christianity and missiology in part due to what happened to Asian culture and history when White missionaries came to convert us. White missionaries came to different parts of Asia and told Asians that our culture and religions were evil and should be subordinate to the Western world and White Christianity. When White American missionaries went to Korea, they built Western homes, ate Western foods, and used Western appliances; they built their own communities and lived better than most Koreans, leading many Koreans to desire life like the Americans. As a result, some Koreans were drawn to Christianity for materialistic, and not only for spiritual, gains.

White supremacy spreads the message of the inferiority of non-White cultures and religions. White missionaries told Asians that our ancestor worship, festivals, and holidays were not acceptable and should be eliminated. Such efforts did not just end in Asia, but affected Asian immigrants all over the world, where they took the teaching of White missionaries to their new homes. For example, many Asian immigrants in North America practiced and worshipped the way missionaries taught them, and as a result held deep within them biases against their own culture. My own immigrant parents were affected, told by missionaries that Jesus and God were White. Asians were taught to remove anything Asian from their lives to advance in society, including relinquishing their own culture, religion, and practices for the sake of believing in the superiority of White Christianity. In many cases, after the work of White missionaries, many Asians have perceived scholars researching World Christianity like another imperial tool to colonize the world under the banner of White supremacy.

This mode of thinking is so far from Todd's scholarship, writing, and practice. Reviewing Todd's scholarly work and collaborating with him on *Christianity in North America* has made me realize the depth, compassion, empathy, and understanding that he has for World Christianity. Many White male scholars will examine global Christianity through the lens of colonialism, Westernization, and imperialism. This view only leads to destruction and devastation of communities outside of the West. However, Todd's experience of living in Singapore and Thailand has helped him bring a different understanding to global Christianity that isn't blurred by White Western perspectives. Rather than operating from White imperialism, Todd has a keen understanding of non-White cultures, religions, and contexts and particularly welcomes Asian heritages and histories. He is sensitive to the issues pertaining to regions and countries around the world and has a lens to appropriately critique the influence of White superiority in Christianity. He is fully aware of the problems caused by White Christians around the globe, and actively seeks to uplift marginalized voices and make them more prominent. He works to decolonize the harmful ways that White Christianity has influenced World Christianity and teaches others to do the same.

## Conclusion

From his different world perspectives, Todd comes to see the world as interdependent, which has led him to faithfully contribute to the growing scholarship on global Christianity by publishing monographs, atlases, articles, and encyclopedias as well as co-directing the Center for the Study of Global Christianity at Gordon-Conwell Theological Seminary. His work is appreciated by so many people around the globe and his non-Euro-centric perspective has been helpful to Christians everywhere. In addition to his scholarship, it is his genuine kindness, thoughtfulness, and warmth that make him so special. Todd's scholarship on global Christianity is important, powerful, and impactful.

It has been a deep joy to work with Todd on *Christianity in North America* and I have come to respect and admire him in so many ways. I appreciate his work ethic, as he put so much effort and time into making our volume a fabulous scholarly work as well as a book for all who are interested in Christianity in North America in all of its diversity. Todd's work is meticulous, thoughtful, and meaningful. His compassion abounds as he works to understand the Other, and as a White man, empathize with other's experiences of social injustice. He understands the problems that women of color experience by reading and heeding their voices and mentors and works with many such women. He provides room for them to speak, teach, write, and share. I really admire this about him. Perhaps most importantly, Todd takes time to dream with people to envision a better world to come.

# Chapter 18: How Are You? What Is Your Name?
## Hospitality and Friendship in Mission and World Christianity

*Feruza Krason*

Hi, how are you? What is your name? Until one has lived in a foreign country and has felt loneliness and disconnect that comes from feeling displaced, one won't know how welcome these questions can be. This is how I met Tricia Johnson at a playground at Gordon-Conwell Theological Seminary. I was surprised by her friendliness and excitement to meet someone from Uzbekistan. In fact, she was so eager for her husband, Todd Johnson, to meet our family that they had us over for dinner soon after that first meeting. I clearly remember that evening of fellowship and warmth; I was a stranger and they welcomed me. Tricia called her dad, missiologist Ralph Winter, and shared the news of meeting a Muslim background follower of Jesus, which seemed over the top until I heard how much her family had been involved in spreading the good news among Muslims all over the world. The friendship I have enjoyed with Todd and Tricia is an answer to a prayer that I had before I even started following Jesus. I had asked God how I would survive if my family and friends rejected me because of my faith in Jesus, but God promised that that he would give me hundreds of brothers and sisters. Todd and Tricia are a big part of that fulfilled promise. That afternoon at the playground, I found a new sister and a brother because of Tricia's sensitivity and her love for the foreigner.

It has been 20 years since that beautiful summer day on the playground and even some of my family and friends in Uzbekistan have had the privilege of meeting Todd and Tricia. My brother, sister, and their spouses where astonished when they met and shared a meal with the Johnsons; their heart for others was so beautiful, their dedication and love for the church was clear from their utter devotion to the Lord, the Creator of all. This devotion has taken Todd and Tricia to places all over the world as witnesses of God's faithfulness. They lead a study abroad course on religions on the Silk Road in Central Asia, teaching students not only facts and figures about the past, but also guiding students to experience the thoughtfulness and partnership that Todd and Tricia demonstrate toward one another. Those who witness the deep respect that Todd and Tricia have for each other gain much more than academic knowledge. In their relationship, the Johnsons model what it means to be a husband-and-wife team. Their spiritual gifts are complementary, and these gifts are used to bring growth not only to the spiritual lives of their family and friends, but also growth in emotional intelligence. In their desire to honor God and those whom they serve, they show patience, kindness, goodness, and faithfulness to all who come across their path on this life's journey. By doing so, they show the world what it means to have the fruits of the Spirit so clearly exhibited in one's life. As they love, they reveal the ultimate love that was displayed on the cross by Jesus and Father God. As they so graciously navigate life's challenges, we witness how God is central to everything they are and do.

We see how God has gifted Todd in his academic accomplishments featured in journals, books, online forums, and conferences. What we don't see, but those who are close to Todd know, is that in Tricia, he has a partner in life who has supported him throughout the years and who has been a solid rock as Todd and his team keep enlightening the world with their wealth of knowledge at the Center for Study of Global Christianity and beyond. Tricia's behind the scenes work of ministering to those around her has been an example of how we, Christians, should be ready to answer the call of God to bring glory to him in all we think, do and say. Whether it is teaching English, hosting, teaching life skills, leading a Bible study or serving on the missions committee, Tricia approaches every task as if she is serving Christ himself. With a wife like that, how can Todd not be great!

Todd and Tricia's awareness of cultures of the world and their life-long commitment to honor those around them is something I aspire to be and do. I remember being at a conference where Todd and I were both presenting. Todd had just given a lecture on the importance of contextualizing in missions, both global and local. He has a way of bringing numbers to life as he tells us of how the church is changing all around the world. He had shown the importance of humility in the church as sacrificial servants for the sake of the kingdom of God. After that brilliant lecture followed by a coffee break, I noticed Todd sitting by himself in the large hall and I sat right next to him. The hall was practically empty, I could have sat anywhere! As I sat down, Todd, ever the teacher, said, "Do you see what you did?" I was clueless as to what he meant, but he said, "Being Uzbek, you didn't want me to sit by myself. But, being of Scandinavian heritage, I had chosen to sit by myself." I had not even been conscious of my decision, yet Todd quickly analyzed the scenario and used that moment to teach me how we make choices based on our cultural context and how these subtle patterns nudge us in our daily, if not hourly, decisions. He helped me become aware of the importance of even the smallest decisions and how to react to situations when we are pushed beyond our comfort zone. Now I realize that Todd might have been seeking privacy at that moment, but being sensitive to my culture, he saw that my need was to make sure that nobody would sit alone, and he accommodated that need. In that conversation, I mentioned that the Uzbek language doesn't even have a word for "privacy," and he incorporated that into our conversation of the different dynamics of Western vs. Eastern cultures. The situation we found ourselves in clearly demonstrated what he had been teaching in that morning's lecture and by reacting to the situation in a most gracious way, he proved to me that he lives what he preaches. In both Todd and Tricia, I found teachers whom I can follow. I can be confident that I can do what they do, not only what they teach!

# Chapter 19: The Power of Curiosity and Generosity

*Sandra S.K. Lee*

I had little idea of the Lord's plans to re-form and re-frame my vision of myself and of the world when I first arrived at Gordon-Conwell Theological Seminary in the winter of 2001. I was a burnt-out high school Social Studies teacher and Youth and English Ministry leader from my father's Korean immigrant church, with an irresistible call from God to lead and educate ministry leaders, and to prepare through study on the "Holy Hill" nestled in the sleepy, affluent New England town of South Hamilton, Massachusetts. There were many times during my seminary studies I wondered why God led me there to study, when ostensibly I did not fit in the surrounding community, nor within the school, as one of the few women in the Masters of Divinity program, and one of even fewer women of color.

I keenly felt myself navigating in liminal spaces—between mainstream White American and immigrant church life, Eastern/Western, urban/suburban, and local/global. In my final year of seminary, I felt called and focused my studies on global missions. It was in this context that I had the privilege of being introduced to Todd Johnson through Timothy Tennent, professor of world mission, and Doug Birdsall, executive chair of the Lausanne Movement. I immensely enjoyed studying and co-authoring pieces with Todd—with someone who masterfully understood and simultaneously bridged and navigated liminal spaces. I was thrilled with the additional opportunity to be seconded to the Center for Study of Global Christianity (CSGC) as the managing editor for the *Atlas of Global Christianity* (Edinburgh University Press, 2009). These years with Todd were providential, as he became an academic and professional mentor. Moreover, his character and *how* he led profoundly informed how I continue to engage in ministry today as an ordained pastor in the Evangelical Covenant Church.

One of my earliest memories of Todd was seeing him running around town—literally! There he was, day after day, in his running gear, at a steady pace along the winding, wooded roads of South Hamilton. He was as reliable as the late Haddon Robinson, in his mid-70s, still exercising daily on the elliptical at the Bennett Center at Gordon College at 6am. If you didn't see Todd running on the sidewalks of South Hamilton, you could catch him at the local Starbucks early in the morning (5am!), reading everything from the *Wall Street Journal* to Jared Diamond's *Guns, Germs, and Steel*. He often described the early morning as his most productive time of day, where he had the space to think clearly, expansively, and creatively. His discipline across many spheres of life allows him the structure and space to step out onto the proverbial balcony to gain wider perspectives and deeper insights. With this same discipline, Todd gives meticulous attention to his intellectual inquiries and endeavors. Details matter not for their own sake and perfection, but because behind each detail is a person and a life, and each person and life matters.

Todd not only works with detail, depth, and breadth of the global church, but also labors with a perseverance marked by faith, vision, and prayer. His work began in a church basement in Richmond, Virginia, working with and then carrying on the statistical work of David Barrett to enumerate the global church. In faith, in 2003 Todd moved the CSGC to Gordon-Conwell into the first floor of a student apartment building. Deep in prayer, he understood the potential impact of being on a major seminary campus and near a global, intellectual city, in partnership with other scholars and institutions in the Boston area, including the Boston Theological Interreligious Consortium. From Richmond, Virginia to the CSGC, Todd and his team saved books and irreplaceable files from consistent floods and water damage, practiced patience during decades-long unfulfilled promises of funding, and at times ran on little more than faith and prayer. Nevertheless, Todd continually testified to God's provision and faithfulness in answering prayer. There was always a deep non-anxious presence and abiding joy that came with walking alongside Todd as he stepped forward in faith. Each staff meeting concluded in communal prayer for the work of the CSGC and its impact on the global church. It took nearly 20 years, amid the COVID-19 pandemic, for the full realization of the Center for the Study of Global Christianity as the heart of Gordon-Conwell, after its move into a renovated lecture hall in the Goddard Library building in 2020. The world has irrevocably changed due to the pandemic and the future of Gordon-Conwell's South Hamilton campus is now uncertain; yet, there is no question that although modalities may change, the way forward for Todd continues to be discernment through prayer and faith, building and equipping an empowered team and community of inquiry with vision and purpose.

**Portrait of a Leader**

A few of Todd's outstanding characteristics are his humility, hospitality, and curiosity—all inextricably linked. His humility and curiosity inform his global perspective and his uncanny ability to connect with people, as well as connect the seemingly intangible with the tangible. Todd's warmth, hospitality, and listening posture create an inviting space to explore new connections, questions, and terrains. Within this welcoming space and listening posture, Todd enters into dialogue and into the stories, worlds, and perspectives of others.

It is said, the shortest distance between two people is a story—and Todd can not only listen well to stories, but also tell stories! One of my favorites is when he got his first smartphone. He went out with his family to their favorite local restaurant, and he was fascinated with exploring all the apps, particularly the weather app. To his horror, he saw a massive storm brewing in their area on the app and he informed his family, "There's a huge storm heading right toward us!" His daughters exclaimed, "Daddy! Look out the window!" As he lifted his eyes up from his phone and looked outside, trees were bent nearly to the ground by wind and rain was pouring down in sheets. He often shares this story to illustrate that we need to look up and all around, beyond the little screens that are right in front of us.

As Christians, we cannot solely be preoccupied with "the little screens" immediately before us. The focus is not just the global Protestant church, but the global church of all Christians, and the global community of both religious and secular communities. Todd is ever curious about people, their stories, and their histories. His curiosity is not just informed from his near photographic memory (although I'm sure that helps, especially when locating citations in his vast library!); nor from searching for treasures in used bookstores. It arises from his humility and genuine desire to connect with and learn from people. Todd asks what is important, not only to his inquiry but also to the person in front of him. Todd also asks how best to communicate to specific audiences in their specific contexts. He is a rare scholar who can seamlessly segue in his PowerPoint presentations from Star Wars references to contemporary Asian artists like He Qi, to the Silk Road across Central Asia, to dialoguing with preeminent Muslim scholars, to the Vatican. Todd reminds us that we must be globally-minded Christians as well as globally-minded citizens—ever curious about the people and the world around us—as we are all ultimately connected.

For Todd, this connection extends beyond the world around us right now to all those who have come before us and those who come after us. Todd is ever desirous to honor his mentor, David Barrett, and his father-in-law, missiologist Ralph Winter, and the scores of scholars around the world who have come before him. He is not only mindful of the past, but also driven to equip and empower the next generation of leaders who not only reflect the current reality of the church, but who also will set the tone to lead the next generation.

Todd has gone beyond merely speaking for over 20 years about the future of the global church as ethnically diverse and female as a theoretical talking point; he also has actively sought to identify, empower, and partner with women and people of color through recruiting, collaborating, and co-authoring articles, chapters, and books with them, myself included. He has often said, "If we want to reach the whole world, we've got to listen to women." Global Christianity is majority female, and the church's task is too large for over half the church to be ignored and disempowered. Todd is driven by both the demographic reality of gender in the world church as well as a father of three daughters. He consistently demonstrates, through mentorship and partnership, how to leverage his own privilege to bring women and people of color a proverbial seat at the table, as well as give them the ability to reconfigure the table and go in the kitchen to decide the menu of what's actually to be served at the table. He models, not just in thought, but through strategic action, how to move the needle one step closer to bringing about God's kingdom "on earth, as it is in heaven."

Todd's life and work have left an indelible mark upon mine in how I endeavor to live and to minister. His imprint has been *life* upon *life*. I've long aspired to press on as faithfully in prayer and discipline, but I fall woefully short and feel hopelessly scattered. Todd's final words to me before leaving Gordon-Conwell after getting married were the immortal words of Rev. Dr. Martin Luther King, Jr. in his 1960 address to Spelman College, a historic Black college for women: "If you can't fly then run, if you can't run then walk, if you can't walk then crawl, but whatever you do, you have to keep moving forward." These words of encouragement continue to carry me through each phase of life. Like Dr. King, Todd exemplifies deep faith, vision, and purpose for God's kingdom. His words continue to reverberate in and through me—to lift my eyes and look around, think humbly and globally, to devote myself to being curious about the world and those around me, to honor those who have gone before me and conscientiously and generously create space for those beside and behind me.

My time and work with Todd were not just providential, but transformative. It transformed a young Korean American woman who was scared of her own voice and felt invisible navigating in liminal spaces into someone who recognizes her own voice, story, and place as central and essential to the great story of God and his people. It transformed me further into one who, like Todd, empowers others, amplifies voices, and creates and facilitates spaces and opportunities for all to be woven in as central pieces of God's redeeming kin-dom work. With this spirit, I continue to minister to pastors, congregations, and ministries in a regional denominational office. I learned from someone who I am privileged to call both mentor and friend—ever faithful, prayerful, humble, hospitable, curious, globally-minded, and generous. Ever leveraging my privilege to bring others whose presence and voices have been traditionally absent, invisible, or silenced to the proverbial table (and to the kitchen!) to prepare for that great Revelation 7 kingdom celebration to come.

# Chapter 20: Intellectual Work
## Reflections on 30 Years of Mission Research

*Justin Long*

My work in missions began in the early 1990s, at a small missions network then called the Association for International Mission Services (AIMS), which served mission agencies from a Pentecostal-Charismatic perspective. There, among other things, I was responsible for assisting the Operation Unreached department—the part of AIMS that focused on helping to mobilize workers to unreached peoples and places.

In those pre-Internet days, we frequently received letters from people who wanted to know which of our member agencies worked in particular parts of the world, with questions like, "I'm interested in working in Ethiopia, who should I contact?" Prior to AIMS, I had worked with various political organizations in IT to build donor databases, and it was a very small leap to apply this technical knowledge to create a database of AIMS member agencies and where they worked, and then be able to generate reports for such requests on a more automated basis. Without realizing the implications, I had created a "work among" database for agencies that leaned toward the Pentecostal-Charismatic world, the first of its kind.

At the same time, AIMS was formulating the idea of international desks, since a partner agency wanted to create a China desk within AIMS, and it seemed natural enough to extend this into a Middle East desk, an Africa desk, an Eastern Europe desk, and so forth. The individuals in these desks would help to foster projects and mobilize people for those regions of the world.

The Middle East desk was to be handled by a man from the United Kingdom, and on his visit to Virginia Beach, where AIMS was located, I was asked to show him around. He told me he knew Dr. David Barrett and the team producing the second edition of the *World Christian Encyclopedia*. He took me to Richmond to meet them, and that's how I became involved with Drs. Barrett and Johnson—or, as they soon became to me, David and Todd. In 1995, when my wife, Heidi, and I married, the *Encyclopedia* team invited us to come work with them, and we accepted. We were part of the team from 1995 to 1999, which was a pivotal period that profoundly shaped my life.

### Intellectual Work

One of my earliest memories of Todd is a bit vague, and yet it formed an impression that stuck with me and marked my later years. I had been asked to do an analysis of a field in a database used in the *World Christian Encyclopedia*. While doing it, a computer crashed and the program I had been working on was lost, with no backup. Todd came in to see how it was going and, on learning what had happened, commiserated with me over "the loss of all the intellectual work" I had done to that point. For me, it was simply a nuisance, just several hours of coding that I would have to recreate. Yet, without realizing it, I subconsciously created a dichotomy. I thought of the coding as having little value, and the analysis of the output as the valuable thing. But Todd's comment made me see it in a different light. The labor involved in writing the code was in its own way just as valuable as the analysis. The work I was doing wasn't just idle speculation or mindless grunt work—there was intellectual work in the coding itself. This recognition led me to realize that intellectual work—working with my mind, including exploring random trails through the databases—was important and desirable. Explorations of the data would lead us to new discoveries that could be valuable, and this affirmation released me into a greater calling in missions research.

**The Monday Morning Reality Check**

In the late 1990s, the World Wide Web became more accessible and CrossConnect (xc.org) created the first missionary email lists. I felt at the time that the *World Christian Encyclopedia* team did not have the opportunity to widely share any of the amazing information it was gathering. The team had a bias to not publish before they were ready, but at the same time I felt like we ought to share a few things, especially since the project was taking longer than anticipated. Through a series of discussions, we began to publish one small factoid on a regular basis and the Monday Morning Reality Check was born, delivered via an email mailing list through CrossConnect.

I remember Todd's concern that we should not allow a weekly publication to distract us from the greater work of the *Encyclopedia*. At the time I was young, inexperienced, and enthusiastic, and hadn't fully come to grasp how creating a regular publication was a different creature from a one-off article. I later came to understand I was creating a content monster that would have to be fed. Todd and David helped me shape the Reality Check into a single statistic published once a week, which kept the monster tamed. Even with that, I quickly came to see how easily even something small could devour hours of time—and I have been mindful ever since to not start something without a clear plan to maintain it over an indefinite period of time.

**The AD 2025 Global Monitor**

Some months later, Todd approached me with the idea of revising and updating the research team's print newsletter. The *AD 2000 Global Monitor* had once been published as a four-page summary of research findings they were encountering in the course of their work. Todd had served as the managing editor during its publication run. His thought was to now revive it, updating the title and making it an eight-page, with me serving as the managing editor. I was excited, and a bit nervous at stepping into a role that Todd had once held. I was also mindful of what I had already learned from the Reality Check, since this would be an even larger endeavor. I was impressed by how thoughtfully and intellectually Todd approached the boundaries of the Monitor's goals and the inclusion criteria for articles.

We began producing the newsletter on a bi-monthly basis (careful of that content monster), and I learned a lot about the tasks of article recruitment and writing, editing, publication design, delivering it to a printer, and getting it mailed out. Through the course of creating the newsletter, I was amazed by how much meaning the research team managed to pack into a one-page article. The pages of every newsletter were stuffed full of data and analysis.

Also, over the course of several issues, we returned to designing one-page infographics that highlighted a single concept. One of those, Global Religious Dynamics, which charted the ebb and flow of population, evangelization, conversion, and defection, is a diagram I draw to this day whenever I teach lesson nine (the Remaining Task) for the Perspectives on the World Christian Movement course. It's the defining piece of data that never fails to envision and stirs people by bringing into sharp relief the concept of the unevangelized.

The combination of the Monday Morning Reality Check and the *AD 2025 Global Monitor* influenced my thinking about subsequent publications. From 2004–2008 I helped to create an online magazine called *Momentum*. Like the *Monitor*, *Momentum* had a carefully defined mission, selected sections, and a maximum length. Unlike the *Monitor*, but like the Reality Check, I avoided the pain and cost of printing and mailing by publishing it in a PDF online. Throughout, I remembered the lessons about providing high impact content and tried to limit most articles in *Momentum* to just a few pages packed with value. Some years later, I returned to publishing a regular email, called the Weekly Roundup, this time, calling back to my roots in the Monday Morning Reality Check coupled with Todd's own New Books section in the *Monitor*. The Weekly Roundup contains an annotated list of links to articles about events in the world of the unreached, like how Todd's New Book section in the *Monitor* contained a list of new books with very brief reviews of how each influences missiological thinking and practice. The Weekly Roundup goes to nearly 1,500 mission leaders and activists worldwide, who frequently tell me it's one of the key resources they read each week. It's shaped in large part by my experiences with the *Encyclopedia*.

**Live Edit**

About halfway through our time working on the *Encyclopedia*, I followed a thread of curiosity and wrote a program to analyze the notes field of the peoples database. It contained a code describing the religious affiliation of an individual people group often in the form of, for example, R[religion]=30% Christian, 70% Muslim. We were still in an early draft, but my analysis showed the religious affiliation information in the peoples database didn't match up to the religious affiliation information in the religions database. In some places they were close, in others they were markedly apart. I printed out reams of tables and analyses, temporarily taping them up on a wall, and Todd inspected it. Making Todd or David stop, think, and deeply consider something was something of an intellectual trophy for me; it meant I'd discovered something new, the hallmark of a researcher. Todd realized that we would have to reconcile the religions database, denominations database, and peoples database together.

Some days later he came back to me with an idea. Could we write a program that would enable him to view all the related data for specific countries in the various databases, with a live total of, for example, the various religions, or for Christians, or for a population? Could he use that program to update the figures, which would then recalculate the totals until they all matched? This program came to be called LiveEdit, a version of which is still being used today at the Center for the Study of Global Christianity, and it remains a crucial way that data are reconciled for analysis and publication. I also have a LiveEdit program for my own databases, which uses much of the same approach to reconcile different databases with each other and bring the totals to match.

The process of coding the program brought me to a deep understanding of how Todd used different perspectives of data (countries, cities, provinces, languages, peoples, religious demography, denominational data) to inform, clarify, and correct one's understanding of a critical fact (like the percentage of a place or people who follow Christ). Further research was necessary when data for one perspective (such as from a government census) didn't agree with data from another perspective (such as from a denomination). It is a major red flag in research to have just one perspective on a particular problem; a second and third perspective of the same situation to confirm or challenge the first produces far more confidence in the analysis.

The process of developing the LiveEdit program provided me a deeper understanding of how programs could be useful tools for people. I frequently sat with Todd, watching while he edited the data, seeing how he interacted with the program, and conversed about potential new improvements and upgrades. To this day, I still help with various information technology projects and programs in my current organization. I work much in the same way I did with Todd, by staying close to the people who use the tools, watch how they are regularly utilized, and try to make them as error-free and beneficial as possible.

**Books, Books, and More Books**

Toward the end of our time at the *Encyclopedia* project, Heidi and I had our first child. A month or two before she was due to give birth, we were over at Todd's house for dinner with his family. He showed me his massive attic library: I had never before seen that many books in a person's house. Every corner was crammed. Shelves of books had been worked into the smallest of spaces. Learning of my own love for science fiction, he pulled out some of his favorites for me to borrow and introduced me to several new authors. His love for books and book sales was infectious. I can't remember if I'd ever heard of a library book sale before that night, but ever since then my wife and I have attended book sales at every opportunity. My own appreciation for a good collection of books grew through Todd's influence, and while I don't have a library quite the same size, I do have more than one bookshelf, and regularly keep notes on what I'm reading.

**The Goal**

Todd does not pursue intellectual work for its own sake. He and David embedded in me a passion for the unevangelized. They helped me understand the reality that billions of people are born, live, and die without having access to the Good News. Yet, Todd also helped me grasp the idea that I could use my own skills in thinking, analyzing, and communicating to change that reality, which has become a defining element of my work. I have spent the better part of 30 years collaborating with networks and mission agencies to see more resources directed toward those with least access to the gospel. Today, I spend half of my time researching and documenting rapidly growing movements to Christ and places where gospel access is rapidly expanding to understand why these networks are growing and how we can help them to spread into other areas. The other half of my time is spent mobilizing more cross-cultural missionaries to bring the gospel to the unevangelized. Because of this work, thousands of additional people are aware of the unevangelized, and dozens of people are now on the field working to start movements to reach them. I look forward to the day when hundreds more will join them. Todd's impact on the lives of many has made me consider my own legacy. As I pass the age of 50, I think more intensely about who I am empowering, raising up, encouraging, and paving the way for. Todd passed on many things that made me a better worker and a better person and I hope to be doing the same for others.

# Chapter 21: The Transforming Power of Images, Memories, and Words on Local Church Mission

*Brian McAtee*

There are many images, memories, and words that I have shared time and again in the past 20 years coming from my four years working for and with Dr. Todd Johnson. The first image comes from the very first time my then wife, Claire, and I tried to meet Todd. It was an early November weekday morning. We had no reason to think anything was out of the ordinary until we learned the entire Boston metro traffic grid was one big parking lot due to a sudden flash freeze that had glazed the roads. A snow squall moved in during the predawn hours while it was 34 degrees. The temperature dropped below freezing as the squall ended and wet, untreated roads glazed over instantly, sending cars sliding all over the highways. People were stuck in their cars much of the day. Our meeting was postponed a few days. It seemed quite a fitting start for a South Carolinian and his Texan wife to begin their journey with a guy from Minnesota.

Claire and I had been serving international students at Boston University the previous four years with our mission sending agency, the Cooperative Baptist Fellowship (CBF). The CBF wanted us to work with Todd as he moved up from Richmond, Virginia and established the new Center for the Study of Global Christianity (CSGC) at Gordon-Conwell Theological Seminary. We were to help him open the CSGC, assist him in his research efforts, and provide strategic data to direct the agency's work among the unreached. Claire had a passion for the unreached, my parents had served among them, and I loved all things global. I also liked numbers. It was a good fit for us.

When the roads thawed enough for southerners to drive on them safely, we met with Todd and began our work with him in February 2004. Because his temporary office was in a small room next to the library, Claire and I would meet there with Todd as needed before finding a place in the library to do our work. Before long, the first floor of a student apartment building (a former preschool) became available, and we helped Todd move all of his books down the hill into their new home. We assembled those many bookshelves, placed the books where Todd wanted them, and made the space a home for conducive research.

The Transforming Power of Images, Memories, and Words on Local Church Mission   133

## A Map That Frames the World

One of the many things I love about Todd is the way he presents something new. It's hard to quantify in words. There's a rise and excitement in his voice, a sparkle in his eye, and a lift in his step. Too many of us present our new things with haughtiness and over-excitement. Todd manages to do it with humility and directs attention to whatever it is, so you are buying into it also. My first encounter with him in such a moment came without warning, as most life shaping moments occur. He came to Claire and me one morning with a simple piece of paper that had a map on it. "I want to show you this thing I have been working on," he said. "OK," I thought; nothing too amazing about this I suspected. I was wrong.

Todd had plotted the center of Christian population around single points on the globe throughout the church's history since the church began. When he told me what it was, I was stunned. "This is the kind of guy we are working with?! Wow," I thought to myself. I don't know if his motive was to provide a framework for all we would do there, but it worked. Not only did it frame our work there, it framed everything else since then. Later in my days as a missions minister, as I read and listened to others discuss the state of the church here in the United States and elsewhere, I saw this map (figure 1). I saw that black line ending in Timbuktu, Mali. I wonder where the black line has gone these past 15 years since I left the CSGC.

I have discussed the map many times in various settings. After spending two years with Todd onsite at Gordon-Conwell, various circumstances led Claire and I to move to the First Baptist Church of Oklahoma City, Oklahoma. I continued working with Todd, gathering church congregation and membership records for all the denominations in the *World Christian Database* for the year 2005 that would appear in the *Atlas of Global Christianity*. I had multiple opportunities to present on the status of global Christianity in ordinary congregational settings. This map was always a centerpiece of my presentations.

Recently I attended a fellowship held in the home of a member of my new church, also in Oklahoma City. We were going about the room with each person sharing things about themselves. After I finished, the host of the party, Larry, spoke up and said, "I remember a talk Brian gave about 15 years ago when he was working on that global Christianity stuff. He had this map that really stood out to me. It showed where all the Christians that have ever been lived! Or something like that. Is that right Brian?"

Larry did a great job explaining something that had happened over a decade ago; something I hardly remember doing! But of course, I remembered the map! And I was fascinated that a man well into his 70s remembered a map from that far back and something about it. So, for the next few moments, I told the story of Todd's map yet again to a room of a dozen adults. Their fascination at the methodology and story it tells of our world and church undoubtedly left a strong impression on them. Larry isn't the only person who has come up to me remembering that map years after hearing me tell them about it. Other ordinary Oklahoma Baptists have built a new missions framework for themselves as well, from a turbulent, black line traced on a globe.

**American Church Statistics That Are Sadly True**

When I left Boston for Oklahoma City in 2006, I had a true passion for helping the average church member understand global missions and engaging them directly among the unreached. As a good Baptist, I had a true love for the local church. I knew that our local autonomous churches, who had more opportunities to engage in direct global missions, were not prepared to do so because agencies had always done it for them. They needed what Todd offered. Todd was game for helping as best he could in this endeavor. The pastor at First Baptist Church of Oklahoma City at that time, Dr. Tom Ogburn, was supportive and passionate about it also and he gave me a position to launch the effort.

*Figure 1. Statistical center of gravity of Christianity, 33–2100*

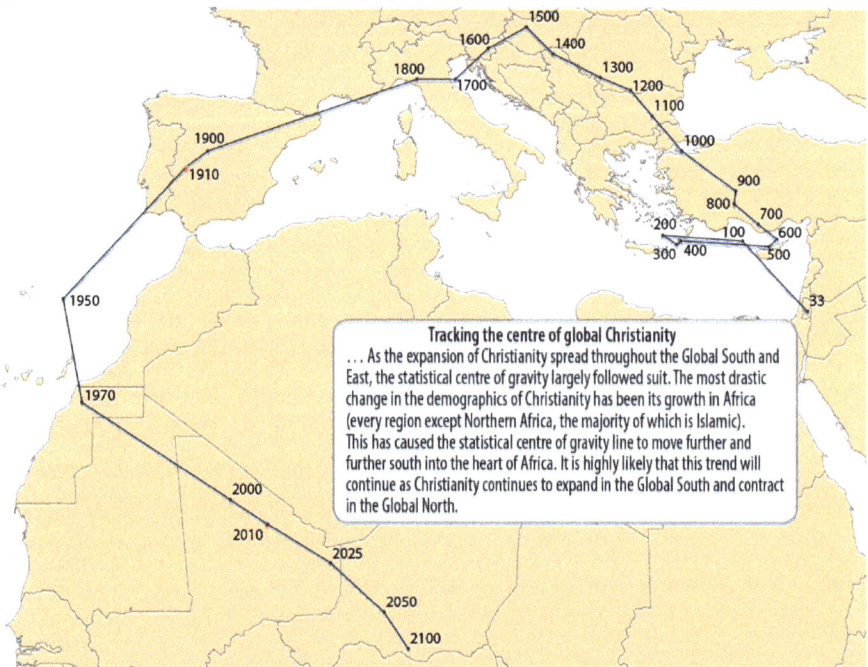

Source: Todd M. Johnson and Kenneth R. Ross eds., *Atlas of Global Christianity 1910–2010* (Edinburgh: Edinburgh University Press, 2009), 53.

# The Transforming Power of Images, Memories, and Words on Local Church Mission

At the time Claire and I began working with Todd, he had a lengthy PowerPoint that included some rather devastating statistics about the American church's place in the global effort to reach the unreached. For having worked in a place like the CSGC, I don't have a great memory for numbers. However, there are two that have stayed with me all these years.

1. More money is stolen from churches than is given to global missions.
2. The global church spends far more on itself and its own people than it does on global missions.

My naïve passions for and about the local church ran into these hard cold walls of reality. I would say that these realities, today, are shaped by the institutional church's desire to survive the march of Todd's black line further and further away from it, deeper south and east into Africa. (I suspect that's where it's still going!) Money is the blood of the institutional church; if it drains out and dries up, the church dies; or so goes the thinking and the behaviors follow suit. People on mission committees see hungry people pouring through their food pantries and sleeping on their church steps and decide they cannot send their missions money overseas when this faces them every day. Churches cut missions staff members from payrolls and jeopardize their mission programs and partners when budgets must be reduced but keep as much in place as possible for their traditional membership and programs. And fraud? It isn't so big and fancy. It's smaller stuff here and there and falls under the rationales of "Oh, it's just this one time. No one will ever see it. It's just a receipt."

I wish I had taken that presentation of Todd's to heart and more personally than I did at the start. It would have better prepared me for reality and saved me some real pain when I encountered it. I would have done a better job of speaking into it. Perhaps I still can. Or perhaps others can read this and do it better for me. Without a doubt, churches are a hard, unreached place in their own way. But the next image I have from my days with Todd give me hope.

## The Global Faces of Jesus

Todd has a collection of depictions of Jesus from all over the world, reflecting the cultures from which they came. I am sure many are familiar with it and I can only imagine how much the collection has grown in the past 15 years. I have had many occasions to reference Todd's collection in local church settings, both formal and informal settings. The topic at hand, often serendipitously, is along the lines of what Jesus looked like, or being able to recognize Jesus if we saw him today or when we get to heaven. I will mention Todd's collection and people are fascinated. Many have never given thought that someone from Asia or Africa visualizes Jesus differently. They've always assumed everyone sees a brown-haired, blue-eyed Jesus in a medieval robe like they do. It suddenly dawns on them that the images of Jesus they've always seen in their Southern Baptist Sunday School literature is not the same image seen around the world. They go, "Humph," and their worldview is changed for the better.

When my work ended with the CSGC in the summer of 2008, I joined the staff of First Baptist Church of Oklahoma City to minister among newly arriving Chin refugees from Myanmar. Our church warmly greeted about 36 of them in July of that year on a Sunday morning. I can only think that my time working with Todd and sharing these and other images from the CSGC prepared our church for their arrival to some degree. In the coming years, we would hold joint worship services with them on Sunday mornings in our main sanctuary; some elements in English, some elements in Burmese or one of the Chin tribal languages. Soon after, believing refugees from Sudan brought their small faith community into our building, and Arabic became a new language in our joint services. Then, a Hispanic ministry started and Spanish was brought into the fold. We saw the many faces and voices of Jesus being seen and heard among us, faces and voices that did not look or sound like ours.

Our church responded beautifully with their coming. I give credit to the images and words that Todd and the mission of the CSGC engrained in me that I could hand off to them. Today, there are several indigenous Chin tribal churches scattered about the Oklahoma City area. Virtually all of them were birthed by that mother church that we started at First Baptist Church in 2009. Had Todd not allowed me to come to Oklahoma City, I would have never had the opportunity to work among refugees and those churches may not have started. The church I served would not have had the opportunity to expand its global frame of reference. Future mission partners the church still has around the globe may not have formed. The quantitative images, numbers, words, and messages Todd and his staff identify and teach have practical and life-changing implications in seen and unseen ways.

# Chapter 22: A Collaborative Approach

*Bryan Nicholson*

Before the *Atlas of Global Christianity* was published, Todd Johnson visited Colorado Springs with printouts of the draft page layouts. I had been working at Global Mapping International (GMI) as a cartographer for only a few years and was invited with other colleagues to give feedback on the maps, colors, and overall design. Todd explained the scope of the *Atlas* and the design techniques that were used "to comprehensively map 'global Christianity,' to describe it in its entirety."[1] We passed around the printouts full of large maps covering multiple pages, detailed tables and charts, and written narrative. It was an exercise in collaboration that is a marker of Todd's scholarly work.

In addition to the detailed analysis from the team at the Center for the Study of Global Christianity (CSGC), the *Atlas* contains essays from dozens of contributors, experts in their subject areas, to bring a depth of insight to the book. Likewise, each of the 10 volumes in the Edinburgh Companions to Global Christianity series includes essays by 35 contributors on countries, major Christian traditions, and key themes. The combination of individual voices and experience from across the global church, authoritative data from the CSGC, and visual analysis with maps and charts make these reference works truly unique.

Maps are dependent on the quality of the data. As a cartographer, I use geographic information systems (GIS) to design maps. Each piece of geography (country, province, city, etc.) is linked to a table of attributes, so the accuracy of the thematic map is determined by quality of the underlying figures. There are only a handful of global datasets on religious demography. The *World Christian Database* (Brill), edited by Todd Johnson and Gina Zurlo, has a long academic history, input from multiple and varied sources, and is well-cited among academics and journalists. It is broad, comprehensive, and constantly updated, representing an authoritative source for maps on global religious demography.

The work of Todd and his team is also set in clear, historical context. The *Atlas of Global Christianity* "is inspired by the centenary of Edinburgh [World Missionary Conference] 1910" and includes comparisons throughout the various data themes from 1910 and 2010.[2] The latest *World Christian Encyclopedia* 3rd edition (Edinburgh University Press, 2019) includes tables of figures for each country for 1900, 1970, 2000, 2015, 2020, and 2050. The maps

---

1 Todd M. Johnson and Kenneth R. Ross, eds., *Atlas of Global Christianity, 1910–2010* (Edinburgh: Edinburgh University Press, 2009), x.
2 Johnson and Ross, *Atlas of Global Christianity*, x.

and charts in the Edinburgh Companions to Global Christianity (2017–2025) show the changes from 1970 to 2025. The availability of standardized, time-series data allows for the development of impactful map designs.

In a design meeting for the final volume of the Edinburgh Companions to Global Christianity series, a compact atlas, Todd and the team had stacks of CSGC books as well as other statistical atlases and infographic works on the table. We were gathering input on design ideas from multiple sources and proposing new ideas for the upcoming publication. A member of the team was sharing a live draft layout of the upcoming volume, incorporating team input in real time. We discussed how this volume would fit in the larger series and in the context of what the CSGC had previously published. Working on the design team at the CSGC since 2015, I've had the privilege to see firsthand the impact of Todd's work and his collaborative approach, authoritative data, and awareness of historical context.

**Works Cited**

Johnson, Todd M., and Kenneth R. Ross, eds. *Atlas of Global Christianity, 1910–2010*. Edinburgh: Edinburgh University Press, 2009.

# Chapter 23: Fairest Lord Jesus, Ruler of the Nations

*Sujin Park*

I remember regularly sitting in Todd's office at the Center for Study of Global Christianity (CSGC) at Gordon-Conwell Theological Seminary for meetings as his Byington scholar. We would go over class schedules, organize his itineraries of approaching international and domestic trips, or talk about what to prepare for upcoming events and deadlines; then, our meeting would often turn into mind-nourishing conversations and heart-warming fellowship. I learned so much from him, not only from reading his books and listening to his lectures, but from watching him live, pray, and serve. This fervent, humble servant of God has influenced my world substantially over the past decade while my world has been expanded.

**Data, Missions, and a Global God**

The moment I was called to mission was an afternoon nearly two decades ago, watching a Korean missionary from Wycliffe giving a presentation on TV. He was categorizing different people groups for mission and using numbers and diagrams to explain his points. I cried that afternoon, listening to his presentation. With concrete data, the reality hit me with stronger impact, clarity, and urgency, and after a while I met Todd and discovered where those numbers had come from.

To some people, data and numbers may seem dry and lifeless, but nothing speaks more powerfully to someone trying to understand an issue and to motivate them to care about it than exact numbers and accurate data. While I would define myself primarily as a musician and creator, sometimes I need more than sentimental appeals or abstract impressions, despite how very strong they may be. My introduction to global Christianity was one of the most pivotal points of my life and ministry, and I never realized the full significance of numbers, data, and the tiring work of counting and research until I met Todd and his team.

I hadn't realized before attending and assisting Todd's NGOs and Development in Mission class that almost any topic or issue is related to global Christianity and mission. It was from that course that I learned of a publication titled, *Encyclopedia of World Problems and Human Potential*, with approximately 57,000 different entries of world problems and a list of 32,000 global strategies to address them. Never could have I imagined that the study of global Christianity and Christian efforts to alleviate social injustices would encompass such a wide range of subjects including globalization, religion, poverty, human trafficking, persecution, war, creation care, climate control, diaspora, refugees, unreached people groups, and reconciliation, among others. Yet, beyond these common topics, Todd would also discuss less frequently discussed issues, such as the removal of land mines or the urban poor. It was fascinating to see how these realities were somehow interrelated. As a result, my years with Todd were eye-opening, mind-blowing, and purpose-renewing, full of learning, unlearning, and relearning that slowly impacted and changed my life, ministry, and music. I learned that Christianity was about the global God who is the God of all realms, all fields, all topics, and all vocations.

As a Korean American Christian artist in ministry, born in South Korea and raised in the US, I always hoped to share the gospel and take part in realizing God's kingdom on earth, making peace between lived experiences, cultures, and communities. The teachings of Todd further expanded my sight to the full spectrum of God's kingdom and the wholeness of the gospel. It was about the kingdom of God where all nations, peoples, cultures, languages, and histories are harmoniously present and complete each other, rather than any one nation or continent with a particular cultural background or linguistic tradition being superior. Just because something was right and true in my own standard and culture, didn't mean it would be true for someone with a different background. While this would be true within your own culture and people, it would be even more so in another country or society. This broader perspective later helped me in actual ministry situations as I met and worked with all kinds of people from different countries and regions. Realizing the full potential of the global God was the most exciting and essential thing, critical for being sent out to meet global families.

**Arts, Music, and Media**

With a background in both music and theology, I always sought different ways to communicate various messages through music, arts, and media, and Todd's love for arts was another blessing. I was often motivated and nourished by his extensive knowledge of arts and music. His artistic and cultural library is huge and, of course, global. My conversations with Todd included his beloved lists of recommended books, music, and movies, and I especially appreciated when he introduced me to new music I had never encountered before. Although it's been many years, I will never forget the day he told me about the Silk Road Project initiated by the world-famous cellist Yo-Yo Ma, the global movement and collection of music inspired by the historical Silk

Road in collaboration with musicians from around the world. I wrote down all of Todd's recommendations on my phone, and years later I still haven't been able to check them all off—it will remain a lifelong study guide in global arts. I once heard that his ultimate dream is to have a section at the CSGC for art and music from around the world, and I doubt that I'm the only one who wishes to see this dream come true.

**Relationship and Friendship in Mission**

I learned far more from Todd than academic knowledge about global Christianity and world religions—I learned about people. His work involves counting and categorizing people, but at the heart was always about loving and serving them. It was only for a short period of time that I worked as his Byington scholar at Gordon-Conwell, and I must confess, I feel like I offered him very little actual assistance. Nevertheless, Todd cherished fellowship with his students and colleagues more than anyone's accomplishments, and this is one of the most important things I absorbed from working with him. I'm thankful to have learned to make people my top priority.

Todd has called me a friend from the moment I graduated seminary. It might be too high of a comparison, but his friendship reminds me of how Jesus called us his friends. Within this friendship, Todd taught me without words how genuine relationships are the most valuable thing in life. I experienced the joy of sharing food and life together while joining his family for dinner at the local Korean restaurant, where we shared *bibimbap*, *bulgogi*, Korean-style fried chicken, and *japchae*. From these experiences I learned how to celebrate the unity in diversity of the body of Christ, as well as simple enjoyment of each other's presence, without pretense.

For 18 years I was unable to travel outside the US, and I met Todd just as my personal situation changed and God opened up the world to me to experience first-hand. My interactions with him made me more equipped to meet people around the world than what I could have prepared for myself. I learned it was more important to listen than to talk; I learned it was more valuable to ask questions than try to give answers. I especially knew that this education was a blessing when the time came that I spent six months of the year on the road doing ministry—I was prepared to be humble, repentant, patient, and self-giving.

I stretched these muscles on winter corners in Harvard Square, sharing songs and words with the homeless, as well as providing food, clothes, socks, and sleeping bags. One winter, I visited this community weekly and met with teenagers who refused to go home even though they had families. I befriended them as they ate, slept, took substances, and even became pregnant on the street. Sometimes I would sit on the corner in their place, watching their money box as they ran to use the toilet. I learned so much during this time because it was the real-life application of what I learned in Todd's NGOs and Development in Mission course.

In Cairo, Jerusalem, Wales, Kolkata, Fukuoka, Shanghai, and Addis Ababa I held concerts, songwriting workshops, arts programs, and lecture series at churches, homes, shelters, public schools, and on the streets. In these places I experienced the essence of worship, faith, and life. One of my most meaningful experiences was visiting the Zabbaleen ("garbage collectors") district in Egypt where I held a small concert for them—people who had no experience of ever attending a concert. Even though they were living in a restricted, underprivileged environment, I could see God's glory and honor (Revelation 21:26) embedded in them. While it wasn't possible for me to comprehend their culture in its entirety, I showed my heart by playing from memory a famous Egyptian contemporary song. Although it wasn't perfect, it provided us a small connection.

In downtown Cairo, I met with local Egyptian teenagers who loved K-pop and K-drama—and even watched more K-dramas than me! I was able to approach them more relationally because of our shared interests. I asked questions about their traditional music and culture instead of trying to feed them what I knew from my own small world. As a result, they opened their hearts and shared personal stories more quickly than I expected.

None of these experiences would have been the same without the guidance and wisdom I gained from Todd. Many people approach these scenarios believing a certain culture or people is inferior to another, and overlook the hard work of listening, learning, and waiting. Because of my training, I was able to perceive diverse settings and respond in a transformed way—all thanks to God and His faithful servants who taught me this in and outside of classrooms.

**Faithful Witness, Faithful Servant**

I have witnessed over the years that Todd lives a life of focus and self-control for the sake of his divine calling to serve the global church. He never loses sight of the purpose of Christ and simplicity of life, despite all the busyness of classes, lectures, research, back-to-back trips, speaking engagements, and writing due dates. It was my greatest privilege and inspiration to know someone with such pure and deep faith, amid hardships and uncertainties. He is a person who faces all times with faithful and humble prayer. Every time faith, obedience, courage, or patience was demanded of him, he wholeheartedly sought the Lord for direction and provision, and was always sure to share those insights with others. He consistently showed me over the years the importance of prayer and devotion as part of my daily routine. I know he lived this in his own life because I often received emails that began with this phrase: "As I was praying for you this morning…"

Knowing Todd is a constant reminder that our song and our worship must not only be global, but also universal and eternal. Worship is always about eternity, but it is also about everyday saints learning to sing a new song (Revelation 14:3) as they walk toward the wholeness of God and his kingdom. I'm honored to have a humble friend and be an eyewitness of a servant scholar and his family who walk along the path toward an eternal calling.

In 2020, I had the honor of attending the installment service of Todd as the Paul E. and Eva B. Toms Distinguished Professor of Mission and Global Christianity at Gordon-Conwell Theological Seminary. At the event, I was asked by Todd to share a specific song: "Fairest Lord, Jesus," his favorite hymn since youth:

*Beautiful Savior!*

*Lord of all the nations!*

*Son of God and Son of Man!*

*Glory and honor, praise, adoration,*

*now and forevermore be Thine.*

Amen.

# Chapter 24: Living Global Christianity in Thailand

*Eva M. Pascal*

Dr. Todd Johnson is not only a leading demographer documenting the shift of Christianity to the global South, he also embodies this shift in his teaching, his engagements as a global citizen, and as a Christian. Todd is well-traveled, gives invited talks, and attends conferences all over the world. But he has also made deep and lasting connections abroad, especially in Thailand, where we first met. Our meeting began a long journey of mentorship and collaboration, and he has profoundly shaped the direction of my scholarship and widened my appreciation of Christianity as a global family.

I was teaching theology and world religions at the McGilvary Divinity College of Payap University in Chiang Mai, Thailand when I first met Todd. My four years in Thailand were a period of vocational discernment. I had completed a Master of Divinity at Harvard Divinity School, but I was not ready to pursue a PhD. My studies at Harvard were heavily theological, but I learned mainly about Western theology and the concerns of the church in the global North. Yet, I grew up in the Caribbean, on the Bay Islands of Honduras, and I had an interest in international travel and learning about different cultures.

A mentor at Harvard, Donald Swearer, suggested I go to Thailand to learn more about Buddhism, Christianity, and the interaction between the two in Southeast Asia. He had suggested I take a position at Payap University, which might open some new possibilities for scholarship. So, to Thailand, I went. However, when there, I become fairly frustrated with my narrow theological training. So many of the thinkers I knew about were concerned with things that seem very foreign to Christianity in the Caribbean and very strange to the students that I was teaching in Thailand. My students were from Thailand, Myanmar, Nepal, Cambodia, Laos, China, and other countries in Asia. These students were contending with very different issues from the kind of theological debates that preoccupied the halls of Harvard, which did not much address or take seriously Christianity outside the West.

Through a forum on World Christianity, I invited Todd to speak in one of my courses on world religions when he was in Chiang Mai. I did not yet fully appreciate the great diversity of Christianity, nor grasp the seismic shift of Christianity's center of gravity to the global South. I certainly did not reflect on the cultural and theological implications of the shift, either. Todd changed my perspective with a single presentation. Using his work on the *Atlas of Global Christianity*, which documented demographic changes in Christianity from 1910–2010, he presented the shift to the global South visually in colorful and powerful graphs and images. Particularly effective was a map of changes in Christian populations from 1910, contrasted with a map of Christian populations in 2010. We could "see" Christianity now present in significant numbers in Latin America, Africa, and Asia. Christianity was now present in places it had not thrived before, like Sub-Saharan Africa and China. Both my students and I were awakened to a new way of looking at Christianity as a truly global religion. The presentation made real for students living outside the West the reality of global Christianity. This was an important didactic lesson not only for myself as a budding scholar, but also for my Asian students. We buzzed with questions after Todd's presentation and reflected on the implications of this major shift. One important question that came up, and still does in my teaching, is: to whom does Christianity belong? Certainly, Christianity is no longer primarily a Western religion. Christians in the global church matter, as do their questions and concerns.

Todd's presentation was the beginning of years of collaboration and the event that sparked his mentorship of me as an up-and-coming doctoral student. I helped arrange the launch of the *Atlas of Global Christianity* on the Payap campus, which was attended by many local Thai Christians, missionaries living in Thailand from places like Germany, South Korea, and the United States, and scholars in Chiang Mai. The launch was a success—and fitting, given that the book detailing the shift of global Christianity to the South was inaugurated in a country *in* the global South.

My scholarly horizon opened up to the field of global Christianity, thanks to Todd. He had a significant impact in directing me to Boston University and introducing me to my doctoral advisor, Dr. Dana Robert. I also studied under Todd in the global Christianity course he taught at Boston University. There, he helped guide my interest in issues of Christianity in Thailand in areas of Christianity and development, and the intersection of Christianity and Buddhism.

Todd and I have a shared interest in Christian mission and development studies, and he helped me write a chapter on Christian non-governmental organizations using case studies from Thailand. This experience laid the groundwork for me to assist him on several study abroad tours in the country. He constructed a two-week residency study program in Chiang Mai that focused on global Christianity and development for Doctor of Ministry students at Gordon-Conwell Theological Seminary. I had the privilege of assisting him and this team on three occasions, most recently in January 2020, building an in-depth and hands-on experience with local Christian organizations in the city. Todd's Global Christianity and Development residency for Doctor of Ministry students is a very unique program, and to my knowledge, no similar program exists anywhere in higher theological education. This residency is emblematic of Todd's life and work as a scholar: interdisciplinary, global, and relational. The reason this program works—that so many local service organizations would welcome a large traveling team from the United States—is because Todd has lived and worked among them in Chiang Mai, he respects them personally and professionally, and because he has built strong relationships with them over many years. It is this kind of character that continues to inspire my own research and scholarship as I, too, participate in global Christianity wherever I am, whether it is Boston, Chiang Mai, the Bay Islands, or Vermont, where I currently reside. I captured the vision for global Christianity from Todd in Thailand—a vision I continue to cast for my students today.

# Chapter 25: Working on Religious Demography with Todd M. Johnson
Not Only Quantities but Quality and Values

*Kenneth R. Ross*

I first became aware of Todd Johnson in the early 2000s when I acquired a copy of the *World Christian Encyclopedia* (Oxford University Press, 2001), which looked like a handy reference tool for my work at that time as General Secretary of the Church of Scotland Board of World Mission, based in Edinburgh.[1] I was intrigued a few years later when I received a message from its co-author asking if we could arrange a call. Little did I guess that some 20 years of close collaboration lay ahead, nor that we would come to be in contact on a near-daily basis.

To provide the context for the call, I need to wind back to 1999. This was the time when the upcoming new millennium was stimulating the imagination. In collaboration with my University of Edinburgh colleague David Kerr, we had invited John Pobee of Ghana to deliver a lecture series on Christianity in the Next Millennium. While he was in Edinburgh, on the sidelines of the public lectures, Pobee delivered a solemn charge to David and me. He believed that the centenary of the Edinburgh 1910 World Missionary Conference, at that time ten years in the future, would be an enormously significant moment for World Christianity. It was incumbent upon us, since we were based in Edinburgh, to lose no time in making preparations. Pobee was persuasive; we were convinced we had to act.

By the following year we had formed a "Towards 2010 Council" with membership drawn from churches, mission agencies, and academic institutions. In 2001, it launched an annual lecture series, each year inviting two distinguished scholars of World Christianity to address, one by one, the eight Commissions that reported to Edinburgh 1910.[2] This proved to be the catalyst for the formation of an international network that in 2005 began to plan seriously for the centenary. Soon an international study process was underway that fed into a centenary conference hosted in Edinburgh in 2010. This was

---
1 This unique and exhaustive work of reference is now in its third edition: Todd M. Johnson and Gina A. Zurlo, *World Christian Encyclopedia*, 3rd ed. (Edinburgh: Edinburgh University Press, 2019).
2 These annual lectures were eventually published as David A. Kerr and Kenneth R. Ross (eds), *Edinburgh 2010: Mission Then and Now* (Oxford: Regnum, 2009). This book turned out to be the first in the 37-volume Regnum Edinburgh 2010 Series, possibly the most extensive attempt to take account of Christian mission at the start of the 21st century. See Kenneth R. Ross, "Review of the Series: Major Findings and Key Trends (Regnum Edinburgh 2010 Series)," *Transformation: An International Journal of Holistic Mission* 33, no. 4 (2016): 297–299.

one of a number of major conferences that marked the centenary.³ It was not the largest but was recognized as the one that was most fully representative of World Christianity in all its various expressions.⁴

## Creating the *Atlas of Global Christianity 1910–2010*

Meanwhile, the Edinburgh centenary had also caught the attention of Todd Johnson on the other side of the Atlantic. He was looking at it from a particular angle. In addition to its eight Commissions which reported on different aspects of missionary work, Edinburgh 1910 commissioned James Dennis to produce a *Statistical Atlas of World Missions*.⁵ This was a ground-breaking work at the time, its maps graphically illustrating the progress of the worldwide missionary movement as well as demonstrating how much remained to be done. Should the centenary not be marked by the production of a new atlas? With his commitment to the demographic study of World Christianity, this was an enticing question for Todd.

He soon realized, however, that a like-for-like atlas would not do justice to the situation that had emerged during the 100 years since the Edinburgh conference. The 1910 atlas plotted the outposts of the Western Protestant missionary movement dotted across the vast expanses of Asia and Africa. By the early 21st century, however, it was clear that the presence and profile of World Christianity had greatly changed through an unprecedented demographic shift that had resulted in its strength increasingly being found in Africa, Latin America, and parts of Asia—often in areas where it was little known a century earlier.⁶ The task of an atlas in 2010 would therefore be to map the extraordinary transformation that had taken place.

It was also apparent that Christianity had increasingly taken on a diversity of expression in the course of the century. For example, Pentecostals, who scarcely registered at Edinburgh 1910, now numbered more than 614 million and this

---

3 See Allen Yeh, *Polycentric Missiology: Twenty-First Century Mission From Everyone to Everywhere* (Downers Grove IL: IVP Academic, 2016).
4 See Kirsteen Kim and Andrew Anderson, eds., *Edinburgh 2010: Mission Today and Tomorrow* (Oxford: Regnum, 2011).
5 *Statistical Atlas of Christian Missions: Containing a Directory of Missionary Societies, a Classified Summary of Statistics, an Index of Mission Stations, and a Series of Specially Prepared Maps of Mission Fields. Compiled by Sub-committees of Commission I, 'On Carrying the Gospel to All the Non-Christian World,' As an Integral Part of Its Report to the World Missionary Conference, Edinburgh, June 14–23, 1910* (Edinburgh: World Missionary Conference, 1910).
6 For a vivid account of this development, which draws on the findings of the *Atlas of Global Christianity*, see Wesley Granberg-Michaelson, *From Times Square to Timbuktu: The Post-Christian West Meets the Non-Western Church* (Grand Rapids, MI: Eerdmans, 2013).

number was continuing to grow.[7] At the same time, older Christian churches, such as the Orthodox and the Catholic, had undergone significant renewal in many contexts. It was clear that in contrast to the strictly Protestant parameters that defined Edinburgh 1910, the new atlas would need to be fully ecumenical in scope. It would therefore need to recognize the principal fault lines within worldwide Christianity and attempt to do justice to each of the main traditions or confessions.

At the same time, Todd's work was guided by an understanding that there is an unmistakable commonality that makes it still meaningful to speak of Christianity in the singular. Present in an astonishing variety of circumstances and in a dazzling diversity of cultural forms, Christian faith is nonetheless marked by an irreducible unity and coherence that demands that we consider a *global* Christianity. The aim of the proposed new atlas was therefore to take a fully ecumenical approach in mapping and describing the worldwide Christian faith.

Another concern in the mind of Todd, formed through his long experience of studying religious demography, was that there are limits to how far the presence of Christianity can be interpreted through the presentation of demographic data alone. Such data can often be very revealing, so Todd was highly motivated to draw on his extensive demographic research to inform the preparation of a new atlas. But he saw the need for the quantitative data to be complemented by qualitative interpretation. This was the reason for his call to me. By 2005 I was immersed in the business of using the Edinburgh centenary as an opportunity to take account of Christian mission on a global basis. Todd's question to me was whether I could be interested in coordinating the qualitative, interpretative side of the preparation of the atlas. I did not need to be asked twice. Soon I was visiting the Center for the Study of Global Christianity at Gordon-Conwell Theological Seminary just north of Boston, where Todd was director, and starting the search for the authors who could bring analytical depth to the text of the atlas.

It was an exhilarating experience. We had the sense that we might be able to make an original contribution to scholarship while at the same time offering a unique resource to the worldwide Christian missionary movement as it approached a milestone in its history. It was ambitious—aiming to provide an accurate portrayal of the presence of Christianity in every part of the world, to complement demographic data with insightful analysis, and to exploit new possibilities in desktop publishing to present the results in an attractive form. While Todd worked on this conception in Boston, I negotiated with Edinburgh

---

7 Todd M. Johnson and Kenneth R. Ross, eds., *Atlas of Global Christianity 1910–2010* (Edinburgh: Edinburgh University Press, 2009), 103.

University Press, which caught the vision and agreed to publish the volume. Four years later, the vision had become a reality. Through its maps, tables, graphs, and charts, supported by 52 interpretative essays, the *Atlas* traced the story of the spread of Christianity in every part of the world in the years since 1910. This involved recognizing extraordinary growth in some regions, as well as decline or stagnation in others.[8]

The *Atlas* was soon recognized as an original and extraordinarily valuable resource. Catholic theologian Peter Phan commented: "A book of breathtaking beauty and publishing virtuosity, it is an absolute treasure-trove of information on contemporary global Christianity and supersedes all previous encyclopedias and factbooks on world Christianity, barred none."[9] Historian Charles Farhadian suggested that, "The *Atlas of Global Christianity* is a masterful presentation of the geographical spread of Christian faith through text and visually attractive colored maps, tables, and graphs…. This marvelous book represents a tremendous achievement and should be a part of college, university, or seminary library collections."[10] The *Atlas* was also highly successful from the point of view of its publisher, Edinburgh University Press, offering a distinctive and original book, and proving to be a best-seller.

**Not Quantities but Values**

Essential to the task of producing the *Atlas* was, of course, quantitative work. This rested on the day-in-day-out commitment to creating and continuously updating the *World Christian Database* (Brill), which has been the core project of the Center for the Study of Global Christianity, under Todd's direction. The genius of the *Atlas* was to transform the columns of numbers into beautiful maps and a variety of user-friendly formats to convey statistical data in accessible ways. However, my memory of the *Atlas* years is not so much a matter of quantities as of values. Todd built a team that included some trusty colleagues who had been working together on the *World Christian Database* but also a cohort of younger members who brought fresh ideas and a sense of the *zeitgeist*. What united the whole team was a shared sense of values.

Data analyst Peter Crossing, text editor Bert Hickman, and desktop publisher Chris Guidry were seasoned colleagues who brought their skills to the challenge of the Atlas. Crucially, however, Todd also recruited younger members to the

---

8  See Kenneth R. Ross and Todd M. Johnson, "The Making of the *Atlas of Global Christianity*," *International Bulletin of Missionary Research* 34, no. 1 (2010): 12–16.

9  Peter C. Phan, "World Christianities: Transcontinental Connections," *Journal of World Christianity* 6, no. 1 (2016): 205–16.

10  Charles Farhadian, "Review of *Atlas of Global Christianity*," *Missiology: An International Review* 38, no. 3 (2010): 357–58.

team, such as managing editor Sandra Lee, information designer Bradley Coon, and senior editorial assistant Gina Zurlo. As the project advanced, he strategically drew on his networks to bring in Darrell Dorr as an additional editor and William Duggin to work on the electronic version of the book. In addition to this core team, there was also need for the larger team coming from every part of the world who could write the interpretative essays. We made a commitment to indigenous authorship—each region of the world would be described and analyzed by a scholar from the region rather than a Western expert. This meant that the 64 contributing authors were highly diverse and international in their composition. This wide circle of authors, scattered across the face of the earth, became a community of shared endeavor. Often there were adversities to be overcome, whether academic, institutional, or more personal. There was need to build the morale and momentum that would carry to completion a project that often called for sacrificial commitment.

What held the team together was a set of values modeled by Todd himself. Mutual respect was at the heart of it. Everyone counted and every idea that was suggested was taken seriously. Hospitality was another core value. Todd and his wife Tricia were endlessly generous in opening their home to visitors who came to share a meal or to spend the night. This built rapport at the human level, which created the convivial and uplifting atmosphere that sustained the literary project. As it reached the decisive point, Todd brought the core team to Edinburgh for a week, to stay at the St. Colm's International House where some of the influential delegates to the World Missionary Conference had been accommodated a century earlier. Such experiences were highly motivational and did much to create the momentum that carried the project to a successful conclusion. Positivity is a quality that Todd has continued to exemplify as we have gone on to embrace further challenges. If I have ever been tempted to throw in the towel when things seemed to be going against us, Todd has always been there with his unquenchable positive spirit—and we have always found a way through.

## The Edinburgh Companions to Global Christianity

The success of the *Atlas* prompted a conversation between the publisher and the editors about whether there was any way that the approach that it pioneered could be taken further. By 2013 a proposal emerged to take the analysis of worldwide Christianity to a deeper level of detail. The idea was that a series of volumes might be developed, each devoted to a continent or sub-continent and offering, along the lines of the *Atlas*, both reliable demographic information and original interpretative essays from indigenous scholars and practitioners.

Following the methodology of the *Atlas*, each would employ statistical data and in-depth scholarly analysis to present the presence of Christianity on a continent-by-continent basis worldwide. Moving on from the 100-year retrospect of the *Atlas*, it would be contemporary in its focus, seeking to appraise the current status of Christianity globally. The series would be titled the Edinburgh Companions to Global Christianity.

Somewhat along the lines of the *Atlas*, each volume would have three sections. The first would be geographical, offering country-level demography and analysis. Indigenous scholars would contribute interpretative essays that would offer a "critical insider" perspective on the way in which Christianity is finding expression in their context. The second section would be concerned with the main traditions or confessions in which Christianity presents itself. Five types of church would be considered: Orthodox, Catholic, Protestant, Anglican, and Independent. In addition, the Evangelical and Pentecostal/Charismatic movements, which cut across ecclesial affiliation, would be examined. These essays would be objective, historical, and analytic, but each would be written from the perspective of someone within the tradition rather than that of an external commentator. The third section would be thematic or topical, with each volume examining the eight themes of faith and culture, worship and spirituality, theology, mission and evangelism, social and political context, gender, inter-religious relations, and religious freedom. Additionally, for each volume three or four further themes would be selected to take account of issues that are of particular relevance in the area being considered.

The scale of the project called for the creation of a large team of scholars to deliver it. Some 350 interpretative essays would be required to complete the ten volumes. At editorial level, Todd and I could continue the technique we had developed with the *Atlas*—he would lead on the demography while I would lead on the interpretative essays. We realized, however, that for each volume we would need the specialist knowledge of a scholar with intimate knowledge of the region(s) being considered. This third editor role has successively been filled by J. Kwabena Asamoah-Gyadu (Sub-Saharan Africa), Mariz Tadros (North Africa and West Asia), Daniel Jeyaraj (South and Central Asia), Francis Alvarez, SJ (East and Southeast Asia), Katalina Tahaafe-Williams (Oceania), Ana María Bidegain (Latin America and the Caribbean), Grace Ji-Sun Kim (North America), Annemarie Mayer (Western and Northern Europe), Marian Simeon (Eastern and Southern Europe), and Gina Zurlo (Compact Atlas of Global Christianity).

Additionally, for each volume the three editors have been supported by an Editorial Advisory Board made up of senior scholars with authoritative knowledge of the field in question, who have been consulted on particular issues. For each volume Gina Zurlo, now co-director of the Center for the Study of Global Christianity, has led a demographic team comprising Peter Crossing, Justin Long, and Bryan Nicholson. Bert Hickman has continued to offer the editorial skills that he honed with his work on the *Atlas* while the managing editor role has successively been filled by highly capable student researchers at the CSGC: Jennifer Lee, Katherine Hampson, Julia Kim, Nadia Andrilenas, Alejandra Fontecha, Danielle DeLong, Shela Chan, Judith Sonya Wang, and Michael Haegeland. The set of values that was cultivated through the preparation of the *Atlas* has been applied to similar effect in forming, motivating, and uniting the large teams that have been needed to create each successive volume of the Companions series. At the time of writing, six of the projected ten volumes have been published, while the remaining four are at various stages of preparation.[11]

**Micro and Macro in the Interpretation of World Christianity**

My own experience of global Christianity dates from 1988 when, very wet behind the ears, I set out from Scotland to begin service as a mission partner in Malawi. The next decade was one of immersion in the Malawi context—learning a new language, a new culture, and a new context. It was an enriching and life-changing experience, as it has been for so many who have spent time in cross-cultural mission. Besides the new horizons that opened up with exposure to a new culture, for me it also involved a great expansion of my ecumenical experience. Having grown up in the sectarian west of Scotland where, as a Protestant, I had very little social contact with Catholics, now at the University of Malawi my Head of Department and close colleague, Joseph Chakanza, was a Catholic priest. When he went on sabbatical leave a year after I arrived, I found that I was teaching his "Islam I" course—another stretching of the horizons. To a great extent, my formation as a scholar and practitioner of World Christianity occurred during the decade that I spent teaching at the University of Malawi and ministering in a local church near Zomba. For that period, I was much absorbed by the Malawi context and thinking through the meaning of Christian faith in relation to what the country was passing through at that time.[12]

---

11  Kenneth R. Ross, J. Kwabena Asamoah-Gyadu, and Todd M. Johnson, eds., *Christianity in Sub-Saharan Africa* (Edinburgh: Edinburgh University Press, 2017); Kenneth R. Ross, Mariz Tadros, and Todd M. Johnson, eds., *Christianity in North Africa and West Asia* (Edinburgh: Edinburgh University Press, 2018); Kenneth R. Ross, Daniel Jeyaraj, and Todd M. Johnson, eds., *Christianity in South and Central Asia* (Edinburgh: Edinburgh University Press, 2019); Kenneth R. Ross, Francis D. Alvarez, SJ, and Todd M. Johnson, eds., *Christianity in East and Southeast Asia* (Edinburgh: Edinburgh University Press, 2020); Kenneth R. Ross, Katalina Tahaafe-Williams, and Todd M. Johnson, eds., *Christianity in Oceania* (Edinburgh: Edinburgh University Press, 2021); Kenneth R. Ross, Ana María Bidegain, and Todd M. Johnson, eds., *Christianity in Latin America and the Caribbean* (Edinburgh: Edinburgh University Press, 2022).

12  See, for example, Kenneth R. Ross, *Gospel Ferment in Malawi: Theological Essays* (Gweru: Mambo-Kachere, 1995); Kenneth R. Ross, *Here Comes Your King! Christ, Church and Nation in Malawi* (Blantyre: CLAIM-Kachere, 1998).

When I returned to Scotland in 1998 to become General Secretary of the Church of Scotland Board of World Mission, it meant extending my geographical reach. Now "the world was my parish" and I was on a rapid learning curve in regard to such contexts as the Middle East, South Asia, and the Caribbean, as well as coming to terms again with my native continent of Europe. Though Scotland is a small country, its people have been migrants. In its day, it also contributed disproportionately to the global missionary movement. Hence its connections are wide and various; now I found myself in the middle of them. It was while I was struggling with all this that my connection with Todd Johnson began as we worked together on the *Atlas*. It was intellectually invigorating as well as professionally satisfying to be able to interpret my experience of World Christianity through the lens of a disciplined study of demographic trends. For example, I knew from first-hand experience at the micro level in Malawi that something very significant was happening with the rise of African Christianity. The demographic analysis of the *Atlas* demonstrated its magnitude on a continent-wide scale as it recorded that the numbers of Christians rose from 11.7 million in 1910 to 494.7 million in 2010.[13] Both the big picture indicated by these numbers and the microscopic analysis yielded by local field research were needed to explain what was taking place.

This interplay between the micro and the macro became for me an interpretative maneuver with endless application and limitless analytical value. As I was engaged with different contexts around the world I was drawn into the intricacies of the "micro" but discovered that often these could only be fully understood against the background of the "macro." Getting clarity on empirical realities and demographic trends helped to understand what was happening in local contexts. Meanwhile, a deeper appreciation of local dynamics helped to interpret broad demographic developments. This dialectic between micro and macro was of great value to me as I sought to interpret current realities in missiological terms.

It also came to form the distinctive chemistry of the Edinburgh Companions series, as we sought to combine the big picture offered by the demographic data with detailed country-by-country studies by indigenous scholars with intimate knowledge of their individual contexts. Commenting on the volume about Oceania, historian Hugh Morrison aptly captured what we were aiming to achieve: "This significant volume is a definitive contribution to Oceanic Christian self-understanding. It is impressive both in its scope and its fine-grained attention to the nuances and diversities of Pacific belief and practice. Sensitively framed critical insider analysis provides a local voice, rendering it

---

13 Johnson and Ross, *Atlas of Global Christianity*, 112.

an accessible and valuable regional and global resource."[14] The combination of the broad scope of the "macro" with the fine-grained attention to the "micro" was what brought distinctive quality to the Edinburgh Companions.

I returned to Malawi in 2019, making it the base for my work as a theological educator with the Church of Scotland. Much of my "macro" work on the Edinburgh Companions has been done while I was engaged on a day-to-day basis with the "micro" context of Malawi. I hope that growing appreciation of the richness of this one specific situation has heightened my sensitivity to the distinctive features of other particular contexts. Meanwhile, the significance of what is transpiring in each is set in a broader context by the big picture painted by the demographic research that Todd has pursued to remarkable effect. Yet I have come to appreciate that his scholarly achievement rests not only on outstanding quantitative work but also on interpretative quality and inspirational values.

**Works Cited**

Farhadian, Charles. "Review of Atlas of Global Christianity." *Missiology: An International Review* 38, no. 3 (2010): 357–58.

Granberg-Michaelson, Wesley. *From Times Square to Timbuktu: The Post-Christian West Meets the Non-Western Church*. Grand Rapids, MI: Eerdmans, 2013.

Johnson, Todd M., and Kenneth R. Ross, eds. *Atlas of Global Christianity 1910–2010*. Edinburgh: Edinburgh University Press, 2009.

Johnson, Todd M., and Gina A. Zurlo. *World Christian Encyclopedia*, 3rd ed. Edinburgh: Edinburgh University Press, 2019.

Kerr, David A., and Kenneth R. Ross, eds. *Edinburgh 2010: Mission Then and Now*. Oxford: Regnum, 2009.

Kim, Kirsteen, and Andrew Anderson, eds. *Edinburgh 2010: Mission Today and Tomorrow*. Oxford: Regnum, 2011.

Phan, Peter C. "World Christianities: Transcontinental Connections." *Journal of World Christianity* 6, no. 1 (2016): 205–16.

Ross, Kenneth R. *Gospel Ferment in Malawi: Theological Essays*. Gweru: Mambo-Kachere, 1995.

Ross, Kenneth R. *Here Comes Your King! Christ, Church and Nation in Malawi*. Blantyre: CLAIM-Kachere, 1998.

Ross, Kenneth R. "Review of the Series: Major Findings and Key Trends (Regnum Edinburgh 2010 Series)." *Transformation: An International Journal of Holistic Mission* 33, no. 4 (2016): 297–99.

---

14 Hugh Morrison, endorsement, Ross, Tahaafe-Williams, and Johnson, *Christianity in Oceania*, back cover.

Ross, Kenneth R., and Todd M. Johnson. "The Making of the *Atlas of Global Christianity*." *International Bulletin of Missionary Research* 34, no. 1 (2010): 12–16.

Ross, Kenneth R., Francis D. Alvarez, SJ, and Todd M. Johnson, eds. *Christianity in East and Southeast Asia.* Edinburgh: Edinburgh University Press, 2020.

Ross, Kenneth R., J. Kwabena Asamoah-Gyadu, and Todd M. Johnson, eds. *Christianity in Sub-Saharan Africa.* Edinburgh: Edinburgh University Press, 2017.

Ross, Kenneth R., Ana María Bidegain, and Todd M. Johnson, eds. *Christianity in Latin America and the Caribbean.* Edinburgh: Edinburgh University Press, 2022.

Ross, Kenneth R., Daniel Jeyaraj, and Todd M. Johnson, eds. *Christianity in South and Central Asia.* Edinburgh: Edinburgh University Press, 2019.

Ross, Kenneth R., Mariz Tadros, and Todd M. Johnson, eds. *Christianity in North Africa and West Asia.* Edinburgh: Edinburgh University Press, 2018.

Ross, Kenneth R., Katalina Tahaafe-Williams, and Todd M. Johnson, eds. *Christianity in Oceania.* Edinburgh: Edinburgh University Press, 2021.

*Statistical Atlas of Christian Missions: Containing a Directory of Missionary Societies, a Classified Summary of Statistics, an Index of Mission Stations, and a Series of Specially Prepared Maps of Mission Fields.* Compiled by Sub-committees of Commission I, "On Carrying the Gospel to All the Non-Christian World," As an Integral Part of Its Report to the World Missionary Conference, Edinburgh, June 14–23, 1910. Edinburgh: World Missionary Conference, 1910.

Yeh, Allen. *Polycentric Missiology: Twenty-First Century Mission From Everyone to Everywhere.* Downers Grove, IL: IVP Academic, 2016.

# Chapter 26: Listen, Empower, Enjoy, and Think

*Justin Schell*

I first benefited from the life, work, and ministry of Dr. Todd Johnson long before we met. Work done by the Center for the Study of Global Christianity informed the ministries that had helped disciple me to Christ and prepare me for what I thought would be a life-long vocation of cross-cultural mission. I didn't know it in 1999, but my debt to him was only beginning.

It was through attending Gordon-Conwell Theological Seminary that I met Todd and I began to see that debt growing in earnest. I arrived with a heart to see Muslim men and women come to know Christ, a passion he shares. What I was not expecting upon arrival was to see my heart for the global church begin to expand. I assumed I was preparing to proclaim Christ where he was least known, not to love and serve the church where he was already well known. But I found in Todd, and increasingly in my own heart, that those two things are not mutually exclusive.

Indeed, the more I began to see the reality of the global church, the more my love for her grew. I loved her diversity—from the small hidden peoples who had turned to Christ in Papua New Guinea to churches popping up in major urban centers like Mexico City and Tokyo. I loved her courage—facing down opposition from militant religions, authoritarian governments, and the spiritual forces of darkness. I loved her love—she poured out her life for those who might persecute her. I loved her Jesus who often looked more like the second person of the Trinity found in Scripture than what passed for Jesus in my Western context.

Toward the end of my time in seminary, a recurring prayer was growing in me, "Lord, use me somehow to lift up, support, and strengthen the Majority World church. Let me spend my life and energy empowering her to fruitful ministry." The Lord used many people, books, and resources in this process, and Todd played a key role in that, in four major ways.

**Learning to Listen**

I had the privilege of serving as a research assistant to Todd for two years. During that time, work on the *Atlas of Global Christianity* was ongoing. I was one of many trained to take a country of the world and find every resource possible on the reality of religion in that country. I thought I was being trained to do a simple task in a massive project. While that was true, I was also being trained to do research of other kinds.

Todd taught me that if I were going to say something about a country, if I were going to make statements about the number of religious adherents or a shift in demographics, I had to first listen. I had to hear every voice possible so that I might join the conversation as a helpful dialogue partner. This is true of religious statistics. It's also true when engaging the book of Romans or the theology of baptism or evangelistic practices or, really, anything.

Listening takes humility. It takes humility to admit that you don't know everything. It takes humility to rely on the research of others. It takes humility to recognize the contributions of others in your field. It takes humility to recommend the work of others. I've never met someone who so enjoyed introducing others to the work and writings that he had found helpful than Todd.

Today, my work requires understanding a complex issue in global mission and suggesting a helpful response. Or, I may need to help two or more organizations think through how to collaborate with one another. Or, I may interact with a younger, emerging leader seeking advice about their calling. All three scenarios require that I listen, that I try to emulate that joyful humility that I witnessed working with Todd.

**Learning to Empower**

Todd isn't interested in having his name stand alone on an article or book. He co-published articles with some of my classmates during seminary and invited them to a process wherein they learned, made real contributions, and saw their first article published. He wasn't looking for someone who had arrived at the peak of their profession, he'd much rather lend someone a hand, see them grow, and eventually see them flourish on their own.

I still call him when I need a recommendation. Often these conversations begin with, "Do you know someone who's able to speak on topic X?" Sometimes the topic I ask about is something within his own expertise, but he is always more excited to introduce me to some, possibly unknown, person instead of being the person on the platform or the project. Because of this example, when others seek my input, I consider who else I might suggest, someone who may be unknown but gifted and simply waiting for an opportunity.

When I sent an early draft of a manuscript to Todd for feedback, he included a gentle rebuke, "I think you could draw more from scholarship in the global South." His statement was a reminder that I have asked the Lord to use me to encourage, support, and strengthen his people in the Majority World. I learned that even works cited pages and bibliographies are a chance to point to, lift up, and recognize others ready to make new and wonderful contributions.

## Learning to Enjoy

No one loves the world's diversity of art, food, dance, music, and people more than Todd. Rarely a conversation would happen at seminary in which he didn't share a video beautifully displaying some aspect of another culture or about a new Thai restaurant in town. Rarely would a lecture finish without being exposed to something beautiful around the world that I had not thought of or heard of. Todd seemed to relish finding the good and beautiful in the world and sharing it with others.

In my work with the Lausanne Movement, almost every project requires seeing Christians from very different places and backgrounds learn to work together. Understanding the differences between warm and cold-climate cultures, or time and event-oriented cultures, or guilt and shame-based cultures is important. Those things can help us learn to understand each other better. Nevertheless, I find that most headway in real trust comes when we begin to enjoy each other's cultures. When I am introduced to the delicious cuisine or lovely art of a new colleague's culture, our hearts are bound together just a little bit more; we become friends, we want each other to succeed, and we love each other.

## Learning to Think

I remember Todd saying something to the effect that, early in his own vocation, he was looking for a way to use math for God's glory among the nations. He had a natural inclination and ability with numbers. One might be surprised to find that someone as inclined toward the empirical as Todd is also extremely warm-hearted, which is why he's so good at what he does. On the one hand, without the heart, without recognizing what is most important in life—love for God and the world—we will not deploy our minds very well. On the other hand, Christians are notorious for making bad decisions based on a desire to love and help. Todd embodies what I often describe as "using our heads in the service of our hearts." He understands what's important in life—the good, the beautiful, the true—and so he can heartily engage his whole-mind in service to that cause. Right belief plus a right heart lead to right practice.

As I consult churches, ministries, or organizations, I often think of Todd. Some of these groups have big hearts, and my hope is to help them think clearly and strategically about the issues that they are trying to tackle. Others of these groups have good minds, and I need to help remind them of what is most important, to deploy their minds more fully on what most moves God's heart. Rarely have I known someone who combines intellect and love like Todd.

Someone who has laid their mind on the altar of God and said, "I want to love you with all of that…with all of me." These lifelong lessons from Todd have made me not only a better mission leader for my work with the Lausanne Movement and Union, but they also continue to help make me a better person. They affect the way I lead, the way I train others, the way I share the gospel and teach God's word, and the way I serve the church.

# Chapter 27: Humility, Kindness, and Music
## Reflection for Todd Johnson

*Jennifer Lee Shin*

My relationship with Todd Johnson goes back to 2015, when I was pursuing a Master of Theology (ThM) in Old Testament at Gordon-Conwell Theological Seminary. I was his Byington Scholar from 2015 to 2016, working as a managing editor for *Christianity in Sub-Saharan Africa,* the first volume of the 10-volume Edinburgh Companions to Global Christianity series (Edinburgh University Press, 2017). I also helped as a research assistant during those years at the Center for the Study of Global Christianity (CSGC).

When I look back to the times I worked with Todd, several memories stand out to me. The first that comes to mind is Todd's deep kindness. In every meeting with me, he expressed gratitude and encouragement for the small tasks I had accomplished. The second snapshot is my husband and I spotting Todd several times at Starbucks right around the time they opened at 5am. The streets were still dark, and the coffee shop was almost empty, but he was there working diligently. My third memory is from his office at the CSGC. The sound of foreign music would come out from his speakers, matching the exotic objects that he brought from various parts of the world. If you are aware of South Hamilton, Massachusetts, you might agree that the town is perhaps one of the least "global" places in the United States. Yet, Todd brought the world into his office, and it was refreshing to be in that space. The fourth memory is the unforgettably delicious apple pie that his wife, Tricia, baked when the Johnson family invited people working at the CSGC to their house. Until now, that remains the best apple pie I have ever had, and I fondly remember the Johnson family's hospitality and friendship to me and my husband.

My interactions with Todd continue to have deep influence in my life. His life and personality showed his enthusiasm for the global church. His humility in approaching different people from different backgrounds has been a model for me. He has also expanded my understanding of Christianity through his publications and presentations that I was able to attend when I was at Gordon-Conwell. Many students from Gordon-Conwell, including myself, were shaped by Todd to think globally and engage with Christianity worldwide. Todd's global mindset and engagement with non-Western voices have also been an influence in my current study. I am working on my doctoral degree in Old Testament at Wheaton College, focusing on "eating, drinking, and rejoicing" in Ecclesiastes in relation to similar themes in other parts of the Old Testament. Although my dissertation is not directly related to an interpretation of Ecclesiastes from a global perspective, I try to incorporate some insights as a Korean female writer. Todd always cherished voices from non-Western writers and I am thankful that his works encourage many to listen to people from various backgrounds.

# Chapter 28: Confronted with the Facts
## 86% of Hindus, Buddhists, and Muslims Have Relatively Little Contact with Christians

*Benjamin P. Thomas*

The finding of this reflection's title, this statistic, this reality, researched and articulated by Dr. Todd Johnson, has deeply reshaped the trajectory of my life's work.[1] I met Todd in 2013 at a critical time in my life. My wife had just been readmitted to the hospital after her initial round of chemotherapy, 10 months after her craniotomy to remove a baseball-sized tumor from her brain. I had called Todd to inform him I would have to drop out of the Doctor of Ministry program at Gordon-Conwell Theological Seminary, since I couldn't give it the time it deserved. He calmly encouraged me to see if this intense season would pass, and I might have more time in a few weeks or months.

Shortly after, our young family of six traveled from Ohio to Massachusetts to attend my first residency of the Global Christianity and Development program, with Todd's graciousness to overlook the required pre-reading. During those two weeks, it was clear to me that learning from Todd and Doug Birdsall was exactly where I needed to be. The DMin cohort focused on global Christianity and the power of Christians around the world to be a blessing in the world. Todd emphasized learning from leaders from the global South, and pointed us away from traditional American and European resources that overlooked diverse perspectives.

It was during this residency that I came across the statistic that changed my life: 86% of Hindus, Buddhists, and Muslims have relatively little contact with Christians. I was floored. How could this be? How far away was the global church from Jesus's command to love and serve the least of these? In many ways, this statistic reaffirmed my doubts as a leader within a large Christian mission organization. Too often, we focused on the already-Christian, and spent a vast amount of resources in gospel-saturated areas.

As a result of Todd's leadership and teaching, our family made the decision to move to the global South. In 2014, with two DMin residencies under my belt, I moved our family to Kigali, Rwanda. I became head of the Kigali International Community School (KICS). KICS is a Christ-centered and missional school with a diverse study body, home to Christians, Muslims, Buddhists, and Hindus. As I deepened my leadership at KICS and my studies in global Christianity,

---
1 Todd M. Johnson and Kenneth R. Ross, eds., *Atlas of Global Christianity 1910–2010* (Edinburgh: Edinburgh University Press, 2009), 316–17.

I began to realize the uniqueness of KICS. Most Christian schools do not offer spaces for people of other faiths. Yet at KICS, part of our DNA is for all students, regardless of religion, to experience God's love. Over my eight years there, some of our biggest supporters and vocal proponents were our non-Christian families, such as Muslims from Yemen and Sudan, Hindus from India and Tanzania, Buddhists from Korea, and non-religious families from the United States.

Todd's teaching and personal life equipped me to lead strongly in the multi-religious setting of KICS. We launched an educational non-profit, B2THEWORLD, that focuses on bringing a similar style of transformative education to other countries recovering from war. Numerous countries with little access to the gospel have also experienced the tragedy and challenges of warfare. B2THEWORLD was fundamentally shaped by my education at Gordon-Conwell in global Christianity and development, such as the values of human flourishing, global leadership, and faithful presence. We relish in our global partnerships in participating in God's mission worldwide.

On a trip to Iraq in 2022, I was hosted by Catholic and Evangelical leaders from five different cities. I couldn't help but chuckle and think, without Todd's influence and support, I would not have been prepared for these opportunities to exercise grace and experience Christian diversity. His impact on my life continues to be significant. He helped me heal through my wife's cancer, showed the love of God and helped clarify God's call on my life, and helped equip me to create a loving and beautiful ministry for people of all faiths to encounter Jesus. He has encouraged me to publish, to share my story, and I know he is always a call, text, or email away for encouragement and friendship. He is world-class. He is also a true Christian and an expert in his field. He has championed global Christianity and I have no doubt he will help raise up many more young ministers like myself in the years to come. I am thankful for Todd's life and leadership, and thankful to call him my mentor and friend. I have keenly felt his impact in the decade I've known him, and I know his impact will continue to grow in the years ahead.

**Works Cited**

Johnson, Todd M., and Kenneth R. Ross, eds. *Atlas of Global Christianity 1910–2010*. Edinburgh: Edinburgh University Press, 2009.

# Chapter 29: "One of the Excellent People Struggling for the Faith"
## A Personal Reflection on the Life of Todd Johnson

*Charles Tieszen*

There is an account of a 9th-century debate between a Christian nobleman and a Muslim sheikh wherein, after a long theological exchange, the two reached an impasse. The Christian suggested they pause the debate and return the next day, at which point he would bring along with him a secret weapon. The next day the sheikh made his way to the place where the nobleman waited to resume the debate. When he arrived, he found that standing next to the Christian was a priest. But this was not just any priest. For the author of the account added a colorful flourish: this was a priest "with a mighty beard."[1]

Clearly the Christian nobleman intended the priest to function as a superior opponent to the Muslim sheikh. The "mighty beard" brings with it dramatic effect, but in the late antique and early medieval Mediterranean world, a beard like this signified an especially holy man. And nearness to such an individual, whether one was Christian or Muslim, meant that his holiness and the theological acuity that accompanied it, would inevitably rub off onto you, too.

As far as I am aware, Todd Johnson has never had a beard, mighty or otherwise. And yet I could not help but feel a certain gravitational pull coming from the small office he first occupied when he arrived at Gordon-Conwell Theological Seminary 20 years ago. When he gave a lecture series that essentially introduced him, his work, and what would become the Center for the Study of Global Christianity (CSGC) to the seminary community, I was transfixed. I had never heard an academic lecture that was at once scholarly, engaging, and entertaining. He drew from ancient sources and popular culture. He quoted Church Mothers and Fathers, grunge musicians, and Swahili-speaking women. I was not the only one attending those lectures who learned something but also laughed, cried, and experienced paradigm shifts. I wondered what it would be like to know Todd personally, to be a bit closer to him so that some of whatever it was he had might rub off onto me, too.

It was not very long after those lectures that Todd moved most of the CSGC down the hill from the library to what had been a daycare and preschool on the ground floor of one of the seminary's apartment buildings. I was delighted

---

1 *Hadīth Wāsil al-Dimashqī*, ed. and trans. Sidney H. Griffith and Larry B. Miller, in S. Griffith, "Bashīr/Bēsēr: Boon Companion of the Byzantine Emperor Leo III: The Islamic Recension of his Story in *Leiden Oriental MS 951 (2)*," *Le Muséon* 103 (1990): 318–19.

to make my way there one afternoon to discuss the possibility of becoming a research assistant. I thought I was sitting for an interview, but after some conversation Todd hired me immediately. When I mentioned that my wife, Sarah, was also looking for work, he hired her in the same instant, too. Todd then promptly left the country for a conference, and we found ourselves in the new CSGC, putting together shelves, organizing thousands of books, filing away some of a million pages of documents, and taking calls from journalists located all over the world. I was both intimidated and overjoyed.

What I quickly learned was that Todd did not see us as mere employees. By virtue of our association with him, we were instantly colleagues, co-authors, and co-conspirators. When he delivered a lecture, we went along and were introduced as team members involved in cutting-edge research. When he wrote an article, we participated in the research and writing, and our names appeared alongside his in publication. When someone visited the CSGC, whether a monsignor, a Buddhist monk, or the seminary's president, we were sure to give Todd plenty of warning so he could reduce the volume of whatever pop or world music he was blaring at that moment.

The sense that we were joined to Todd by proximity and shared vocation became most vivid for me one morning when the CSGC front desk phone rang. I answered and found myself speaking with David Barrett, the originator of the research, living in Richmond, Virginia. Of course, I knew who David was and had heard much about him. Up until that point, I had encountered among the CSGC archives hundreds of pages of David's original research documenting the growth of indigenous Christian communities in East Africa. I had filed away numerous photographs of David, many with various dignitaries like Pope John Paul II standing next to him. So, I was a bit starstruck on the phone that morning. But David spoke as if this was the thing that normally happened every day. He immediately launched into a discussion of his cosmology research, much of which we were transcribing. The discussion, however, did not focus on whether I could read his handwriting or if I had any questions. Instead, he had cosmological questions for me. I discovered then that Todd's way of treating me like a colleague may have its origins in David. What I was to Todd in that moment, Todd had been to David. Todd stepped into the work David began and was part of its legacy. Now I, too, was part of that legacy. This discovery jolted me with an abiding sense of seriousness for the work I was doing at the CSGC, which remains with me to this day even though my scholarship has journeyed into adjacent fields.

There were other ways in which my time near Todd helped to shape the manner in which I continue to approach scholarship and interacting with other students and colleagues. I still see students as having something to contribute to scholarly conversation in the same way that other peers enter that discussion. While it is true that part of my responsibility is to help shape students so that they might enter these conversations with greater skill and precision, at the same time, I am still learning, too, often from those for whom I am trying to offer guidance.

There are times when scholarly discussion involves disagreement. This reality need not involve marginalization. When I worked at the CSGC it was not uncommon to come across a document, receive a phone call, or overhear a discussion in which Todd's definition of martyrs, martyrdom, or some other concern over statistical vocabulary was called into question. Todd always received this criticism with grace. He even welcomed it. But he often responded with a challenge. Instead of simply lobbing disagreement at him, he encouraged dissenters to join the conversation—present or publish an alternative view. Only in this kind of exchange can we sharpen perspectives and the ones who hold them. One of the harshest pieces of criticism I have received was from a scholar responding to the published version of my doctoral thesis. This criticism, especially in the form in which it was offered, was difficult to receive. But before my imposter syndrome could flare too wildly, I remembered Todd. Both my critic and I were participating in a conversation. We might do that with greater or lesser degrees of magnanimity, but we remained peers on the same playing field in pursuit of the virtue of knowledge.

One of the most enduring things that rubbed off on me during my time with Todd was how he reimagined the ways in which Christian and other religious communities engaged one another. One of my first publications was a short essay in which Todd and I reflected on the implications for estimates of personal contact between Christians and adherents of other religions.[2] This was something that Todd had already begun to think about, and he pulled me alongside him when it came time to formalize and publish the research. What we sensed anecdotally could be estimated statistically: religious communities—and non-religious communities, too—suffer deeply from tribalism as relatively few people are in personal contact with those from outside their religious groups.

This research galvanized a developing vocation for me that emphasized proximity to others, especially those not traditionally centered in my traditions. This further pushed me towards the field in which I currently work, thinking about the history, theology, and practice of Christian-Muslim relations. But it also helped me to see common pitfalls in the ways we often tend to describe inter-religious contact. For example, while global Muslims

---

2 Todd M. Johnson and Charles L. Tieszen, "Personal Contact: The *sin qua non* of Twenty-first Century Christian Mission," *Evangelical Missions Quarterly* 43, no. 4 (October 2007): 494–501.

and Christians share core religious values that one might collectively label Islam or Christianity, these terms mask and generalize what is in fact wide-ranging diversity. They make it difficult to see the vast number of traditions, cultures, and languages found within these religions, such that we are often better off speaking of Islams and Christianities. In the same way, we ought to be wary of constructs like "Islam and the West." Which Islam? What, exactly, of the West? Why compare a diverse religion with a nebulous geographic region? Other phrases, such as "Muslim world," also become suspect. While there are geographic regions that we might consider traditional homelands of Islam in its earliest development, the earliest Muslim communities inhabited vast geographic regions and comprised a variety of languages and cultures. This historic reality is even truer today since Muslim communities can be found in every major geographic region. Where, indeed, is the "Muslim world"? Similar questions might be posed for Christianity. What imprecisions lie behind the ways in which we equate Christianity with the West? What traditions do we fail to see when our study of Christian history avoids the ancient Christian East and the Majority World almost entirely? What do we fail to realize when we neglect the enormous implications of both Christianity's and Islam's shifting centers of statistical gravity?

Much of what I have mentioned here comprises the ways in which Todd has helped to shape my life as a scholar and a teacher. But my relationship with Todd went much further than intellectual mentoring. Every now and then, maybe during a break for lunch or tea or during a moment of relaxation, Todd would share something personal, and I would see the ways in which his travel and scholarship had shaped him as a person of faith. When Todd and his wife, Tricia, invited my wife, Sarah, and I to live in their basement for a few months before we moved to England, I also saw how the Johnson's global awareness had permeated their entire family. Todd showed me that scholarship was not just theory. This was personal.

It was about another, likely bearded Mediterranean holy man named Al-'Utbī l-Qurṭubī whose biographers wrote, "*min ahl al-jihād wa-l-khayr*"; one of the excellent people struggling for the faith.[3] I am grateful to have been near enough to Todd so that some of the ways in which he approaches scholarship and postures himself toward others might rub off onto me, too. And I am grateful to know him, like many of the holy ones who have gone before us, as one of the excellent people struggling for the faith.

---

3 See Juan Pedro Monferrer-Sala, "Al-'Utbī l-Qurṭubī," in *Christian-Muslim Relations, a Bibliographical History, Volume 1 (600–900)*, ed. David Thomas and Barbara Roggema (Leiden: Brill, 2009), 734.

## Works Cited

*Hadīth Wāsil al-Dimashqī*, edited and translated by Sidney H. Griffith and Larry B. Miller, in S. Griffith, "Bashīr/Bēsēr: Boon Companion of the Byzantine Emperor Leo III: The Islamic Recension of his Story in *Leiden Oriental MS 951 (2)*." *Le Muséon* 103 (1990): 318–19.

Johnson, Todd M., and Charles L. Tieszen. "Personal Contact: The *sin qua non* of Twenty-first Century Christian Mission." *Evangelical Missions Quarterly* 43, no. 4 (October 2007): 494–501.

Monferrer-Sala, Juan Pedro. "Al-'Utbī l-Qurṭubī." In *Christian-Muslim Relations. A Bibliographical History, Volume 1 (600–900)*, edited by David Thomas and Barbara Roggema, 115–922. Leiden: Brill, 2009.

# Chapter 30: By the Numbers

*Cindy M. Wu*

In the fall of 2012, I received a most unexpected phone call. Dr. Todd M. Johnson, one of my former seminary professors at Gordon-Conwell Theological Seminary (GCTS), was inviting me to co-author a book on global Christianity. Caving into my feelings of insecurity, my immediate thought was to say I would pray about it for one week, and then respectfully decline. There was also that minor detail of having my hands full while being immersed in homeschooling my three children. But my husband (and, of course, the Holy Spirit) would not let me back out so easily. Todd and I went on to publish *Our Global Families: Christians Embracing Common Identity in a Changing World* (Baker Academic, 2015), a book about how Christians see themselves and the work God calls them to do in the world through the framework of belonging to both a human family and a Christian faith family.

I view the experience of publishing *Our Global Families* with Todd as a key turning point in my life. But even greater than the milestone of publishing a book was gaining a friendship with someone as inspiring as Todd. He is well regarded as one of the world's foremost religious demographers, but on a personal level, he is also a caring friend. I credit Todd with imparting to me all kinds of knowledge and wisdom, including an important life lesson: numbers tell a story! Statistics can be misleading unless you understand their context. Charts and tables are not dull at all if you understand the bigger picture behind those axis labels. As I reflect on the impact of Todd's scholarship and personal example, I am compelled to use three numbers to express the legacy of Todd Johnson on my life: 27 million, 55, and 2022.

**27 Million**

Early on in my Christian journey, I felt called to global missions, whether that involved evangelism and church planting abroad or befriending internationals in my local context. My studies at Gordon-Conwell inspired and helped solidify my calling to work cross culturally and care for some of the world's most marginalized and persecuted people—refugees. For the past decade I have served as a missions mobilizer, recruiting, educating, and equipping volunteers to welcome refugees to the United States. My passion is to foster theological understanding of our special mandate as followers of Jesus to welcome the stranger, and to do so with cultural sensitivity and agility.

God used my time at GCTS to stir my heart so strongly for refugee ministry that I decided to do my final integrative project (similar to a master's thesis) on the global refugee crisis. At the time of my project, completed in 2011, there were 11 million refugees in the world. Today that number has ballooned to a staggering 27 million. During my final semester at GCTS, I asked Todd to serve as my project advisor, and rather than do a research paper, I chose to write a curriculum that would incorporate biblical teaching, theological reflection, and practical advice to mobilize the American church to welcome refugees. At the time, I wrote my workbook for an audience of one (Todd) with the goal of completing my graduation requirement. Six years later, at the height of the Syrian refugee crisis, I published *A Better Country: Embracing the Refugees in Our Midst* (William Carey Library, 2017) as a small group Bible study.

In the past decade since graduating from GCTS, my calling and desire to serve refugees has evolved but never waned, and I credit much of that clarity to both the academic study and mentorship I received under professors like Todd. Sadly, the number of refugees has increased starkly and attitudes towards refugees and immigrants have become so politicized as to create more need for refugee ministries in the United States. The current climate has prompted me to work on a revised edition of my workbook to hopefully inspire more Christians to respond biblically to what God is doing through forced migration—bringing the nations to our country.

This phenomenon is the focus of my ministry. In my recent capacity as a program manager for a non-profit called Houston Welcomes Refugees, my job included pairing volunteer Welcome Teams with refugee arrivals. Welcome Teams walk alongside refugees in friendship for six months, and my role was to provide support and resources to volunteers during that period of engagement. One of my most important tasks was to orient teams to their assigned refugee family's situation. Sometimes I would have nothing more than a name, arrival date, and flight number, and it would be up to the team to uncover the family's narrative. Unraveling refugees' stories was typically tragic yet fascinating. Their personal journey was always tied to a story far outside their immediate experience; sometimes that story traversed national boundaries and straddled decades. A refugee arriving in Houston might be fleeing conflict that occurred five years ago, or maybe 20; refugees might claim one nationality but never have set foot within the boundaries of that nation.

People involved in refugee resettlement are keenly aware of how resettlement is constantly being shaped by global trends. Whenever a conflict breaks out half a world away, those of us in resettlement start imagining what direct impact the resultant migration will have on our job in the near future, as was the case following the Taliban takeover of Kabul in August 2021 when Houston received a record-shattering influx of Afghan refugees. There have been many moments when I have drawn upon my former studies at GCTS to contemplate how to best facilitate integration for refugees. Perspectives on what God is doing in and through the global church and a vision for diaspora ministry influence my missiology and praxis as it pertains to my approach to refugee ministry. An appreciation for what the non-Western world has to offer churches in the West infuses my mindset and values. I have also developed a sensitivity toward methodologies that concentrate or sustain power in the hands of Westerners. These are themes I revisit daily in my work, and I still have much to learn.

## 55

A few years ago, I was doing some research on the number of religious affiliations accounted for in Houston. I reached out to the director of interfaith relations at Houston's most prominent interfaith organization for the answer, and he somehow landed on the number 55. Of course, it depends, we chuckled, on how you define "religious affiliation" and "accounted for" and "in Houston." As any demographer will tell you, the methodology of counting is tricky! While the interfaith director may not have arrived at an accurate number, I do know I'm blessed to live in a city where the correct answer is always "a lot," thus providing many opportunities for ecumenical and interfaith engagement.

My time at Gordon-Conwell not only equipped me to participate in engagement with people who share different—even opposing—theological stances, it also taught me not to fear such interactions. Through Todd, I was exposed to the ecumenical movement in the Boston area. I greatly appreciated how Todd invited representatives of many Christian traditions to speak to our class and have them describe their beliefs on their own terms. Todd taught us to honor and appreciate other traditions for what they have to offer the global Church, not to eye them with suspicion as I had been taught to do in some Evangelical circles. Through the Boston Theological Interreligious Consortium, of which Todd has been a fixture, I took classes with students holding an even broader range of theological convictions than what GCTS already had to offer.

When I returned home to Houston after seminary, I started regularly attending interfaith dinners and conversations. These exposed me to new communities of people I never knew existed in my hometown. As I started working in resettlement and making contacts among the consortium of refugee-focused non-profit organizations, I saw the good work people of all faiths were doing within the refugee community. Rather than seeking to limit partnership to a narrow range of Christians just like me, I felt led to expand my network for the sake of bearing Christian witness and to better provide comprehensive services to refugees.

In *Our Global Families*, Todd and I write about our human and our Christian families. We belong to both families, and both are broader than we are often led to believe. Whereas I was once suspicious of certain religious others, today I am less intimidated because I have seen the beauty of expanding one's definition of family.

## 2022

The year 2021 held the most major life transitions in any given year for me. During that season of change, I felt God stirring something within me, a feeling that it was time for me to transition out of my job and pursue a vocation more in sync with my calling and gifts. As I sorted through my doubts and convictions, I consulted Todd. Many of the themes we had written on in the past were rising to the surface in my current situation and speaking with Todd helped confirm what I was sensing.

In the end I left my job and in 2022 I made the leap to co-labor with my husband in developing Mosaic Formation, a spiritual formation ministry. The vision of Mosaic Formation is to see diverse peoples transformed into Christ's image. We seek to promote spiritual formation among leaders who minister to marginalized and under-resourced communities. We aim to approach spiritual formation with a culturally inclusive lens, one that involves a greater embodiment of global voices and fosters mutual learning, resulting in richer theology and spiritual practice. These values were very much instilled in me through my studies of global Christianity.

Also that year, I was ordained to word and service with the Evangelical Covenant Church. Before attending GCTS I held to a default belief that only men could preach or hold senior pastoral positions. Sitting under stellar female professors and attending an egalitarian church during seminary resulted in a massive paradigm shift for this Texas girl from the Southern Baptist megachurch capital of the country. At GCTS I also encountered male professors who leveraged their privilege to empower women, especially women of color. Todd is among those who instilled courage and confidence in me. The empowerment I experienced at Gordon-Conwell lit a spark to lean into God's calling on my life in a way I had not dared to pursue before.

## Windows and Doors

Ultimately, the fruit of studying global Christianity and other world religions is beholding a great and boundless God. Through his research, classes, and publications, Todd opened a window for me to view and study global Christianity as I had never fully appreciated before, thus expanding my understanding of God, the reconciling work of Jesus Christ, and the ministry of the Holy Spirit. Before seminary, I had a narrow understanding of who belonged to my global Christian family, and Todd helped expand that for me in ways that felt more faithful to the gospel.

Besides opening a window to broader scholarship, Todd also opened a door for me. Co-authoring *Our Global Families* led to invitations to speak before audiences with whom I otherwise would not have had inroads. Over the years, Todd has continued to open doors for me by inviting me to co-author articles and co-teach webinars on global Christianity and refugees. He and Dr. Gina Zurlo asked me to contribute to the *World Christian Encyclopedia*, 3rd edition (Edinburgh University Press, 2019) as an editorial assistant, and Todd has referred me to others for writing and speaking opportunities. When it was time for me to find a publisher for *A Better Country*, my workbook on refugees, it was Todd who connected me.

Todd's impressive intellect could tempt him to be arrogant and standoffish, yet he is one of the most unassuming and approachable professors I have ever met. Todd is not merely a world class scholar, he is a devotee of his subject matter, as any visit to his office will prove to you. His walls are decked with photos and artwork from around the globe, world music playing softly in the background. The last time I visited him, the only framed photo on his desk was of Thai royalty to remind him of the hospitality he received while living in Thailand. He travels the world researching and teaching, has an adventurous palate, and, along with his wife, Tricia, is intentional about bringing international students into their home. I have been the recipient of their warm hospitality several times.

Recently, I was teased by friends over a memory: when I presented on migration at a Perspectives on the World Christian Movement class in Houston a few years ago, I entered the room clutching my oversized *Atlas of Global Christianity*, of which Todd is an editor, eager to expose the students to this recently published resource. The class organizers eventually became friends of mine, and they recalled how I had included graphics from the *Atlas* in my slide deck and afterwards invited students to flip through the book on their own. I don't recall if anyone actually looked at it. (I still struggle to understand why not everyone shares my admiration for the *Atlas*.) I was eager to share it because I knew how much effort and heart had gone into producing it; I knew it contained fresh data and unique perspectives on God's mission in the world; and the enthusiasm for the subject matter had rubbed off on me in such an indelible way I could not help but share it.

Todd's contribution to the field of global Christianity is impossible to measure, even by one as good at numbers as he. As one who knows him personally, I am most impressed not by his numerous publications or the sum of his gifts, but by the integrity and authenticity of his life. In knowing Todd, I have gained an understanding and appreciation of a God who is bigger than my imagination and a church that is broader than my boundaries. I have also gained a brother in Christ whom I am blessed and humbled to call mentor, colleague, and friend.

# Chapter 31: Belonging

*Kenneth Young*

The beginning of something new is always daunting, but leaving home and moving several states away can be downright horrific. Nevertheless, several years ago I vowed to follow God wherever I was sent, regardless of location. When the Isaiah moment arrived, I followed God from Georgia to the North Shore of Boston, Massachusetts. My sister and I packed all my belongings into a Pontiac G5 and headed north for roughly 21 hours. We made stops on the way up Interstate 95, experienced many traffic jams and a loss of direction in the Washington, DC area. Our excitement was palpable upon seeing the sign, "Welcome to Massachusetts." Life can sometimes feel like a long road trip: long and tiring, but also exciting and intriguing, with plenty of twists and turns, traffic jams and toll roads, fast and slow lanes to get to your destination. Making it to Gordon-Conwell Theological Seminary was the goal, and I did it.

The rolling hills of the North Shore were beyond what words could articulate; the area is beautiful and spectacular, nearly other worldly for those born and reared in the South. The many mansions and weekly polo match on Sunday afternoons were beyond my wildest dreams. How could a guy from Georgia fit into this highly affluent area? How could I belong in a place like South Hamilton, Massachusetts? It is difficult to shake that sinking feeling of standing out. I was not prepared to be a Black man at a primarily White Evangelical seminary, emersed in a foreign culture and discussions of lobsters, John Calvin, and Boston lager beer. Even the opportunity to travel on trains presented a new world that I would have to explore on my own. I quickly realized that studying and living in this place would take grit and gall.

"What have I gotten myself into?" I asked myself walking down the hall of the main Kerr building on campus. I wondered if anyone in Phippen Hall, the men's dorm, was willing to hear my story or considered me important enough to be interested in me. Nestled on top of one of the highest hills in Essex County, the seminary seems to be excluded from the rest of society. I could not fathom staying full-time in such an isolated place—fine for a getaway, but not to live.

I took several classes at Gordon-Conwell that did not seem to fit the Evangelical narrative, as they were primarily centered on solely a White American Evangelical story. The classes seemed to be focused on a literal reading of the scriptures, Calvinism vs. Arminianism, or church growth. I was excited to register for Dr. Todd Johnson's Global Pentecostalism course; the syllabus was intriguing, exciting, and seemed different from the other courses at the seminary. Furthermore, I was unsure if I had ever experienced a professor speaking directly to the Pentecostal tradition in a positive way. Other perspectives on campus seemed to put the Holy Spirit in a box, a package tucked away somewhere in a storage room. I really had no idea what to expect. Todd appeared to represent the culture of Gordon-Conwell as an older, White male professor. Yet, he had a keen ability to make students who did not "fit" the mainstream feel like they truly belonged. Belonging allows people to let down their walls and no longer wear façades. For me, veneers and masks had become my personal self-survival tactic in rooms full of mostly White students. Upon coming to Gordon-Conwell, I had to learn how to change my language to fit in the community.

Todd began his first lecture by explaining the different definitions of Pentecostalism. He used familiar phrasing such as, "When did you get saved?" I had never heard any of my professors define salvation as an experiential moment in the life of a Christian until that day. That language felt familiar to me and made me feel like perhaps I could belong there. He continued to describe the gospel as something that people experience versus something that is intellectualized—a welcome breath of fresh air. I learned that the church is increasing in the global South, and many of these new Christians were Pentecostals. I sat in my chair, shocked, unable to articulate this deep feeling of satisfaction and recognition. Other classes did not know how to classify the Black Church in the United States, wanting to put it in either a mainline Protestant or Evangelical box, but Black Christianity is its own thing, not the same as White Christian traditions. Gordon-Conwell professors apparently had little knowledge of the Black Church's history, uniqueness, and culture. Yet, Todd understood that at the core of the Black Church was experiential faith. Gospel lyrics such as, "Do you have good religion? Certainly, Lord!" articulate an experience that Blacks have with God.

In Todd's Pentecostalism class, I could finally take a deep breath and read books about people's experiences *with* God, not just people's thoughts *about* God. The books assigned included people that looked and sounded like me, and it made me feel like I could truly be myself, for the first time. In class, I was unashamed of my background, could speak about the Black Church, and could share freely about the Pentecostal movement, such as its interracial beginnings at the 1906 Azusa Street Revival. Todd was clear about what happened during this revival in America, he understood the nuances of Black Pentecostal theology (such as the Church of God in Christ), and the class was able to see me and my people, perhaps for the first time. All of this made the classroom less hostile and more accessible. There was no need to pontificate over five-point Calvinism; instead, we had impactful conversations about lives being changed by the power of the Holy Spirit. Todd shared with us movements of the Holy Spirit and I was inspired by his in-depth knowledge of different revivals worldwide, as the class emphasized Pentecostalism outside of the Western world. I could breathe easy here.

Todd became a favorite professor of many students because he spoke a different language. His courses were not solely focused on narrow Evangelical theology and he made sure to expose students to many different strands of theological thinking. The theology of experience came as a shock to several students, but everyone had freedom in Todd's classroom to learn, explore, dialogue, and arrive at new conclusions to pressing theological questions from a global perspective, not be force-fed particular theological doctrines. It was a joy to navigate global Pentecostalism with Todd, but most importantly, his efforts to make all students feel like they belonged was priceless. Such belonging is key to provide space for students to learn non-defensively, and it is my hope for seminaries worldwide to have gifted professors like Todd to guide them and make them feel welcome.

# Part III

# The Work of Todd M. Johnson: Data

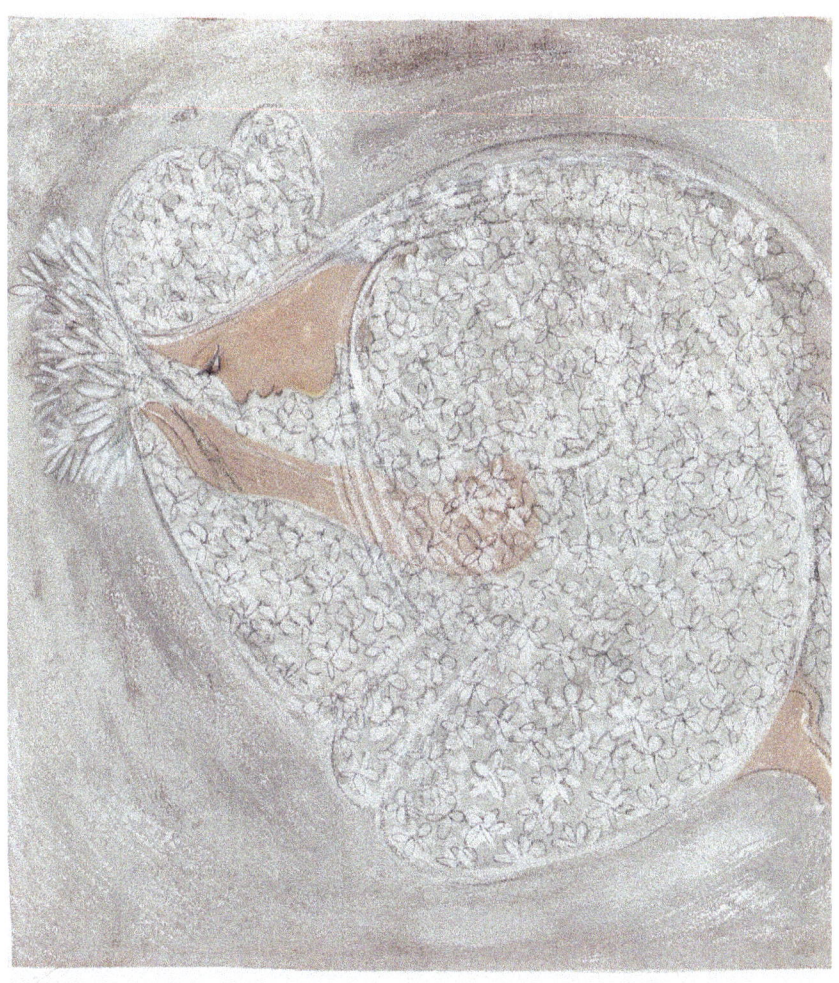

Nalini Jayasuriya (1927–2014), *Silence* (The Worshipper), courtesy of the Overseas Ministries Study Center at Princeton Theological Seminary, Princeton, New Jersey, USA.

Part III includes a series of 185 data tables on Christian martyrdom, world religions, global Christianity, evangelization, mission, and human development. These tables and graphs serve as a quick-reference snapshot for trends in these areas to provide contextual information on changes occurring within global Christianity in the last 120 years, with projections for the future (2050). These tables are largely self-explanatory by the column headings, with just two exceptions: Highest HIV adults per 1,000, 2020 and Highest malaria per 1,000, 2020 each include only highest values (top ten) because the lowest values (bottom ten) are all zero. The source for all tables and line graphs is Todd M. Johnson and Gina A. Zurlo, eds., *World Christian Database* (Leiden/Boston: Brill), accessed May 2022. The baseline year of current data is 2020, except for denominations, which is 2015. These data are based on the 2019 United Nations population revision.

**Contents**

Martyrdom . . . . . . . . . . . . . . . . . . . . . . . . . . . . . . . . . . . . . . . . . . . . . . . . . . . . . . 181

General Country Data . . . . . . . . . . . . . . . . . . . . . . . . . . . . . . . . . . . . . . . . . . . . 183

World Religions . . . . . . . . . . . . . . . . . . . . . . . . . . . . . . . . . . . . . . . . . . . . . . . . . 184

Major Christian Traditions and Movements . . . . . . . . . . . . . . . . . . . . . . . . . 194

Christian Mission . . . . . . . . . . . . . . . . . . . . . . . . . . . . . . . . . . . . . . . . . . . . . . . . 201

Denominations . . . . . . . . . . . . . . . . . . . . . . . . . . . . . . . . . . . . . . . . . . . . . . . . . . 203

Peoples . . . . . . . . . . . . . . . . . . . . . . . . . . . . . . . . . . . . . . . . . . . . . . . . . . . . . . . . . 207

Evangelization by Peoples . . . . . . . . . . . . . . . . . . . . . . . . . . . . . . . . . . . . . . . . . 212

Bible Translation . . . . . . . . . . . . . . . . . . . . . . . . . . . . . . . . . . . . . . . . . . . . . . . . . 214

Cities . . . . . . . . . . . . . . . . . . . . . . . . . . . . . . . . . . . . . . . . . . . . . . . . . . . . . . . . . . . 216

Country Indicators . . . . . . . . . . . . . . . . . . . . . . . . . . . . . . . . . . . . . . . . . . . . . . . 218

# Martyrdom

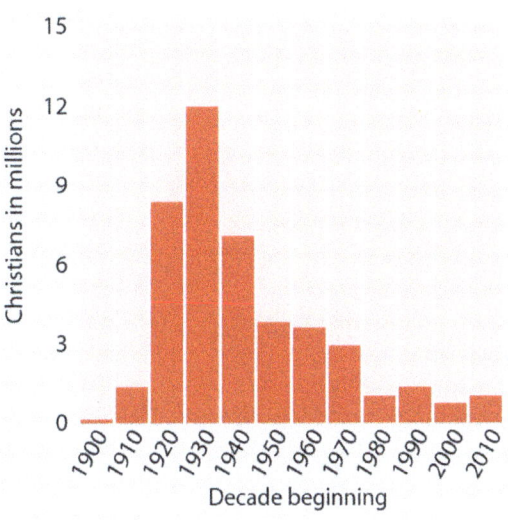

Source: Todd M. Johnson and Gina A. Zurlo, *World Christian Encyclopedia*, 3rd ed. (Edinburgh: Edinburgh University Press, 2019), 34.

Largest martyrdom situations

| | Situation | Martyrs |
|---|---|---|
| 1 | 1921–50, Christians die in Soviet prison camps | 15,000,000 |
| 2 | 1950–80, Christians die in Soviet prison camps | 5,000,000 |
| 3 | 1214, Genghiz Khan massacre | 4,000,000 |
| 4 | 1358, Tamerlane destroys Church of the East | 4,000,000 |
| 5 | 1929–37, Orthodox killed by Stalin | 2,700,000 |
| 6 | 1560, Conquistadors kill Amerindians | 2,200,000 |
| 7 | 1925, Soviets attempt to liquidate Roman Catholics | 1,200,000 |
| 8 | 1258, Baghdad captured in massacre by Hulaku Khan | 1,100,000 |
| 9 | 1937, Nazis kill 1 million Christians | 1,000,000 |
| 10 | 1214, Diocese of Herat sacked by Genghiz Khan | 1,000,000 |

Most severe martyrdom situations

| | Situation | % of local Christians |
|---|---|---|
| 1 | 1624, all 400 Tibetan Christians wiped out | 100.0% |
| 2 | 1938, Nazis exterminate 500,000 Gypsies | 89.7% |
| 3 | 1975, Khmer Rouge slaughter 2 million | 88.8% |
| 4 | 1241, Mongols ravage Hungary killing Christians | 86.7% |
| 5 | 1570, Huguenot corsairs murder 52 Jesuits | 86.7% |
| 6 | 287, Martyrs of Agaunum | 83.3% |
| 7 | 1843, Turks use Kurds to massacre 20,000 Nestorians | 80.0% |
| 8 | 1933, Assyrians (Nestorians) murdered by Iraqi troops | 80.0% |
| 9 | 1970, Massacre of 40,000 Vietnamese Catholics | 76.9% |
| 10 | 1918, Turks massacre 80% of all Syrian Orthodox | 75.0% |

### Persecutors of most martyrs

| | Persecutor | Martyrs |
|---|---|---|
| 1 | State ruling power | 56,760,000 |
| 2 | Atheists | 31,689,000 |
| 3 | Muslims | 9,191,000 |
| 4 | Shamanists | 7,469,000 |
| 5 | Roman Catholics | 5,229,000 |
| 6 | Non-religious (including Nazis) | 2,712,000 |
| 7 | Buddhists | 1,671,000 |
| 8 | Hindus | 677,000 |
| 9 | Zoroastrians | 384,000 |
| 10 | Byzantines | 222,000 |

### Countries with most martyrs (in the past)

| | Country | Martyrs |
|---|---|---|
| 1 | USSR | 23,260,000 |
| 2 | Uzbekistan | 4,000,000 |
| 3 | Ukraine | 3,571,000 |
| 4 | Mexico | 3,283,000 |
| 5 | China | 2,704,000 |
| 6 | Iraq | 1,956,000 |
| 7 | Russia | 1,544,000 |
| 8 | Turkey | 1,047,000 |
| 9 | Poland | 1,005,000 |
| 10 | Afghanistan | 1,001,000 |

### Traditions with most martyrs

| | Tradition | Martyrs |
|---|---|---|
| 1 | Russian Orthodox | 21,626,400 |
| 2 | Assyrian (East Syrian, Messihaye) | 12,379,330 |
| 3 | Latin-rite Catholic | 11,903,256 |
| 4 | Ukrainian Orthodox | 3,500,000 |
| 5 | Armenian Orthodox (Gregorian) | 1,215,100 |
| 6 | Coptic Orthodox | 1,067,900 |
| 7 | Pentecostal (Protestant; Classical Pentecostal) | 1,020,820 |
| 8 | Messianic Jewish | 1,000,000 |
| 9 | Taiping Heavenly Kingdom | 1,000,000 |
| 10 | Anglicans | 998,020 |

### Centuries with most martyrs

| | Century | Martyrs |
|---|---|---|
| 1 | 1900s | 41,367,000 |
| 2 | 1200s | 7,228,000 |
| 3 | 1300s | 4,906,000 |
| 4 | 1500s | 3,618,000 |
| 5 | 1800s | 1,587,000 |
| 6 | 2000s | 907,000 |
| 7 | 300s | 861,000 |
| 8 | 1400s | 763,000 |
| 9 | 400s | 513,000 |
| 10 | 200s | 409,000 |

## General Country Data

### Global Annual Ministry Income

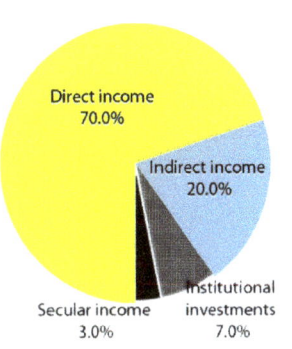

### Global Annual Ministry Expenses

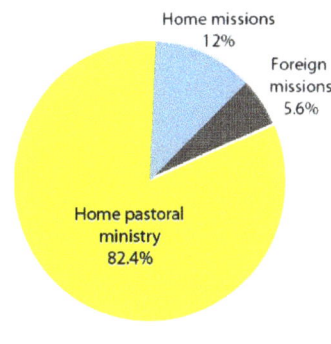

Source: Todd M. Johnson and Kenneth R. Ross, eds., *Atlas of Global Christianity, 1910–2010* (Edinburgh: Edinburgh University Press, 2009), 296.

Largest countries by population, 2020

| | Country | Population |
|---|---|---|
| 1 | China | 1,439,324,000 |
| 2 | India | 1,380,004,000 |
| 3 | United States | 331,003,000 |
| 4 | Indonesia | 273,524,000 |
| 5 | Pakistan | 220,892,000 |
| 6 | Brazil | 212,559,000 |
| 7 | Nigeria | 206,140,000 |
| 8 | Bangladesh | 164,689,000 |
| 9 | Russia | 145,934,000 |
| 10 | Mexico | 128,933,000 |

Most peoples, 2020

| | Country | Number of peoples |
|---|---|---|
| 1 | Papua New Guinea | 916 |
| 2 | Indonesia | 763 |
| 3 | Nigeria | 537 |
| 4 | China | 518 |
| 5 | India | 486 |
| 6 | Mexico | 314 |
| 7 | United States | 314 |
| 8 | Cameroon | 312 |
| 9 | DR Congo | 263 |
| 10 | Australia | 227 |

Most urbanized
(countries over 1 million), 2020

| | Country | % urban |
|---|---|---|
| 1 | Hong Kong | 100.0% |
| 2 | Singapore | 100.0% |
| 3 | Kuwait | 100.0% |
| 4 | Qatar | 99.2% |
| 5 | Belgium | 98.1% |
| 6 | Uruguay | 95.5% |
| 7 | Puerto Rico | 93.6% |
| 8 | Israel | 92.6% |
| 9 | Netherlands | 92.2% |
| 10 | Argentina | 92.1% |

Least urbanized
(countries over 1 million), 2020

| | Country | % urban |
|---|---|---|
| 1 | Papua New Guinea | 13.3% |
| 2 | Burundi | 13.7% |
| 3 | Niger | 16.6% |
| 4 | Malawi | 17.4% |
| 5 | Rwanda | 17.4% |
| 6 | Sri Lanka | 18.7% |
| 7 | South Sudan | 20.2% |
| 8 | Nepal | 20.6% |
| 9 | Ethiopia | 21.7% |
| 10 | Chad | 23.5% |

Most Christian income, 2020

|   | Country | Total Christian income |
|---|---|---|
| 1 | United States | $13,500 billion |
| 2 | Russia | $2,900 billion |
| 3 | Brazil | $2,700 billion |
| 4 | Germany | $2,600 billion |
| 5 | Mexico | $2,100 billion |
| 6 | United Kingdom | $1,800 billion |
| 7 | France | $1,700 billion |
| 8 | Italy | $1,700 billion |
| 9 | China | $1,600 billion |
| 10 | Spain | $1,400 billion |

Least Christian income, 2020

|   | Country | Total Christian income |
|---|---|---|
| 1 | Mayotte | $2,830,000 |
| 2 | Comoros | $6,216,000 |
| 3 | Tokelau | $7,363,000 |
| 4 | Somalia | $8,289,000 |
| 5 | Western Sahara | $8,674,000 |
| 6 | Niue | $9,052,000 |
| 7 | Afghanistan | $13,757,000 |
| 8 | Yemen | $20,472,000 |
| 9 | Maldives | $21,124,000 |
| 10 | Saint Helena | $22,213,000 |

## World Religions[1]

### Religions, 1900–2050

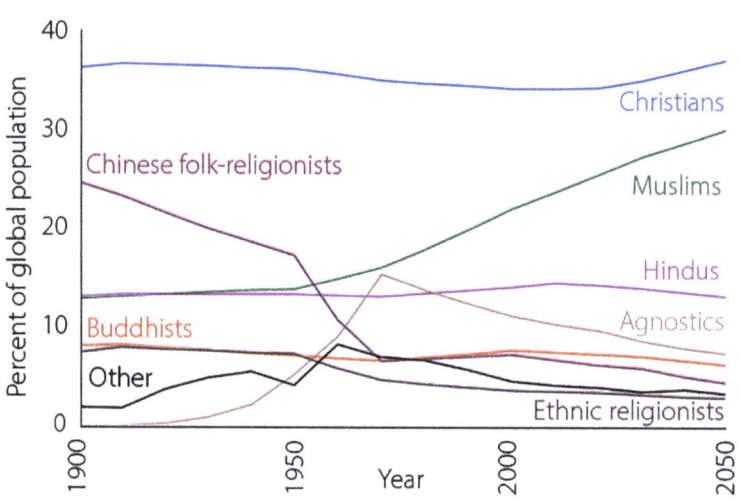

Source: Todd M. Johnson and Gina A. Zurlo, *World Christian Encyclopedia*, 3rd ed. (Edinburgh: Edinburgh University Press, 2019), 28.

---

1 Tables are shown for religions and non-religions over 1%, plus Jews.

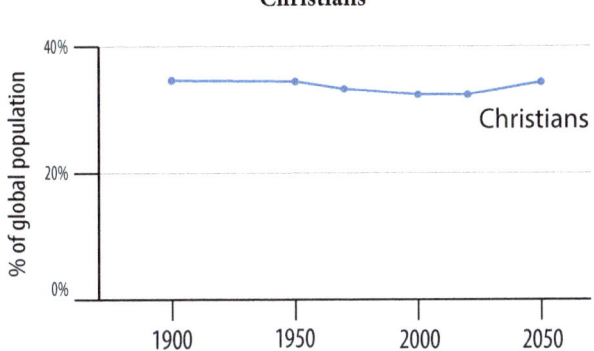

**Christians**

Most Christians in 1900

| | Country | Christians |
|---|---|---|
| 1 | United States | 73,712,000 |
| 2 | Russia | 62,545,000 |
| 3 | Germany | 41,533,000 |
| 4 | France | 40,731,000 |
| 5 | United Kingdom | 37,125,000 |
| 6 | Italy | 32,903,000 |
| 7 | Ukraine | 28,501,000 |
| 8 | Poland | 22,050,000 |
| 9 | Spain | 18,795,000 |
| 10 | Brazil | 17,319,000 |

Highest % Christian in 1900

| | Country | % Christian |
|---|---|---|
| 1 | Finland | 100.0% |
| 2 | Slovenia | 100.0% |
| 3 | Samoa | 100.0% |
| 4 | Barbados | 100.0% |
| 5 | Kiribati | 100.0% |
| 6 | Curaçao | 100.0% |
| 7 | Tonga | 100.0% |
| 8 | Antigua & Barbuda | 100.0% |
| 9 | Aruba | 100.0% |
| 10 | United States Virgin Is | 100.0% |

Most Christians in 2020

| | Country | Christians |
|---|---|---|
| 1 | United States | 245,457,000 |
| 2 | Brazil | 192,939,000 |
| 3 | Mexico | 123,370,000 |
| 4 | Russia | 119,945,000 |
| 5 | China | 106,018,000 |
| 6 | Philippines | 99,307,000 |
| 7 | Nigeria | 95,186,000 |
| 8 | DR Congo | 85,061,000 |
| 9 | Ethiopia | 67,903,000 |
| 10 | India | 66,316,000 |

Highest % Christian in 2020

| | Country | % Christian |
|---|---|---|
| 1 | Holy See | 100.0% |
| 2 | Samoa | 98.8% |
| 3 | Romania | 98.6% |
| 4 | Faeroe Islands | 98.0% |
| 5 | American Samoa | 98.0% |
| 6 | Guatemala | 97.4% |
| 7 | Wallis & Futuna Islands | 97.3% |
| 8 | Moldova | 97.2% |
| 9 | Kiribati | 96.8% |
| 10 | Niue | 96.7% |

Most Christians in 2050

| | Country | Christians |
|---|---|---|
| 1 | United States | 251,376,000 |
| 2 | Brazil | 201,934,000 |
| 3 | China | 200,020,000 |
| 4 | Nigeria | 187,860,000 |
| 5 | DR Congo | 186,316,000 |
| 6 | Mexico | 144,882,000 |
| 7 | Philippines | 130,047,000 |
| 8 | Ethiopia | 128,574,000 |
| 9 | Russia | 109,077,000 |
| 10 | India | 106,500,000 |

Highest % Christian in 2050

| | Country | % Christian |
|---|---|---|
| 1 | Holy See | 100.0% |
| 2 | Romania | 98.8% |
| 3 | Samoa | 98.7% |
| 4 | Moldova | 98.1% |
| 5 | Kiribati | 96.3% |
| 6 | Poland | 96.3% |
| 7 | Guatemala | 96.1% |
| 8 | Burundi | 96.1% |
| 9 | Papua New Guinea | 96.0% |
| 10 | Solomon Islands | 95.8% |

## Muslims

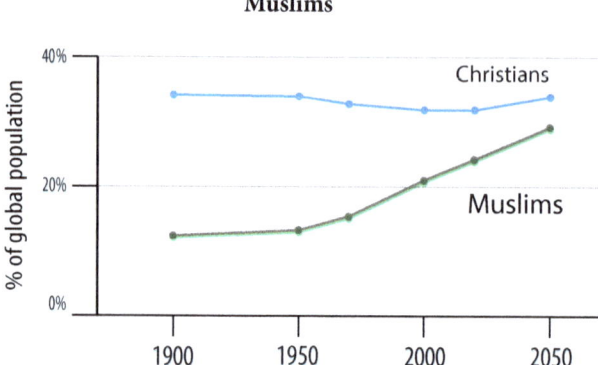

### Most Muslims in 1900

| | Country | Muslims |
|---|---|---|
| 1 | India | 31,552,000 |
| 2 | China | 24,000,000 |
| 3 | Pakistan | 20,911,000 |
| 4 | Bangladesh | 18,807,000 |
| 5 | Indonesia | 15,520,000 |
| 6 | Turkey | 10,958,000 |
| 7 | Iran | 9,324,000 |
| 8 | Egypt | 8,917,000 |
| 9 | Russia | 6,576,000 |
| 10 | Afghanistan | 5,070,000 |

### Highest % Muslim in 1900

| | Country | % Muslim |
|---|---|---|
| 1 | Maldives | 100.0% |
| 2 | Saudi Arabia | 100.0% |
| 3 | Oman | 100.0% |
| 4 | Somalia | 99.9% |
| 5 | Comoros | 99.9% |
| 6 | United Arab Emirates | 99.8% |
| 7 | Kuwait | 99.7% |
| 8 | Mayotte | 99.7% |
| 9 | Bahrain | 99.7% |
| 10 | Qatar | 99.6% |

### Most Muslims in 2020

| | Country | Muslims |
|---|---|---|
| 1 | Indonesia | 216,409,000 |
| 2 | Pakistan | 213,086,000 |
| 3 | India | 198,477,000 |
| 4 | Bangladesh | 146,254,000 |
| 5 | Nigeria | 94,517,000 |
| 6 | Egypt | 92,165,000 |
| 7 | Turkey | 82,996,000 |
| 8 | Iran | 82,770,000 |
| 9 | Algeria | 43,142,000 |
| 10 | Sudan | 40,197,000 |

### Highest % Muslim in 2020

| | Country | % Muslim |
|---|---|---|
| 1 | Afghanistan | 99.9% |
| 2 | Somalia | 99.8% |
| 3 | Morocco | 99.7% |
| 4 | Western Sahara | 99.6% |
| 5 | Tunisia | 99.5% |
| 6 | Yemen | 99.2% |
| 7 | Mauritania | 99.2% |
| 8 | Libya | 99.0% |
| 9 | Mayotte | 98.8% |
| 10 | Maldives | 98.7% |

### Most Muslims in 2050

| | Country | Muslims |
|---|---|---|
| 1 | Pakistan | 328,467,000 |
| 2 | India | 265,000,000 |
| 3 | Indonesia | 263,272,000 |
| 4 | Nigeria | 200,000,000 |
| 5 | Bangladesh | 171,348,000 |
| 6 | Egypt | 147,028,000 |
| 7 | Iran | 101,213,000 |
| 8 | Turkey | 94,812,000 |
| 9 | Sudan | 77,074,000 |
| 10 | Ethiopia | 70,745,000 |

### Highest % Muslim in 2050

| | Country | % Muslim |
|---|---|---|
| 1 | Afghanistan | 99.9% |
| 2 | Somalia | 99.9% |
| 3 | Western Sahara | 99.7% |
| 4 | Morocco | 99.7% |
| 5 | Mauritania | 99.5% |
| 6 | Tunisia | 99.5% |
| 7 | Mayotte | 99.2% |
| 8 | Tajikistan | 99.2% |
| 9 | Yemen | 99.1% |
| 10 | Libya | 98.8% |

## Hindus

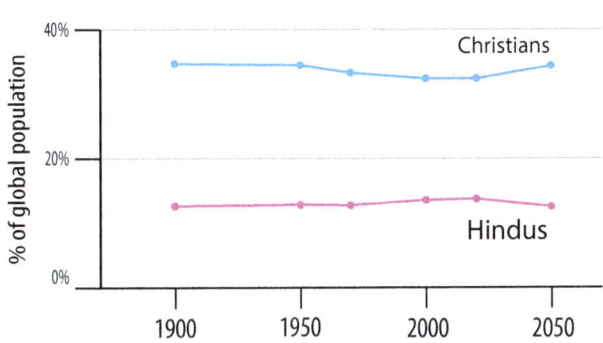

### Most Hindus in 1900

| | Country | Hindus |
|---|---|---|
| 1 | India | 184,023,000 |
| 2 | Bangladesh | 9,371,000 |
| 3 | Pakistan | 3,560,000 |
| 4 | Nepal | 3,410,000 |
| 5 | Sri Lanka | 828,000 |
| 6 | Indonesia | 776,000 |
| 7 | Myanmar | 284,000 |
| 8 | Malaysia | 210,000 |
| 9 | Mauritius | 207,000 |
| 10 | Guyana | 71,200 |

### Highest % Hindu in 1900

| | Country | % Hindu |
|---|---|---|
| 1 | India | 80.0% |
| 2 | Nepal | 77.0% |
| 3 | Mauritius | 54.5% |
| 4 | Bangladesh | 32.7% |
| 5 | Suriname | 26.4% |
| 6 | Trinidad & Tobago | 25.1% |
| 7 | Guyana | 25.0% |
| 8 | Sri Lanka | 23.2% |
| 9 | Bhutan | 15.2% |
| 10 | Pakistan | 14.0% |

### Most Hindus in 2020

| | Country | Hindus |
|---|---|---|
| 1 | India | 999,122,000 |
| 2 | Nepal | 19,173,000 |
| 3 | Bangladesh | 15,447,000 |
| 4 | Indonesia | 4,428,000 |
| 5 | Pakistan | 2,913,000 |
| 6 | Sri Lanka | 2,794,000 |
| 7 | Malaysia | 2,009,000 |
| 8 | United States | 1,603,000 |
| 9 | South Africa | 1,414,000 |
| 10 | Myanmar | 928,000 |

### Highest % Hindu in 2020

| | Country | % Hindu |
|---|---|---|
| 1 | India | 72.4% |
| 2 | Nepal | 65.8% |
| 3 | Mauritius | 44.2% |
| 4 | Guyana | 30.8% |
| 5 | Fiji | 27.7% |
| 6 | Trinidad & Tobago | 24.3% |
| 7 | Suriname | 20.6% |
| 8 | Sri Lanka | 13.0% |
| 9 | Bhutan | 11.4% |
| 10 | Bangladesh | 9.4% |

### Most Hindus in 2050

| | Country | Hindus |
|---|---|---|
| 1 | India | 1,137,232,000 |
| 2 | Nepal | 21,289,000 |
| 3 | Bangladesh | 17,250,000 |
| 4 | Indonesia | 4,900,000 |
| 5 | Pakistan | 3,620,000 |
| 6 | Sri Lanka | 2,800,000 |
| 7 | Malaysia | 2,730,000 |
| 8 | United States | 2,500,000 |
| 9 | South Africa | 1,800,000 |
| 10 | Myanmar | 1,000,000 |

### Highest % Hindu in 2050

| | Country | % Hindu |
|---|---|---|
| 1 | India | 69.4% |
| 2 | Nepal | 60.3% |
| 3 | Mauritius | 38.9% |
| 4 | Guyana | 29.3% |
| 5 | Fiji | 24.3% |
| 6 | Trinidad & Tobago | 22.3% |
| 7 | Suriname | 20.1% |
| 8 | Sri Lanka | 12.8% |
| 9 | Bhutan | 12.2% |
| 10 | Bangladesh | 9.0% |

## Buddhists

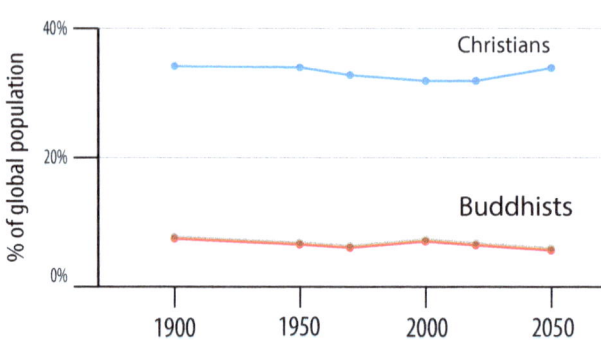

### Most Buddhists in 1900

|    | Country     | Buddhists  |
|----|-------------|------------|
| 1  | China       | 60,000,000 |
| 2  | Japan       | 35,666,000 |
| 3  | Myanmar     | 9,055,000  |
| 4  | Viet Nam    | 7,623,000  |
| 5  | Thailand    | 5,488,000  |
| 6  | Cambodia    | 2,138,000  |
| 7  | Sri Lanka   | 2,105,000  |
| 8  | Laos        | 905,000    |
| 9  | Nepal       | 886,000    |
| 10 | South Korea | 800,000    |

### Highest % Buddhist in 1900

|    | Country   | % Buddhist |
|----|-----------|------------|
| 1  | Thailand  | 90.9%      |
| 2  | Myanmar   | 86.7%      |
| 3  | Cambodia  | 85.5%      |
| 4  | Japan     | 79.6%      |
| 5  | Bhutan    | 78.9%      |
| 6  | Viet Nam  | 69.3%      |
| 7  | Laos      | 60.3%      |
| 8  | Sri Lanka | 58.9%      |
| 9  | Mongolia  | 38.3%      |
| 10 | Nepal     | 20.0%      |

### Most Buddhists in 2020

|    | Country     | Buddhists   |
|----|-------------|-------------|
| 1  | China       | 228,117,000 |
| 2  | Japan       | 70,539,000  |
| 3  | Thailand    | 60,846,000  |
| 4  | Viet Nam    | 47,334,000  |
| 5  | Myanmar     | 40,469,000  |
| 6  | Sri Lanka   | 14,559,000  |
| 7  | Cambodia    | 14,380,000  |
| 8  | South Korea | 12,637,000  |
| 9  | India       | 9,799,000   |
| 10 | Taiwan      | 6,304,000   |

### Highest % Buddhist in 2020

|    | Country   | % Buddhist |
|----|-----------|------------|
| 1  | Thailand  | 87.2%      |
| 2  | Cambodia  | 86.0%      |
| 3  | Bhutan    | 82.7%      |
| 4  | Myanmar   | 74.4%      |
| 5  | Sri Lanka | 68.0%      |
| 6  | Mongolia  | 58.1%      |
| 7  | Japan     | 55.8%      |
| 8  | Laos      | 52.4%      |
| 9  | Viet Nam  | 48.6%      |
| 10 | Taiwan    | 26.5%      |

### Most Buddhists in 2050

|    | Country       | Buddhists   |
|----|---------------|-------------|
| 1  | China         | 260,840,000 |
| 2  | Japan         | 56,495,000  |
| 3  | Thailand      | 55,854,000  |
| 4  | Viet Nam      | 54,803,000  |
| 5  | Myanmar       | 47,717,000  |
| 6  | Cambodia      | 18,375,000  |
| 7  | India         | 14,800,000  |
| 8  | Sri Lanka     | 14,508,000  |
| 9  | South Korea   | 12,700,000  |
| 10 | United States | 7,000,000   |

### Highest % Buddhist in 2050

|    | Country     | % Buddhist |
|----|-------------|------------|
| 1  | Thailand    | 84.7%      |
| 2  | Cambodia    | 84.1%      |
| 3  | Bhutan      | 81.4%      |
| 4  | Myanmar     | 76.6%      |
| 5  | Sri Lanka   | 66.5%      |
| 6  | Mongolia    | 65.0%      |
| 7  | Laos        | 59.6%      |
| 8  | Japan       | 53.4%      |
| 9  | Viet Nam    | 50.0%      |
| 10 | South Korea | 27.1%      |

## Chinese folk-religionists

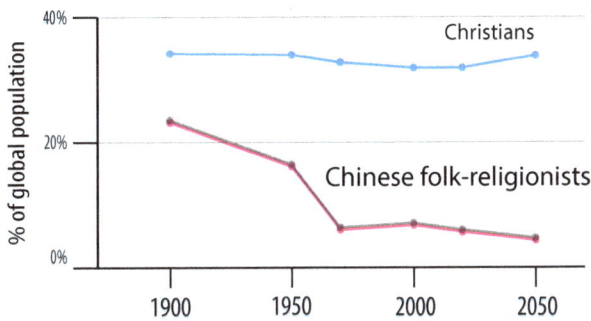

Most Chinese folk-religionists in 1900

|    | Country       | Chinese folk-religionists |
|----|---------------|---------------------------|
| 1  | China         | 375,870,000               |
| 2  | Taiwan        | 2,193,000                 |
| 3  | Malaysia      | 525,000                   |
| 4  | Hong Kong     | 340,000                   |
| 5  | Thailand      | 240,000                   |
| 6  | Viet Nam      | 200,000                   |
| 7  | Indonesia     | 195,000                   |
| 8  | Singapore     | 124,000                   |
| 9  | Cambodia      | 100,000                   |
| 10 | United States | 70,000                    |

Highest % Chinese folk-religionist in 1900

|    | Country   | % Chinese folk-religionist |
|----|-----------|----------------------------|
| 1  | Hong Kong | 89.5%                      |
| 2  | Macao     | 82.2%                      |
| 3  | China     | 79.7%                      |
| 4  | Taiwan    | 68.6%                      |
| 5  | Singapore | 49.5%                      |
| 6  | Malaysia  | 25.0%                      |
| 7  | Brunei    | 6.0%                       |
| 8  | Cambodia  | 4.0%                       |
| 9  | Thailand  | 4.0%                       |
| 10 | Viet Nam  | 1.8%                       |

Most Chinese folk-religionists in 2020

|    | Country   | Chinese folk-religionists |
|----|-----------|---------------------------|
| 1  | China     | 436,922,000               |
| 2  | Taiwan    | 10,225,000                |
| 3  | Malaysia  | 5,948,000                 |
| 4  | Hong Kong | 3,186,000                 |
| 5  | Indonesia | 2,425,000                 |
| 6  | Singapore | 2,194,000                 |
| 7  | Viet Nam  | 973,000                   |
| 8  | Canada    | 687,000                   |
| 9  | Thailand  | 643,000                   |
| 10 | Macao     | 381,000                   |

Highest % Chinese folk-religionist in 2020

|    | Country            | % Chinese folk-religioniss |
|----|--------------------|----------------------------|
| 1  | Macao              | 58.7%                      |
| 2  | Taiwan             | 42.9%                      |
| 3  | Hong Kong          | 42.5%                      |
| 4  | Singapore          | 37.5%                      |
| 5  | China              | 30.4%                      |
| 6  | Malaysia           | 18.4%                      |
| 7  | Nauru              | 10.5%                      |
| 8  | Brunei             | 5.2%                       |
| 9  | Northern Mariana Is| 4.9%                       |
| 10 | French Guiana      | 3.6%                       |

Most Chinese folk-religionists in 2050

|    | Country   | Chinese folk-religionists |
|----|-----------|---------------------------|
| 1  | China     | 428,072,000               |
| 2  | Taiwan    | 9,000,000                 |
| 3  | Malaysia  | 7,500,000                 |
| 4  | Hong Kong | 2,704,000                 |
| 5  | Indonesia | 2,550,000                 |
| 6  | Singapore | 1,853,000                 |
| 7  | Viet Nam  | 1,100,000                 |
| 8  | Canada    | 1,000,000                 |
| 9  | Thailand  | 800,000                   |
| 10 | Cambodia  | 565,000                   |

Highest % Chinese folk-religionist in 2050

|    | Country            | % Chinese folk-religionist |
|----|--------------------|----------------------------|
| 1  | Macao              | 56.4%                      |
| 2  | Taiwan             | 40.2%                      |
| 3  | Hong Kong          | 33.6%                      |
| 4  | China              | 30.5%                      |
| 5  | Singapore          | 28.9%                      |
| 6  | Malaysia           | 18.5%                      |
| 7  | Nauru              | 11.1%                      |
| 8  | Brunei             | 6.4%                       |
| 9  | Northern Mariana Is| 5.5%                       |
| 10 | French Guiana      | 3.1%                       |

### Ethnic religionists

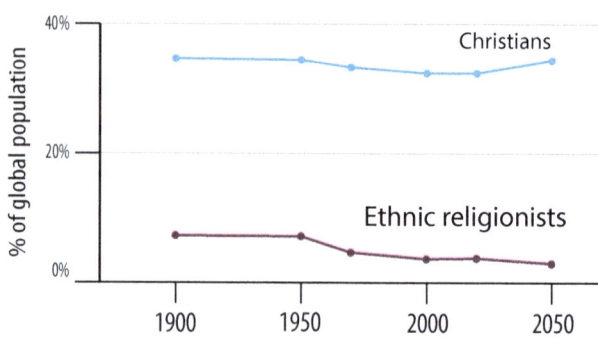

#### Most Ethnic religionists in 1900

| | Country | Ethnic religionists |
|---|---|---|
| 1 | Indonesia | 17,671,000 |
| 2 | Nigeria | 11,824,000 |
| 3 | China | 9,924,000 |
| 4 | DR Congo | 8,865,000 |
| 5 | India | 6,670,000 |
| 6 | South Korea | 6,507,000 |
| 7 | North Korea | 3,766,000 |
| 8 | Tanzania | 3,440,000 |
| 9 | Angola | 2,953,000 |
| 10 | Ethiopia | 2,819,000 |

#### Highest % Ethnic religionist in 1900

| | Country | % Ethnic religionist |
|---|---|---|
| 1 | Rwanda | 99.8% |
| 2 | Burundi | 99.8% |
| 3 | Zambia | 99.7% |
| 4 | Central African Republic | 99.6% |
| 5 | Angola | 99.4% |
| 6 | Eswatini | 99.0% |
| 7 | DR Congo | 98.1% |
| 8 | Congo | 97.5% |
| 9 | São Tomé and Príncipe | 96.9% |
| 10 | Mozambique | 96.3% |

#### Most Ethnic religionists in 2020

| | Country | Ethnic religionists |
|---|---|---|
| 1 | China | 62,084,000 |
| 2 | India | 55,107,000 |
| 3 | Nigeria | 15,730,000 |
| 4 | Madagascar | 10,861,000 |
| 5 | Viet Nam | 10,454,000 |
| 6 | Mozambique | 8,158,000 |
| 7 | South Korea | 7,748,000 |
| 8 | Ethiopia | 7,366,000 |
| 9 | Tanzania | 6,775,000 |
| 10 | Indonesia | 6,347,000 |

#### Highest % Ethnic religionist in 2020

| | Country | % Ethnic religionist |
|---|---|---|
| 1 | Laos | 42.8% |
| 2 | Guinea-Bissau | 41.2% |
| 3 | Liberia | 40.9% |
| 4 | Madagascar | 39.2% |
| 5 | Togo | 33.0% |
| 6 | South Sudan | 32.8% |
| 7 | Benin | 28.5% |
| 8 | Botswana | 28.5% |
| 9 | Mozambique | 26.1% |
| 10 | Côte d'Ivoire | 23.3% |

#### Most Ethnic religionists in 2050

| | Country | Ethnic religionists |
|---|---|---|
| 1 | China | 50,000,000 |
| 2 | India | 45,000,000 |
| 3 | Madagascar | 18,500,000 |
| 4 | Mozambique | 14,203,000 |
| 5 | Nigeria | 12,000,000 |
| 6 | Viet Nam | 10,500,000 |
| 7 | Tanzania | 8,500,000 |
| 8 | Côte d'Ivoire | 8,000,000 |
| 9 | South Korea | 7,700,000 |
| 10 | Cameroon | 6,855,000 |

#### Highest % Ethnic religionist in 2050

| | Country | % Ethnic religionist |
|---|---|---|
| 1 | Liberia | 34.9% |
| 2 | Madagascar | 34.2% |
| 3 | Laos | 33.8% |
| 4 | Guinea-Bissau | 33.7% |
| 5 | Togo | 29.2% |
| 6 | South Sudan | 25.0% |
| 7 | Mozambique | 21.7% |
| 8 | Mongolia | 18.0% |
| 9 | Benin | 16.5% |
| 10 | South Korea | 16.4% |

## Jews

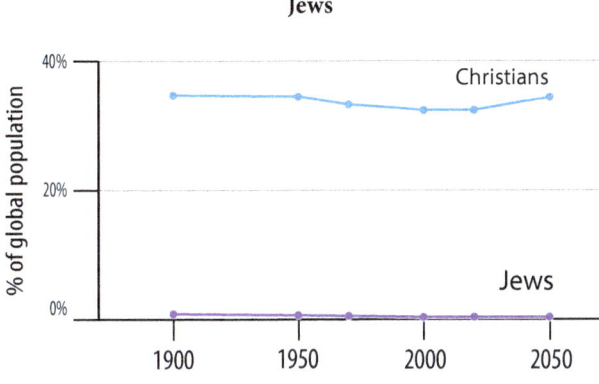

### Most Jews in 1900

| | Country | Jews |
|---|---|---|
| 1 | Russia | 3,470,000 |
| 2 | Poland | 2,120,000 |
| 3 | United States | 1,058,000 |
| 4 | Belarus | 900,000 |
| 5 | Ukraine | 720,000 |
| 6 | Romania | 496,000 |
| 7 | Germany | 480,000 |
| 8 | Hungary | 410,000 |
| 9 | United Kingdom | 235,000 |
| 10 | Czechia | 218,000 |

### Highest % Jewish in 1900

| | Country | % Jewish |
|---|---|---|
| 1 | Belarus | 12.9% |
| 2 | Palestine | 8.8% |
| 3 | Poland | 8.8% |
| 4 | Israel | 8.6% |
| 5 | Hungary | 6.0% |
| 6 | Tunisia | 5.0% |
| 7 | Libya | 5.0% |
| 8 | Russia | 4.7% |
| 9 | Romania | 4.5% |
| 10 | Iraq | 4.0% |

### Most Jews in 2020

| | Country | Jews |
|---|---|---|
| 1 | Israel | 6,215,000 |
| 2 | United States | 5,579,000 |
| 3 | Palestine | 667,000 |
| 4 | France | 442,000 |
| 5 | Canada | 361,000 |
| 6 | United Kingdom | 278,000 |
| 7 | Argentina | 180,000 |
| 8 | Russia | 136,000 |
| 9 | Germany | 127,000 |
| 10 | Australia | 108,000 |

### Highest % Jewish in 2020

| | Country | % Jewish |
|---|---|---|
| 1 | Israel | 71.8% |
| 2 | Palestine | 13.1% |
| 3 | Gibraltar | 1.8% |
| 4 | United States | 1.7% |
| 5 | Monaco | 1.5% |
| 6 | Canada | 1.0% |
| 7 | Cayman Islands | 0.9% |
| 8 | France | 0.7% |
| 9 | Uruguay | 0.6% |
| 10 | Hungary | 0.5% |

### Most Jews in 2050

| | Country | Jews |
|---|---|---|
| 1 | Israel | 8,795,000 |
| 2 | United States | 5,000,000 |
| 3 | Palestine | 1,200,000 |
| 4 | Canada | 390,000 |
| 5 | France | 370,000 |
| 6 | United Kingdom | 250,000 |
| 7 | Argentina | 160,000 |
| 8 | Germany | 140,000 |
| 9 | Australia | 110,000 |
| 10 | Russia | 100,000 |

### Highest % Jewish in 2050

| | Country | % Jewish |
|---|---|---|
| 1 | Israel | 69.1% |
| 2 | Palestine | 13.6% |
| 3 | Gibraltar | 1.8% |
| 4 | United States | 1.3% |
| 5 | Monaco | 1.3% |
| 6 | Canada | 0.9% |
| 7 | Cayman Islands | 0.7% |
| 8 | Uruguay | 0.5% |
| 9 | France | 0.5% |
| 10 | Latvia | 0.5% |

## Agnostics

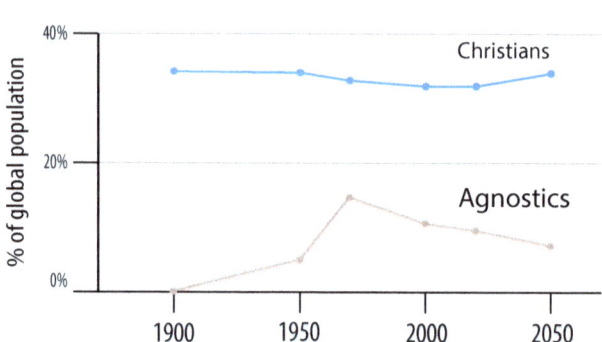

### Most Agnostics in 1900

| | Country | Agnostics |
|---|---|---|
| 1 | United States | 1,000,000 |
| 2 | United Kingdom | 720,000 |
| 3 | Uruguay | 340,000 |
| 4 | Russia | 110,000 |
| 5 | Croatia | 100,000 |
| 6 | France | 92,000 |
| 7 | Germany | 80,000 |
| 8 | Netherlands | 65,000 |
| 9 | Ukraine | 60,000 |
| 10 | Belgium | 50,000 |

### Highest % Agnostic in 1900

| | Country | % Agnostic |
|---|---|---|
| 1 | Uruguay | 37.1% |
| 2 | Croatia | 3.6% |
| 3 | United Kingdom | 1.9% |
| 4 | New Caledonia | 1.8% |
| 5 | United States | 1.3% |
| 6 | Kosovo | 1.3% |
| 7 | Netherlands | 1.3% |
| 8 | Australia | 1.0% |
| 9 | Isle of Man | 1.0% |
| 10 | Sweden | 1.0% |

### Most Agnostics in 2020

| | Country | Agnostics |
|---|---|---|
| 1 | China | 474,394,000 |
| 2 | United States | 55,493,000 |
| 3 | Germany | 19,555,000 |
| 4 | India | 16,345,000 |
| 5 | United Kingdom | 14,845,000 |
| 6 | North Korea | 14,768,000 |
| 7 | Japan | 12,880,000 |
| 8 | France | 12,800,000 |
| 9 | Viet Nam | 12,077,000 |
| 10 | Canada | 8,656,000 |

### Highest % Agnostic in 2020

| | Country | % Agnostic |
|---|---|---|
| 1 | Czechia | 58.5% |
| 2 | Estonia | 57.8% |
| 3 | North Korea | 57.3% |
| 4 | New Zealand | 35.4% |
| 5 | China | 33.0% |
| 6 | Netherlands | 32.3% |
| 7 | Uruguay | 28.8% |
| 8 | Belgium | 25.9% |
| 9 | Australia | 25.3% |
| 10 | Germany | 23.3% |

### Most Agnostics in 2050

| | Country | Agnostics |
|---|---|---|
| 1 | China | 340,000,000 |
| 2 | United States | 78,000,000 |
| 3 | India | 25,000,000 |
| 4 | Germany | 21,625,000 |
| 5 | United Kingdom | 20,480,000 |
| 6 | France | 17,000,000 |
| 7 | North Korea | 16,384,000 |
| 8 | Japan | 13,200,000 |
| 9 | Canada | 13,000,000 |
| 10 | Viet Nam | 12,000,000 |

### Highest % Agnostic in 2050

| | Country | % Agnostic |
|---|---|---|
| 1 | North Korea | 61.7% |
| 2 | Czechia | 57.9% |
| 3 | Estonia | 57.7% |
| 4 | New Zealand | 39.2% |
| 5 | Netherlands | 38.6% |
| 6 | Australia | 33.2% |
| 7 | Uruguay | 30.8% |
| 8 | Canada | 28.5% |
| 9 | United Kingdom | 27.6% |
| 10 | Belgium | 27.0% |

## Atheists

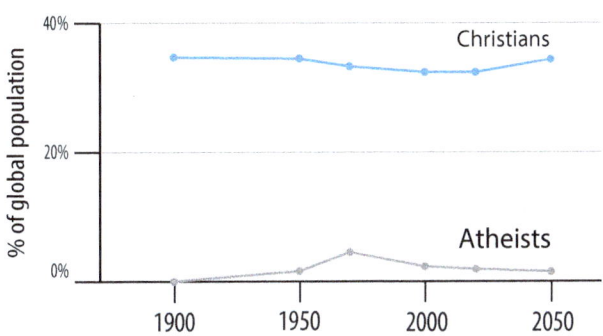

### Most Atheists in 1900

|    | Country        | Atheists |
|----|----------------|----------|
| 1  | Germany        | 40,000   |
| 2  | Russia         | 40,000   |
| 3  | France         | 30,000   |
| 4  | Belgium        | 10,000   |
| 5  | Hungary        | 10,000   |
| 6  | Italy          | 10,000   |
| 7  | Netherlands    | 10,000   |
| 8  | United Kingdom | 10,000   |
| 9  | Czechia        | 8,000    |
| 10 | Romania        | 6,000    |

### Highest % Atheist in 1900

|    | Country     | % Atheist |
|----|-------------|-----------|
| 1  | Netherlands | 0.2%      |
| 2  | Belgium     | 0.1%      |
| 3  | Hungary     | 0.1%      |
| 4  | Argentina   | 0.1%      |
| 5  | Uruguay     | 0.1%      |
| 6  | Czechia     | 0.1%      |
| 7  | Sweden      | 0.1%      |
| 8  | Germany     | 0.1%      |
| 9  | Serbia      | 0.1%      |
| 10 | Denmark     | 0.1%      |

### Most Atheists in 2020

|    | Country       | Atheists    |
|----|---------------|-------------|
| 1  | China         | 100,084,000 |
| 2  | United States | 9,622,000   |
| 3  | Viet Nam      | 6,233,000   |
| 4  | North Korea   | 4,016,000   |
| 5  | Japan         | 3,581,000   |
| 6  | France        | 2,737,000   |
| 7  | India         | 2,186,000   |
| 8  | Italy         | 2,137,000   |
| 9  | Germany       | 2,061,000   |
| 10 | Australia     | 1,660,000   |

### Highest % Atheist in 2020

|    | Country     | % Atheist |
|----|-------------|-----------|
| 1  | North Korea | 15.6%     |
| 2  | Sweden      | 11.0%     |
| 3  | China       | 7.0%      |
| 4  | Uruguay     | 6.6%      |
| 5  | Australia   | 6.5%      |
| 6  | Viet Nam    | 6.4%      |
| 7  | Czechia     | 5.8%      |
| 8  | Estonia     | 4.4%      |
| 9  | Cuba        | 4.3%      |
| 10 | Hungary     | 4.2%      |

### Most Atheists in 2050

|    | Country       | Atheists   |
|----|---------------|------------|
| 1  | China         | 75,000,000 |
| 2  | United States | 20,000,000 |
| 3  | Viet Nam      | 6,400,000  |
| 4  | France        | 4,000,000  |
| 5  | North Korea   | 4,000,000  |
| 6  | Japan         | 3,700,000  |
| 7  | India         | 3,300,000  |
| 8  | Australia     | 3,250,000  |
| 9  | Italy         | 2,750,000  |
| 10 | Germany       | 2,250,000  |

### Highest % Atheist in 2050

|    | Country       | % Atheist |
|----|---------------|-----------|
| 1  | North Korea   | 15.1%     |
| 2  | Sweden        | 14.0%     |
| 3  | Australia     | 9.9%      |
| 4  | Uruguay       | 7.7%      |
| 5  | Czechia       | 6.6%      |
| 6  | France        | 5.9%      |
| 7  | Viet Nam      | 5.8%      |
| 8  | China         | 5.3%      |
| 9  | United States | 5.3%      |
| 10 | Italy         | 5.1%      |

## Major Christian Traditions and Movements

### Christian Traditions 2020

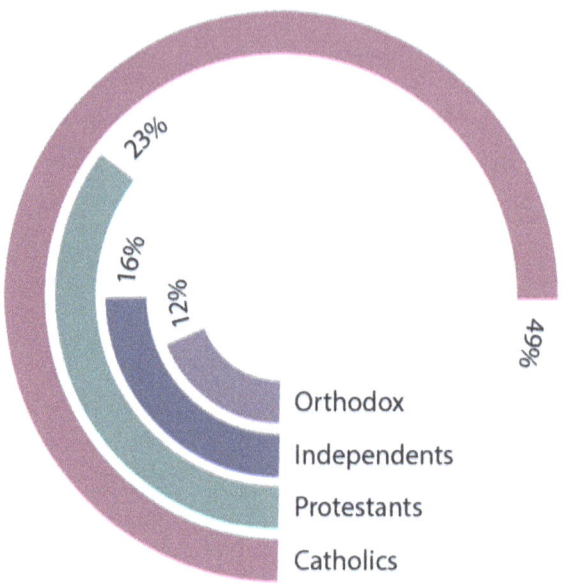

Source: Todd M. Johnson and Gina A. Zurlo, *World Christian Encyclopedia*, 3rd ed. (Edinburgh: Edinburgh University Press, 2019), 7.

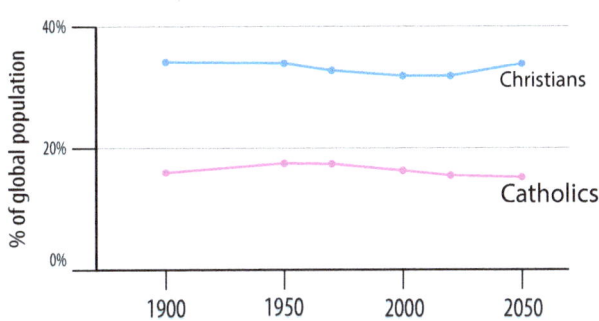

### Catholics

### Most Catholics in 1900

| | Country | Catholics |
|---|---|---|
| 1 | France | 40,215,000 |
| 2 | Italy | 32,903,000 |
| 3 | Spain | 18,794,000 |
| 4 | Poland | 18,717,000 |
| 5 | Brazil | 17,200,000 |
| 6 | Germany | 15,050,000 |
| 7 | Mexico | 12,380,000 |
| 8 | United States | 10,775,000 |
| 9 | Czechia | 6,984,000 |
| 10 | Belgium | 6,518,000 |

### Highest % Catholic in 1900

| | Country | % Catholic |
|---|---|---|
| 1 | San Marino | 100.0% |
| 2 | Holy See | 100.0% |
| 3 | Spain | 100.0% |
| 4 | Portugal | 99.8% |
| 5 | Italy | 99.7% |
| 6 | Puerto Rico | 99.7% |
| 7 | Guam | 99.5% |
| 8 | Costa Rica | 98.9% |
| 9 | France | 98.1% |
| 10 | Cabo Verde | 98.0% |

### Most Catholics in 2020

| | Country | Catholics |
|---|---|---|
| 1 | Brazil | 150,000,000 |
| 2 | Mexico | 115,574,000 |
| 3 | Philippines | 83,000,000 |
| 4 | United States | 73,900,000 |
| 5 | DR Congo | 49,200,000 |
| 6 | Italy | 45,100,000 |
| 7 | Colombia | 43,800,000 |
| 8 | Spain | 39,170,000 |
| 9 | France | 38,540,000 |
| 10 | Argentina | 35,500,000 |

### Highest % Catholic in 2020

| | Country | % Catholic |
|---|---|---|
| 1 | Holy See | 98.8% |
| 2 | Martinique | 95.9% |
| 3 | Wallis & Futuna Islands | 94.6% |
| 4 | Saint Pierre & Miquelon | 91.6% |
| 5 | Poland | 90.1% |
| 6 | Mexico | 89.6% |
| 7 | Cabo Verde | 89.6% |
| 8 | Guadeloupe | 89.2% |
| 9 | Malta | 88.3% |
| 10 | Paraguay | 87.4% |

### Most Catholics in 2050

| | Country | Catholics |
|---|---|---|
| 1 | Brazil | 138,000,000 |
| 2 | Mexico | 125,000,000 |
| 3 | Philippines | 105,500,000 |
| 4 | DR Congo | 103,500,000 |
| 5 | United States | 80,000,000 |
| 6 | Colombia | 46,000,000 |
| 7 | Nigeria | 46,000,000 |
| 8 | Angola | 43,000,000 |
| 9 | Argentina | 38,800,000 |
| 10 | Tanzania | 37,300,000 |

### Highest % Catholic in 2050

| | Country | % Catholic |
|---|---|---|
| 1 | Holy See | 98.1% |
| 2 | Martinique | 91.9% |
| 3 | Poland | 89.8% |
| 4 | Wallis & Futuna Islands | 89.5% |
| 5 | Cabo Verde | 88.3% |
| 6 | Gibraltar | 86.2% |
| 7 | San Marino | 84.7% |
| 8 | Saint Pierre & Miquelon | 84.5% |
| 9 | Malta | 84.4% |
| 10 | Guadeloupe | 83.6% |

## Independents

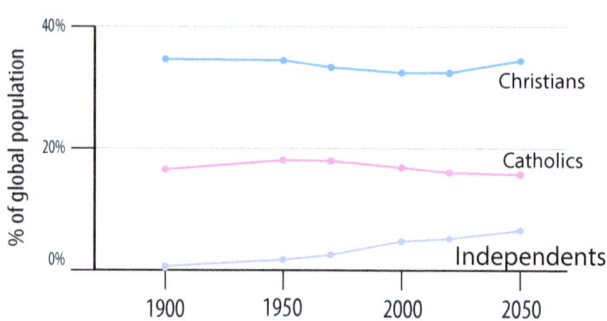

### Most Independents in 1900

|   | Country | Independents |
|---|---|---|
| 1 | United States | 6,650,000 |
| 2 | Philippines | 1,800,000 |
| 3 | India | 90,200 |
| 4 | Romania | 57,000 |
| 5 | Switzerland | 41,000 |
| 6 | Belgium | 28,000 |
| 7 | Austria | 20,000 |
| 8 | Jamaica | 20,000 |
| 9 | Canada | 19,000 |
| 10 | Tonga | 16,400 |

### Highest % Independent in 1900

|   | Country | % Independent |
|---|---|---|
| 1 | Tonga | 81.8% |
| 2 | Philippines | 23.7% |
| 3 | Bermuda | 13.8% |
| 4 | United States | 8.8% |
| 5 | Liberia | 3.6% |
| 6 | Jamaica | 2.8% |
| 7 | French Polynesia | 2.3% |
| 8 | Samoa | 1.3% |
| 9 | Switzerland | 1.2% |
| 10 | Gabon | 1.0% |

### Most Independents in 2020

|   | Country | Independents |
|---|---|---|
| 1 | United States | 63,800,000 |
| 2 | China | 62,000,000 |
| 3 | Nigeria | 28,285,000 |
| 4 | Brazil | 26,000,000 |
| 5 | South Africa | 24,325,000 |
| 6 | DR Congo | 23,930,000 |
| 7 | Philippines | 19,300,000 |
| 8 | India | 18,130,000 |
| 9 | South Korea | 11,330,000 |
| 10 | Kenya | 9,000,000 |

### Highest % Independent in 2020

|   | Country | % Independent |
|---|---|---|
| 1 | Tonga | 79.9% |
| 2 | Eswatini | 54.4% |
| 3 | Zimbabwe | 42.7% |
| 4 | Samoa | 42.3% |
| 5 | South Africa | 41.0% |
| 6 | American Samoa | 39.0% |
| 7 | Botswana | 34.2% |
| 8 | Niue | 28.2% |
| 9 | DR Congo | 26.7% |
| 10 | Saint Vincent | 26.6% |

### Most Independents in 2050

|   | Country | Independents |
|---|---|---|
| 1 | China | 115,000,000 |
| 2 | United States | 72,500,000 |
| 3 | DR Congo | 51,600,000 |
| 4 | Nigeria | 50,000,000 |
| 5 | India | 35,200,000 |
| 6 | Brazil | 35,000,000 |
| 7 | South Africa | 28,120,000 |
| 8 | Philippines | 25,600,000 |
| 9 | Kenya | 15,000,000 |
| 10 | Mexico | 14,000,000 |

### Highest % Independent in 2050

|   | Country | % Independent |
|---|---|---|
| 1 | Tonga | 72.7% |
| 2 | Eswatini | 60.3% |
| 3 | American Samoa | 42.9% |
| 4 | Zimbabwe | 42.0% |
| 5 | Botswana | 38.5% |
| 6 | South Africa | 37.2% |
| 7 | Niue | 33.9% |
| 8 | Samoa | 32.9% |
| 9 | Saint Vincent | 29.1% |
| 10 | DR Congo | 26.5% |

## Orthodox

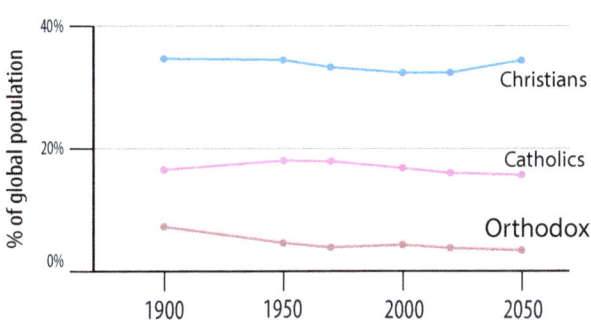

Most Orthodox in 1900

|   | Country | Orthodox |
|---|---------|----------|
| 1 | Russia | 56,710,000 |
| 2 | Ukraine | 20,781,000 |
| 3 | Romania | 9,702,000 |
| 4 | Belarus | 3,937,000 |
| 5 | Turkey | 2,950,000 |
| 6 | Bulgaria | 2,848,000 |
| 7 | Ethiopia | 2,752,000 |
| 8 | Greece | 2,574,000 |
| 9 | Serbia | 2,487,000 |
| 10 | Poland | 2,020,000 |

Highest % Orthodox in 1900

|   | Country | % Orthodox |
|---|---------|------------|
| 1 | Moldova | 88.9% |
| 2 | Montenegro | 88.3% |
| 3 | Romania | 88.2% |
| 4 | Armenia | 87.8% |
| 5 | Georgia | 85.0% |
| 6 | Greece | 84.4% |
| 7 | Cyprus | 77.1% |
| 8 | Russia | 76.9% |
| 9 | Serbia | 76.5% |
| 10 | Bulgaria | 76.1% |

Most Orthodox in 2020

|   | Country | Orthodox |
|---|---------|----------|
| 1 | Russia | 115,700,000 |
| 2 | Ethiopia | 45,600,000 |
| 3 | Ukraine | 31,000,000 |
| 4 | Romania | 17,100,000 |
| 5 | Greece | 9,170,000 |
| 6 | Egypt | 8,800,000 |
| 7 | United States | 7,150,000 |
| 8 | Belarus | 5,650,000 |
| 9 | Bulgaria | 5,620,000 |
| 10 | Serbia | 5,545,000 |

Highest % Orthodox in 2020

|   | Country | % Orthodox |
|---|---------|------------|
| 1 | Moldova | 94.7% |
| 2 | Romania | 88.9% |
| 3 | Greece | 88.0% |
| 4 | Georgia | 84.2% |
| 5 | Armenia | 83.6% |
| 6 | Serbia | 83.5% |
| 7 | Bulgaria | 80.9% |
| 8 | Russia | 79.3% |
| 9 | Montenegro | 71.2% |
| 10 | Ukraine | 70.9% |

Most Orthodox in 2050

|   | Country | Orthodox |
|---|---------|----------|
| 1 | Russia | 104,654,000 |
| 2 | Ethiopia | 91,500,000 |
| 3 | Ukraine | 26,400,000 |
| 4 | Romania | 13,635,000 |
| 5 | Egypt | 11,000,000 |
| 6 | United States | 8,600,000 |
| 7 | Greece | 7,250,000 |
| 8 | India | 6,500,000 |
| 9 | Belarus | 5,592,000 |
| 10 | Kazakhstan | 4,600,000 |

Highest % Orthodox in 2050

|   | Country | % Orthodox |
|---|---------|------------|
| 1 | Moldova | 94.0% |
| 2 | Georgia | 83.9% |
| 3 | Romania | 83.9% |
| 4 | Serbia | 81.4% |
| 5 | Bulgaria | 80.8% |
| 6 | Armenia | 80.6% |
| 7 | Greece | 80.3% |
| 8 | Russia | 77.1% |
| 9 | Ukraine | 75.0% |
| 10 | Montenegro | 68.8% |

## Protestants

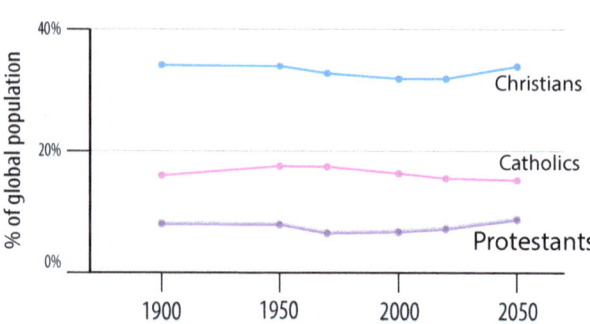

### Most Protestants in 1900

| | Country | Protestants |
|---|---|---|
| 1 | United States | 37,042,000 |
| 2 | United Kingdom | 33,680,000 |
| 3 | Germany | 25,735,000 |
| 4 | Sweden | 5,074,000 |
| 5 | Netherlands | 3,114,000 |
| 6 | Canada | 2,847,000 |
| 7 | Finland | 2,636,000 |
| 8 | Denmark | 2,430,000 |
| 9 | Australia | 2,377,000 |
| 10 | Norway | 2,208,000 |

### Highest % Protestant in 1900

| | Country | % Protestant |
|---|---|---|
| 1 | Faeroe Islands | 100.0% |
| 2 | Tuvalu | 100.0% |
| 3 | Saint Helena | 100.0% |
| 4 | Niue | 100.0% |
| 5 | Tokelau | 100.0% |
| 6 | Iceland | 99.5% |
| 7 | Norway | 99.4% |
| 8 | Denmark | 99.2% |
| 9 | Sweden | 98.8% |
| 10 | Turks & Caicos Is | 98.0% |

### Most Protestants in 2020

| | Country | Protestants |
|---|---|---|
| 1 | Nigeria | 62,059,000 |
| 2 | United States | 54,035,000 |
| 3 | China | 34,000,000 |
| 4 | Brazil | 32,140,000 |
| 5 | United Kingdom | 27,000,000 |
| 6 | Kenya | 26,000,000 |
| 7 | Germany | 25,031,000 |
| 8 | India | 23,000,000 |
| 9 | Indonesia | 20,204,000 |
| 10 | Uganda | 19,300,000 |

### Highest % Protestant in 2020

| | Country | % Protestant |
|---|---|---|
| 1 | Faeroe Islands | 97.5% |
| 2 | Marshall Islands | 84.5% |
| 3 | Montserrat | 84.0% |
| 4 | Tuvalu | 83.1% |
| 5 | Saint Kitts & Nevis | 81.3% |
| 6 | Iceland | 79.4% |
| 7 | Denmark | 77.7% |
| 8 | American Samoa | 76.0% |
| 9 | Bahamas | 75.1% |
| 10 | Vanuatu | 75.1% |

### Most Protestants in 2050

| | Country | Protestants |
|---|---|---|
| 1 | Nigeria | 110,000,000 |
| 2 | China | 65,000,000 |
| 3 | United States | 60,000,000 |
| 4 | Kenya | 44,000,000 |
| 5 | Brazil | 39,000,000 |
| 6 | Tanzania | 38,750,000 |
| 7 | Uganda | 36,000,000 |
| 8 | DR Congo | 35,400,000 |
| 9 | India | 34,000,000 |
| 10 | Ethiopia | 31,202,000 |

### Highest % Protestant in 2050

| | Country | % Protestant |
|---|---|---|
| 1 | Faeroe Islands | 95.4% |
| 2 | Tuvalu | 82.2% |
| 3 | American Samoa | 80.2% |
| 4 | Vanuatu | 76.3% |
| 5 | Montserrat | 76.0% |
| 6 | Saint Kitts & Nevis | 74.8% |
| 7 | Marshall Islands | 74.3% |
| 8 | Iceland | 71.9% |
| 9 | Saint Vincent | 69.6% |
| 10 | Bahamas | 68.8% |

## Evangelicals

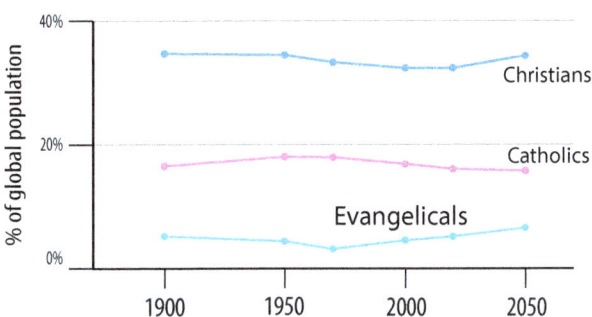

### Most Evangelicals in 1900

|   | Country | Evangelicals |
|---|---|---|
| 1 | United States | 40,020,000 |
| 2 | United Kingdom | 19,158,000 |
| 3 | Germany | 3,932,000 |
| 4 | Sweden | 3,050,000 |
| 5 | Australia | 1,736,000 |
| 6 | Netherlands | 1,571,000 |
| 7 | Canada | 1,504,000 |
| 8 | Norway | 1,344,000 |
| 9 | South Africa | 1,082,000 |
| 10 | Finland | 557,000 |

### Highest % Evangelical in 1900

|   | Country | % Evangelical |
|---|---|---|
| 1 | Isle of Man | 86.6% |
| 2 | Cayman Islands | 77.1% |
| 3 | Samoa | 76.5% |
| 4 | Fiji | 66.0% |
| 5 | French Polynesia | 65.9% |
| 6 | Cook Islands | 62.2% |
| 7 | Norway | 60.5% |
| 8 | Sweden | 59.4% |
| 9 | British Virgin Islands | 57.1% |
| 10 | New Zealand | 55.8% |

### Most Evangelicals in 2020

|   | Country | Evangelicals |
|---|---|---|
| 1 | United States | 69,000,000 |
| 2 | Nigeria | 45,500,000 |
| 3 | China | 35,000,000 |
| 4 | Brazil | 29,000,000 |
| 5 | Ethiopia | 21,500,000 |
| 6 | Kenya | 16,500,000 |
| 7 | South Korea | 12,855,000 |
| 8 | India | 12,200,000 |
| 9 | Indonesia | 9,414,000 |
| 10 | Tanzania | 9,400,000 |

### Highest % Evangelical in 2020

|   | Country | % Evangelical |
|---|---|---|
| 1 | Marshall Islands | 60.1% |
| 2 | Barbados | 39.7% |
| 3 | Vanuatu | 36.1% |
| 4 | Bahamas | 34.6% |
| 5 | Palau | 31.5% |
| 6 | Dominica | 30.7% |
| 7 | Kenya | 30.7% |
| 8 | Central African Republic | 30.0% |
| 9 | Isle of Man | 29.4% |
| 10 | British Virgin Islands | 28.1% |

### Most Evangelicals in 2050

|   | Country | Evangelicals |
|---|---|---|
| 1 | Nigeria | 92,000,000 |
| 2 | United States | 90,000,000 |
| 3 | China | 50,000,000 |
| 4 | Brazil | 40,000,000 |
| 5 | Ethiopia | 38,000,000 |
| 6 | Kenya | 28,000,000 |
| 7 | Tanzania | 23,022,000 |
| 8 | India | 20,000,000 |
| 9 | Uganda | 19,600,000 |
| 10 | Ghana | 14,000,000 |

### Highest % Evangelical in 2050

|   | Country | % Evangelical |
|---|---|---|
| 1 | Marshall Islands | 53.1% |
| 2 | Barbados | 43.3% |
| 3 | Palau | 42.3% |
| 4 | American Samoa | 32.7% |
| 5 | Dominica | 32.6% |
| 6 | Bahamas | 32.4% |
| 7 | Isle of Man | 32.0% |
| 8 | British Virgin Islands | 31.7% |
| 9 | Central African Republic | 31.5% |
| 10 | Montserrat | 31.4% |

## Pentecostals/Charismatics (P/C)

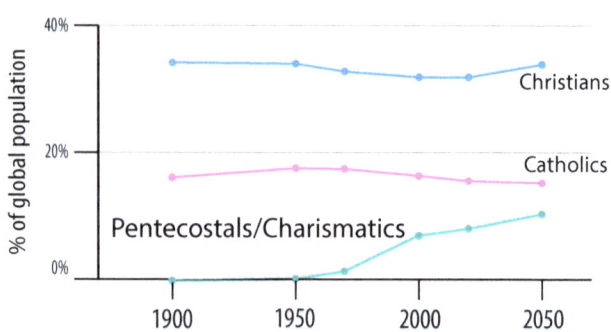

### Most Pentecostals/Charismatics in 1900

|    | Country         | P/C     |
|----|-----------------|---------|
| 1  | South Africa    | 805,000 |
| 2  | Nigeria         | 96,000  |
| 3  | United States   | 46,100  |
| 4  | Germany         | 20,000  |
| 5  | Trinidad & Tobago | 10,000 |
| 6  | China           | 2,000   |
| 7  | India           | 1,800   |
| 8  | South Korea     | 500     |
| 9  | Aruba           | 0       |
| 10 | Armenia         | 0       |

### Highest % P/C in 1900

|    | Country           | % P/C |
|----|-------------------|-------|
| 1  | South Africa      | 16.4% |
| 2  | Trinidad & Tobago | 3.6%  |
| 3  | Nigeria           | 0.6%  |
| 4  | United States     | 0.1%  |
| 5  | Germany           | 0.0%  |
| 6  | South Korea       | 0.0%  |
| 7  | India             | 0.0%  |
| 8  | China             | 0.0%  |
| 9  | Brazil            | 0.0%  |
| 10 | DR Congo          | 0.0%  |

### Most Pentecostals/Charismatics in 2020

|    | Country       | P/C         |
|----|---------------|-------------|
| 1  | Brazil        | 108,000,000 |
| 2  | United States | 65,000,000  |
| 3  | Nigeria       | 60,000,000  |
| 4  | Philippines   | 38,000,000  |
| 5  | China         | 37,000,000  |
| 6  | DR Congo      | 28,000,000  |
| 7  | South Africa  | 27,700,000  |
| 8  | India         | 21,000,000  |
| 9  | Mexico        | 17,450,000  |
| 10 | Kenya         | 17,300,000  |

### Highest % P/C in 2020

|    | Country         | % P/C |
|----|-----------------|-------|
| 1  | Marshall Islands | 63.4% |
| 2  | Zimbabwe        | 62.2% |
| 3  | Puerto Rico     | 57.7% |
| 4  | Eswatini        | 51.3% |
| 5  | Brazil          | 50.8% |
| 6  | Guatemala       | 50.1% |
| 7  | South Africa    | 46.7% |
| 8  | American Samoa  | 42.6% |
| 9  | Ghana           | 37.0% |
| 10 | Vanuatu         | 35.8% |

### Most Pentecostals/Charismatics in 2050

|    | Country       | P/C         |
|----|---------------|-------------|
| 1  | Nigeria       | 130,000,000 |
| 2  | Brazil        | 125,000,000 |
| 3  | United States | 85,000,000  |
| 4  | China         | 70,000,000  |
| 5  | DR Congo      | 58,000,000  |
| 6  | Philippines   | 58,000,000  |
| 7  | India         | 42,000,000  |
| 8  | South Africa  | 35,000,000  |
| 9  | Kenya         | 32,500,000  |
| 10 | Ethiopia      | 27,000,000  |

### Highest % P/C in 2050

|    | Country          | % P/C |
|----|------------------|-------|
| 1  | Puerto Rico      | 69.5% |
| 2  | Zimbabwe         | 62.6% |
| 3  | Marshall Islands | 55.7% |
| 4  | Brazil           | 54.6% |
| 5  | Eswatini         | 52.8% |
| 6  | Guatemala        | 52.0% |
| 7  | American Samoa   | 46.7% |
| 8  | South Africa     | 46.3% |
| 9  | Montserrat       | 41.0% |
| 10 | Ghana            | 40.4% |

# Christian Mission

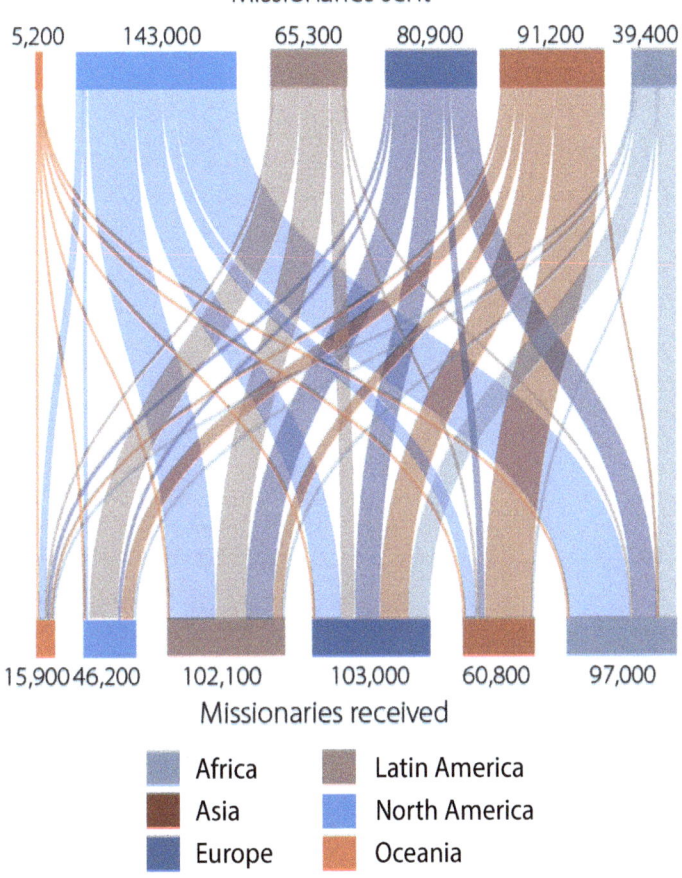

Source: Todd M. Johnson and Gina A. Zurlo, *World Christian Encyclopedia*, 3rd ed. (Edinburgh: Edinburgh University Press, 2019), 32.

### Most missionaries sent, 2020

| | Country | Missionaries |
|---|---|---|
| 1 | United States | 135,000 |
| 2 | Brazil | 40,000 |
| 3 | South Korea | 35,000 |
| 4 | Philippines | 25,000 |
| 5 | Nigeria | 20,000 |
| 6 | China | 15,000 |
| 7 | United Kingdom | 14,000 |
| 8 | Spain | 10,000 |
| 9 | South Africa | 10,000 |
| 10 | Italy | 10,000 |

### Most missionaries received, 2020

| | Country | Missionaries |
|---|---|---|
| 1 | United States | 38,000 |
| 2 | Russia | 25,000 |
| 3 | Brazil | 20,000 |
| 4 | South Africa | 15,000 |
| 5 | DR Congo | 15,000 |
| 6 | United Kingdom | 12,000 |
| 7 | Argentina | 10,000 |
| 8 | Italy | 10,000 |
| 9 | France | 10,000 |
| 10 | Germany | 10,000 |

### Most missionaries sent per million Christians, 2020

| | Country | Missionaries per million |
|---|---|---|
| 1 | Palestine | 4,400 |
| 2 | Mongolia | 2,800 |
| 3 | South Korea | 2,100 |
| 4 | Malta | 1,700 |
| 5 | Samoa | 1,500 |
| 6 | Ireland | 1,100 |
| 7 | Macao | 1,100 |
| 8 | Somalia | 960 |
| 9 | Tonga | 590 |
| 10 | Micronesia | 550 |

### Most missionaries received per million population, 2020

| | Country | Missionaries per million |
|---|---|---|
| 1 | Micronesia | 4,700 |
| 2 | Samoa | 4,000 |
| 3 | Tonga | 3,800 |
| 4 | Guam | 3,000 |
| 5 | Curacao | 2,800 |
| 6 | United States Virgin Is | 1,600 |
| 7 | French Polynesia | 1,600 |
| 8 | Grenada | 1,200 |
| 9 | New Caledonia | 1,200 |
| 10 | Vanuatu | 1,100 |

### Most national workers, 2020

| | Country | Workers |
|---|---|---|
| 1 | United States | 3,922,000 |
| 2 | India | 900,000 |
| 3 | Germany | 730,000 |
| 4 | Ethiopia | 650,000 |
| 5 | Italy | 640,000 |
| 6 | Russia | 480,000 |
| 7 | United Kingdom | 470,000 |
| 8 | France | 460,000 |
| 9 | Spain | 400,000 |
| 10 | Brazil | 350,000 |

### Most national workers per million population, 2020

| | Country | Workers per million |
|---|---|---|
| 1 | Holy See | 865,000 |
| 2 | Tokelau | 141,000 |
| 3 | Niue | 43,300 |
| 4 | Samoa | 25,200 |
| 5 | Tonga | 13,200 |
| 6 | United States | 11,800 |
| 7 | Malta | 11,300 |
| 8 | Guadeloupe | 11,100 |
| 9 | Ireland | 11,100 |
| 10 | Wallis & Futuna Islands | 10,700 |

### Most unevangelized in 2020

| | Country | Unevangelized |
|---|---|---|
| 1 | India | 591,685,000 |
| 2 | China | 466,731,000 |
| 3 | Pakistan | 115,362,000 |
| 4 | Indonesia | 105,131,000 |
| 5 | Bangladesh | 81,581,000 |
| 6 | Iran | 52,838,000 |
| 7 | Turkey | 43,193,000 |
| 8 | Nigeria | 41,812,000 |
| 9 | Egypt | 38,896,000 |
| 10 | Japan | 36,011,000 |

### Most evangelized non-Christians in 2020

| | Country | Evangelized non-Christians |
|---|---|---|
| 1 | China | 866,574,000 |
| 2 | India | 722,004,000 |
| 3 | Indonesia | 134,984,000 |
| 4 | Pakistan | 101,342,000 |
| 5 | Japan | 87,837,000 |
| 6 | Bangladesh | 82,194,000 |
| 7 | United States | 79,671,000 |
| 8 | Nigeria | 69,141,000 |
| 9 | Viet Nam | 62,133,000 |
| 10 | Egypt | 53,965,000 |

## Denominations

### Movements within Christian families, 2015

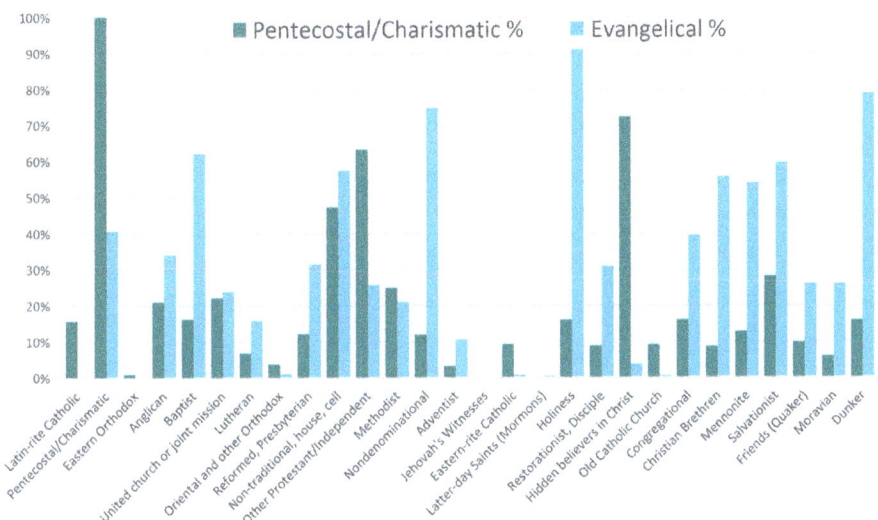

### Largest denominations, 2015

| | Denomination | Country | Affiliated |
|---|---|---|---|
| 1 | Igreja Católica no Brasil | Brazil | 148,550,000 |
| 2 | Russian Orthodox Church | Russia | 110,850,000 |
| 3 | Iglesia Católica en México | Mexico | 110,155,000 |
| 4 | Catholic Church in the Philippines | Philippines | 78,271,000 |
| 5 | Catholic Church in the USA | United States | 72,798,000 |
| 6 | Chiesa Cattolica in Italia | Italy | 45,563,000 |
| 7 | Eglise Catholique au DR Congo | DR Congo | 42,891,000 |
| 8 | Iglesia Católica en Colombia | Colombia | 42,206,000 |
| 9 | Iglesia Católica en España | Spain | 39,377,000 |
| 10 | Ethiopian Orthodox Church | Ethiopia | 39,200,000 |

### Fastest growing denominations, 2015

| | Denomination | Country | Rate |
|---|---|---|---|
| 1 | Calvary Temple | India | 87.04% |
| 2 | Igreja da Coligação Cristã de Angola | Angola | 81.25% |
| 3 | Eglise Le Temps Du Reveil | Martinique | 77.83% |
| 4 | E de JC des Saints des Derniers Jours | Benin | 53.84% |
| 5 | Vietnam Good News Mission Church | Viet Nam | 52.98% |
| 6 | Eglise du Nazarène | Benin | 40.33% |
| 7 | Eglise Luthérienne d'Haiti | Haiti | 30.77% |
| 8 | Ch of Jesus Christ of Latter-day Saints | Laos | 29.04% |
| 9 | E de JC des Saints des Derniers Jours | Togo | 26.83% |
| 10 | Church of the Nazarene | Bangladesh | 26.03% |

Largest Catholic denominations, 2015

| | Denomination | Country | Affiliated |
|---|---|---|---|
| 1 | Igreja Católica no Brasil | Brazil | 148,550,000 |
| 2 | Iglesia Católica en México | Mexico | 110,155,000 |
| 3 | Catholic Church in the Philippines | Philippines | 78,271,000 |
| 4 | Catholic Church in the USA | United States | 72,798,000 |
| 5 | Chiesa Cattolica in Italia | Italy | 45,563,000 |
| 6 | Eglise Catholique au DR Congo | DR Congo | 42,891,000 |
| 7 | Iglesia Católica en Colombia | Colombia | 42,206,000 |
| 8 | Iglesia Católica en España | Spain | 39,377,000 |
| 9 | Eglise Catholique de France | France | 37,926,000 |
| 10 | Catholic Church in Poland | Poland | 34,462,000 |

Fastest growing Catholic denominations, 2015

| | Denomination | Country | Rate |
|---|---|---|---|
| 1 | Catholic Church (VA Arabia North) | Qatar | 13.29% |
| 2 | Catholic Church (AP of Azerbaijan) | Azerbaijan | 10.82% |
| 3 | Catholic Church: mission (sui juris) Turkmenistan | Turkmenistan | 9.68% |
| 4 | Catholic Church in Sierra Leone | Sierra Leone | 9.27% |
| 5 | Catholic Church in Norway | Norway | 7.84% |
| 6 | Catholic Church (VA Arabia South) | United Arab Emirates | 7.61% |
| 7 | Catholic Church in Kuwait (VA Arabia North) | Kuwait | 7.42% |
| 8 | Catholic Church: D Reykjavik | Iceland | 7.07% |
| 9 | Catholic Church: PA Ulaanbaatar | Mongolia | 6.71% |
| 10 | Catholic Church in Greece | Greece | 6.33% |

Largest Independent denominations, 2015

| | Denomination | Country | Affiliated |
|---|---|---|---|
| 1 | Han traditional house churches | China | 20,000,000 |
| 2 | Han house churches Big Five (rural) | China | 19,510,000 |
| 3 | Han emerging urban church networks | China | 15,000,000 |
| 4 | EdeJC sur la Terre par le Prophète SK | DR Congo | 12,000,000 |
| 5 | National Baptist Convention, USA | United States | 9,200,000 |
| 6 | Church of God in Christ | United States | 8,046,000 |
| 7 | Igreja Universal do Reino de Deus | Brazil | 7,500,000 |
| 8 | Ch of Jesus Christ of Latter-day Saints | United States | 6,642,000 |
| 9 | Zion Christian Church | South Africa | 5,000,000 |
| 10 | National Baptist Conv of America | United States | 4,250,000 |

Fastest growing Independent denominations, 2015

| | Denomination | Country | Rate |
|---|---|---|---|
| 1 | Calvary Temple | India | 87.04% |
| 2 | Igreja da Coligação Cristã de Angola | Angola | 81.25% |
| 3 | Eglise Le Temps Du Reveil | Martinique | 77.83% |
| 4 | E de JC des Saints des Derniers Jours | Benin | 53.84% |
| 5 | Vietnam Good News Mission Church | Viet Nam | 52.98% |
| 6 | Ch of Jesus Christ of Latter-day Saints | Laos | 29.04% |
| 7 | E de JC des Saints des Derniers Jours | Togo | 26.83% |
| 8 | Igr de JC dos Santos dos Ultimos Dias | Mozambique | 21.17% |
| 9 | Jehovah's Witnesses | Cambodia | 18.56% |
| 10 | E de JC des Saints des Derniers Jours | Cameroon | 16.97% |

Largest Orthodox denominations, 2015

| | Denomination | Country | Affiliated |
|---|---|---|---|
| 1 | Russian Orthodox Church | Russia | 110,850,000 |
| 2 | Ethiopian Orthodox Church | Ethiopia | 39,200,000 |
| 3 | Romanian Orthodox Church, P Bucuresti | Romania | 17,400,000 |
| 4 | Ukrainian Orthodox Church (P Kyiv) | Ukraine | 16,000,000 |
| 5 | Ukrainian Orthodox Church (P Moscow) | Ukraine | 13,500,000 |
| 6 | Church of Greece | Greece | 8,460,000 |
| 7 | Coptic Orthodox Church | Egypt | 8,400,000 |
| 8 | Bulgarian Orthodox Church | Bulgaria | 5,800,000 |
| 9 | Serbian Orthodox Church | Serbia | 5,611,000 |
| 10 | Belarusian Orthodox Church D Minsk & Belarus | Belarus | 5,400,000 |

Fastest growing Orthodox denominations, 2015

| | Denomination | Country | Rate |
|---|---|---|---|
| 1 | Iglesia Ortodoxa Ucraniana | Spain | 20.30% |
| 2 | Chiesa Ortodossa Romania | Italy | 19.79% |
| 3 | Russian Orthodox Church | Iceland | 16.54% |
| 4 | Orthodox Churches | Norway | 14.43% |
| 5 | Orthodoxe Kirche von Rumänien | Germany | 13.37% |
| 6 | Romanian Orthodox Church | Denmark | 12.99% |
| 7 | Bulgarische Kirche in Deutschland | Germany | 11.11% |
| 8 | Russisch-Orth Kirche (P von Moskau) | Austria | 10.55% |
| 9 | Ukrainian Orthodox Church (P Kyiv) | Ukraine | 9.68% |
| 10 | Serbian Orthodox Church | Iceland | 9.33% |

Largest Protestant denominations, 2015

| | Denomination | Country | Affiliated |
|---|---|---|---|
| 1 | Three-Self Patriotic Movement | China | 30,000,000 |
| 2 | Evangelische Kirche in Deutschland | Germany | 24,450,000 |
| 3 | Church of England | United Kingdom | 23,000,000 |
| 4 | Anglican Church of Nigeria | Nigeria | 22,000,000 |
| 5 | Assembleias de Deus | Brazil | 20,978,000 |
| 6 | Southern Baptist Convention | United States | 18,836,000 |
| 7 | Church of Uganda | Uganda | 14,000,000 |
| 8 | Word of Life Evangelical Church | Ethiopia | 8,500,000 |
| 9 | Evangelical Church Mekane Yesus | Ethiopia | 7,887,000 |
| 10 | United Methodist Church | United States | 7,067,000 |

Fastest growing Protestant denominations, 2015

| | Denomination | Country | Rate |
|---|---|---|---|
| 1 | Eglise du Nazarène | Benin | 40.33% |
| 2 | Eglise Luthérienne d'Haiti | Haiti | 30.77% |
| 3 | Church of the Nazarene | Bangladesh | 26.03% |
| 4 | Seventh-day Adventist Church | Mongolia | 21.25% |
| 5 | Seventh-day Adventist Church | Bhutan | 21.16% |
| 6 | United Pentecostal Church | Nepal | 19.99% |
| 7 | Igreja Evangélica Luterana em Moçambique | Mozambique | 19.46% |
| 8 | Church of the Nazarene | Nepal | 18.72% |
| 9 | Iglesia Episcopal: D Ecuador | Ecuador | 17.04% |
| 10 | Assemblies of God | Laos | 16.59% |

### Largest Evangelical denominations, 2015

| | Denomination | Country | Affiliated |
|---|---|---|---|
| 1 | Assembleias de Deus | Brazil | 20,978,000 |
| 2 | Southern Baptist Convention | United States | 18,836,000 |
| 3 | Han emerging urban church networks | China | 15,000,000 |
| 4 | Han house churches Big Five (rural) | China | 12,505,000 |
| 5 | Anglican Church of Nigeria | Nigeria | 11,000,000 |
| 6 | Word of Life Evangelical Church | Ethiopia | 8,500,000 |
| 7 | Evangelical Church Mekane Yesus | Ethiopia | 7,887,000 |
| 8 | Evangelical Churches Winning All | Nigeria | 6,800,000 |
| 9 | Assemblies of God in Nigeria | Nigeria | 5,964,000 |
| 10 | Church of Uganda | Uganda | 5,600,000 |

### Fastest growing Evangelical denominations, 2015

| | Denomination | Country | Rate |
|---|---|---|---|
| 1 | Han emerging urban church networks | China | 37.17% |
| 2 | Han house churches Big Five (rural) | China | 36.61% |
| 3 | Han traditional house churches | China | 32.70% |
| 4 | National Baptist Convention, USA | United States | 30.08% |
| 5 | Church of God in Christ | United States | 29.70% |
| 6 | Church of South India | India | 29.43% |
| 7 | Gen As of Pres Ch in K GaeHyeok-Reformed | South Korea | 27.63% |
| 8 | National Assoc of Independent Chs | India | 27.40% |
| 9 | Igr Fraternidade Ev de Pentecostes de Afr | Angola | 26.98% |
| 10 | Willow Creek Association of Chs | United States | 26.82% |

### Largest Pentecostal/Charismatic denominations, 2015

| | Denomination | Country | Affiliated |
|---|---|---|---|
| 1 | Igreja Católica no Brasil | Brazil | 59,420,000 |
| 2 | Catholic Church in the Philippines | Philippines | 23,481,000 |
| 3 | Assembleias de Deus | Brazil | 20,978,000 |
| 4 | Catholic Church in the USA | United States | 18,199,000 |
| 5 | Han house churches Big Five (rural) | China | 17,619,000 |
| 6 | Iglesia Católica en Colombia | Colombia | 12,820,000 |
| 7 | EdeJC sur la Terre par le Prophète SK | DR Congo | 12,000,000 |
| 8 | Iglesia Católica en México | Mexico | 10,923,000 |
| 9 | Church of God in Christ | United States | 8,046,000 |
| 10 | Igreja Universal do Reino de Deus | Brazil | 7,500,000 |

### Fastest growing Pentecostal/Charismatic denominations, 2015

| | Denomination | Country | Rate |
|---|---|---|---|
| 1 | Han house churches Big Five (rural) | China | 37.66% |
| 2 | Iglesia Católica en México | Mexico | 36.20% |
| 3 | Igreja Universal do Reino de Deus | Brazil | 35.07% |
| 4 | Iglesia Católica en la Argentina | Argentina | 34.15% |
| 5 | Church of Uganda | Uganda | 33.34% |
| 6 | Han emerging urban church networks | China | 33.00% |
| 7 | The Kingdom of Jesus Christ | Philippines | 32.80% |
| 8 | Iglesia Católica en el Perú | Peru | 32.11% |
| 9 | Eglise Neo-Apostolique | DR Congo | 32.09% |
| 10 | Catholic Church in Kenya | Kenya | 31.88% |

# Peoples

## Ethnic families, 2020

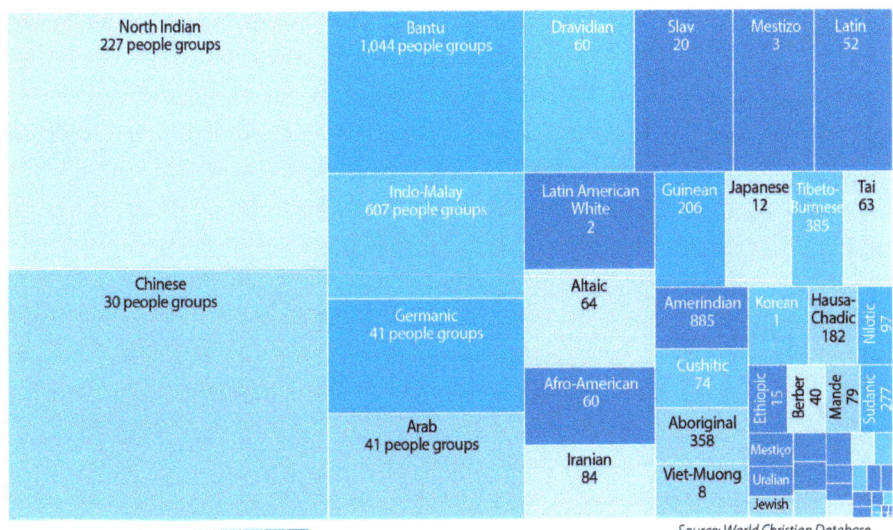

Source: Todd M. Johnson and Gina A. Zurlo, *World Christian Encyclopedia*, 3rd ed. (Edinburgh: Edinburgh University Press, 2019), 31.

## Largest peoples, 2020

|    | People | Country | Population |
|----|--------|---------|------------|
| 1  | Han Chinese (Mandarin) | China | 901,447,000 |
| 2  | USA White | United States | 124,560,000 |
| 3  | Japanese | Japan | 123,361,000 |
| 4  | Russian | Russia | 115,205,000 |
| 5  | Bengali | Bangladesh | 111,431,000 |
| 6  | Brazilian White (Branco) | Brazil | 109,425,000 |
| 7  | Bengali | India | 107,226,000 |
| 8  | Telugu (Andhra, Tolangan) | India | 96,125,000 |
| 9  | Maratha (Maharathi) | India | 93,385,000 |
| 10 | Han Chinese (Wu) | China | 92,532,000 |

## Peoples with greatest number of Christians, 2020

|    | People | Country | Christians |
|----|--------|---------|------------|
| 1  | Russian | Russia | 110,804,000 |
| 2  | Brazilian White (Branco) | Brazil | 98,592,000 |
| 3  | Han Chinese (Mandarin) | China | 85,637,000 |
| 4  | USA White | United States | 80,603,000 |
| 5  | Mexican Mestizo | Mexico | 68,393,000 |
| 6  | Brazilian Mulato | Brazil | 43,957,000 |
| 7  | Polish (Pole, Silesian) | Poland | 34,403,000 |
| 8  | African American (Black) | United States | 32,928,000 |
| 9  | German (High German) | Germany | 32,761,000 |
| 10 | English (British) | United Kingdom | 31,536,000 |

## Peoples with greatest number of Muslims, 2020

|   | People | Country | Muslims |
|---|---|---|---|
| 1 | Bengali | Bangladesh | 111,131,000 |
| 2 | Western Punjabi (Lahnda) | Pakistan | 86,390,000 |
| 3 | Javanese (Orang Jawa) | Indonesia | 70,980,000 |
| 4 | Urdu (Islami, Undri) | India | 65,432,000 |
| 5 | Egyptian Arab | Egypt | 56,692,000 |
| 6 | Turk | Turkey | 51,849,000 |
| 7 | Sundanese (Urang Sunda) | Indonesia | 43,937,000 |
| 8 | Hausa (Hausawa) | Nigeria | 35,009,000 |
| 9 | Bengali | India | 32,168,000 |
| 10 | Persian (Irani) | Iran | 27,606,000 |

## Peoples with greatest number of Hindus, 2020

|   | People | Country | Hindus |
|---|---|---|---|
| 1 | Hindi (High Hindi) | India | 73,771,000 |
| 2 | Telugu (Andhra, Tolangan) | India | 72,670,000 |
| 3 | Bengali | India | 72,378,000 |
| 4 | Maratha (Maharathi) | India | 69,432,000 |
| 5 | Tamil (Madrasi, Tamalsan) | India | 65,482,000 |
| 6 | Hindi (Bazaar, Popular) | India | 64,446,000 |
| 7 | Gujarati | India | 51,246,000 |
| 8 | Kanarese (Canarese) | India | 43,163,000 |
| 9 | Maitili (Maithili, Tharu) | India | 40,841,000 |
| 10 | Bhojpuri Bihari (Deswali) | India | 40,718,000 |

## Peoples with greatest number of Agnostics, 2020

|   | People | Country | Agnostics |
|---|---|---|---|
| 1 | Han Chinese (Mandarin) | China | 353,367,000 |
| 2 | USA White | United States | 35,500,000 |
| 3 | Han Chinese (Jinyu) | China | 34,375,000 |
| 4 | Han Chinese (Kan, Gan) | China | 22,704,000 |
| 5 | Han Chinese (Wu) | China | 18,506,000 |
| 6 | German (High German) | Germany | 14,766,000 |
| 7 | North Korean | North Korea | 14,587,000 |
| 8 | English (British) | United Kingdom | 13,653,000 |
| 9 | Japanese | Japan | 12,842,000 |
| 10 | Vietnamese (Kinh) | Viet Nam | 11,236,000 |

## Peoples with greatest number of Buddhists, 2020

|   | People | Country | Buddhists |
|---|---|---|---|
| 1 | Han Chinese (Mandarin) | China | 168,571,000 |
| 2 | Japanese | Japan | 68,774,000 |
| 3 | Vietnamese (Kinh) | Viet Nam | 43,942,000 |
| 4 | Burmese (Myen, Bhama) | Myanmar | 27,945,000 |
| 5 | Central Thai (Siamese) | Thailand | 22,313,000 |
| 6 | Northeastern Tai (Isan) | Thailand | 18,331,000 |
| 7 | Sinhalese (Singhalese) | Sri Lanka | 14,514,000 |
| 8 | Central Khmer (Cambodian) | Cambodia | 13,844,000 |
| 9 | Han Chinese (Wu) | China | 12,954,000 |
| 10 | Han Chinese (Cantonese) | China | 12,954,000 |

Peoples with greatest number of Chinese folk-religionists, 2020

|   | People | Country | Chinese folk-religionists |
|---|---|---|---|
| 1 | Han Chinese (Mandarin) | China | 196,515,000 |
| 2 | Han Chinese (Wu) | China | 54,409,000 |
| 3 | Han Chinese (Cantonese) | China | 38,279,000 |
| 4 | Han Chinese (Hunanese) | China | 32,578,000 |
| 5 | Han Chinese (Hakka) | China | 30,806,000 |
| 6 | Han Chinese (Min Nan) | China | 21,331,000 |
| 7 | Han Chinese (Kan, Gan) | China | 17,957,000 |
| 8 | Han Chinese (Jinyu) | China | 10,252,000 |
| 9 | Han Chinese (Min Dong) | China | 7,451,000 |
| 10 | Taiwanese (Hoklo) | Taiwan | 5,456,000 |

Peoples with greatest number of Ethnic religionists, 2020

|   | People | Country | Ethnic religionists |
|---|---|---|---|
| 1 | Northern Zhuang (Chwang) | China | 9,851,000 |
| 2 | South Korean | South Korea | 7,691,000 |
| 3 | Tujia (Tuchia) | China | 7,154,000 |
| 4 | Gormati (Banjara, Labhan) | India | 5,941,000 |
| 5 | Central Bhil | India | 5,100,000 |
| 6 | Mina | India | 4,690,000 |
| 7 | Southern Zhuang | China | 3,990,000 |
| 8 | Wagdi (Wagheri, Vaged) | India | 3,266,000 |
| 9 | Eastern Bhil (Vil) | India | 3,260,000 |
| 10 | North Korean | North Korea | 3,166,000 |

Peoples with greatest number of Atheists, 2020

|   | People | Country | Atheists |
|---|---|---|---|
| 1 | Han Chinese (Mandarin) | China | 90,145,000 |
| 2 | Han Chinese (Jinyu) | China | 9,046,000 |
| 3 | USA White | United States | 7,474,000 |
| 4 | Vietnamese (Kinh) | Viet Nam | 6,019,000 |
| 5 | North Korean | North Korea | 3,983,000 |
| 6 | Japanese | Japan | 3,577,000 |
| 7 | French | France | 1,641,000 |
| 8 | German (High German) | Germany | 1,624,000 |
| 9 | Anglo-Australian | Australia | 1,592,000 |
| 10 | English (British) | United Kingdom | 949,000 |

Peoples with greatest number of New religionists, 2020

|   | People | Country | New religionists |
|---|---|---|---|
| 1 | Japanese | Japan | 33,394,000 |
| 2 | Vietnamese (Kinh) | Viet Nam | 10,675,000 |
| 3 | South Korean | South Korea | 6,947,000 |
| 4 | North Korean | North Korea | 3,319,000 |
| 5 | Jakarta Malay (Batavi) | Indonesia | 1,723,000 |
| 6 | Taiwanese (Hoklo) | Taiwan | 1,604,000 |
| 7 | Brazilian White (Branco) | Brazil | 1,313,000 |
| 8 | Sundanese (Urang Sunda) | Indonesia | 906,000 |
| 9 | Javanese (Orang Jawa) | Indonesia | 882,000 |
| 10 | Balinese | Indonesia | 666,000 |

### Peoples with greatest number of Sikhs, 2020

|   | People | Country | Sikhs |
|---|---|---|---|
| 1 | Eastern Punjabi (Gurmukhi) | India | 18,354,000 |
| 2 | Maratha (Maharathi) | India | 1,868,000 |
| 3 | Gujarati | India | 1,190,000 |
| 4 | Western Punjabi | India | 1,066,000 |
| 5 | Hindi (High Hindi) | India | 823,000 |
| 6 | Hindi (Bazaar, Popular) | India | 690,000 |
| 7 | Punjabi | United Kingdom | 448,000 |
| 8 | Punjabi | Canada | 443,000 |
| 9 | Punjabi | United States | 417,000 |
| 10 | Punjabi | Australia | 135,000 |

### Peoples with greatest number of Jews, 2020

|   | People | Country | Jews |
|---|---|---|---|
| 1 | Jewish | United States | 4,844,000 |
| 2 | Israeli Jewish (Sabra) | Israel | 1,230,000 |
| 3 | Jewish (Russian) | Israel | 979,000 |
| 4 | Jewish | Palestine | 550,000 |
| 5 | Jewish (Judeo-German) | United States | 511,000 |
| 6 | Polish Jew | Israel | 491,000 |
| 7 | Arabic Jew | Israel | 475,000 |
| 8 | Romanian Jew | Israel | 456,000 |
| 9 | Moroccan Jew | Israel | 452,000 |
| 10 | Yiddish Jewish | Israel | 378,000 |

### Peoples with greatest number of Spiritists, 2020

|   | People | Country | Spiritists |
|---|---|---|---|
| 1 | Brazilian White (Branco) | Brazil | 3,720,000 |
| 2 | Brazilian Mulato | Brazil | 2,806,000 |
| 3 | Brazilian Black | Brazil | 2,455,000 |
| 4 | Brazilian Mestico | Brazil | 1,275,000 |
| 5 | Mulatto | Cuba | 951,000 |
| 6 | Black | Cuba | 816,000 |
| 7 | Colombian Mulatto | Colombia | 351,000 |
| 8 | Venezuelan Black | Venezuela | 284,000 |
| 9 | Haitian Black | Haiti | 269,000 |
| 10 | Cuban White | Cuba | 179,000 |

### Peoples with greatest number of Daoists, 2020

|   | People | Country | Daoists |
|---|---|---|---|
| 1 | Han Chinese (Mandarin) | China | 5,409,000 |
| 2 | Taiwanese (Hoklo) | Taiwan | 3,005,000 |
| 3 | Puyi (Bouyei, Pu-I) | China | 257,000 |
| 4 | She | China | 151,000 |
| 5 | Biao-Jiao Mien | China | 49,800 |
| 6 | Han Chinese (Fukienese) | United States | 13,200 |
| 7 | Han Chinese (Mandarin) | Australia | 11,800 |
| 8 | Shikou Biao Mien | China | 10,100 |
| 9 | Han Chinese (Mandarin) | New Zealand | 910 |
| 10 | Han Chinese (Mandarin) | Laos | 330 |

Peoples with greatest number of Confucianists, 2020

| | People | Country | Confucianists |
|---|---|---|---|
| 1 | South Korean | South Korea | 5,557,000 |
| 2 | Han Chinese (Mandarin) | China | 1,803,000 |
| 3 | Han Chinese (Mandarin) | Myanmar | 596,000 |
| 4 | Han Chinese | Thailand | 247,000 |
| 5 | Han Chinese (Min Nan) | Myanmar | 176,000 |
| 6 | Korean | Japan | 121,000 |
| 7 | South Korean (Chejumal) | South Korea | 40,200 |
| 8 | Han Chinese (Cantonese) | Australia | 38,300 |
| 9 | Han Chinese | South Africa | 35,600 |
| 10 | Han Chinese (Hakka) | Myanmar | 34,900 |

Peoples with greatest number of Baha'is, 2020

| | People | Country | Baha'is |
|---|---|---|---|
| 1 | Telugu (Andhra, Tolangan) | India | 673,000 |
| 2 | Vietnamese (Kinh) | Viet Nam | 401,000 |
| 3 | Hindi (Bazaar, Popular) | India | 345,000 |
| 4 | Hindi (High Hindi) | India | 329,000 |
| 5 | Persian (Irani) | Iran | 254,000 |
| 6 | Levantine Arab | United States | 159,000 |
| 7 | Bemba | Zambia | 159,000 |
| 8 | USA White | United States | 149,000 |
| 9 | Central Aymara | Bolivia | 145,000 |
| 10 | Gujarati | India | 119,000 |

Peoples with greatest number of Jains, 2020

| | People | Country | Jains |
|---|---|---|---|
| 1 | Maratha (Maharathi) | India | 1,307,000 |
| 2 | Rajasthani (Marwari) | India | 662,000 |
| 3 | Gujarati | India | 595,000 |
| 4 | Rajasthani (Jaipuri) | India | 589,000 |
| 5 | Rajasthani (Mewari) | India | 531,000 |
| 6 | Rajasthani (Mewati) | India | 512,000 |
| 7 | Rajasthani (Shekhawati, Marwari) | India | 393,000 |
| 8 | Godwari | India | 391,000 |
| 9 | Hindi (Bazaar, Popular) | India | 345,000 |
| 10 | Hindi (High Hindi) | India | 329,000 |

Peoples with greatest number of Shintoists, 2020

| | People | Country | Shintoists |
|---|---|---|---|
| 1 | Japanese | Japan | 2,714,000 |
| 2 | Japanese | United States | 66,900 |
| 3 | Japanese | South Korea | 30,800 |
| 4 | Japanese | Brazil | 8,500 |
| 5 | Japanese | Singapore | 1,400 |
| 6 | Japanese | Thailand | 420 |
| 7 | Japanese | New Zealand | 400 |
| 8 | Japanese | Viet Nam | 190 |
| 9 | Japanese | Sri Lanka | 170 |

Peoples with greatest number of Zoroastrians, 2020

|   | People | Country | Zoroastrians |
|---|---|---|---|
| 1 | Parsi | India | 75,900 |
| 2 | Parsi (Parsee, Dari) | Iran | 47,900 |
| 3 | Persian | United States | 18,800 |
| 4 | Gabri | Iran | 16,000 |
| 5 | Persian | Pakistan | 8,100 |
| 6 | Iranian (Persian) | United Kingdom | 5,200 |
| 7 | Persian | Afghanistan | 4,000 |
| 8 | Persian | Australia | 2,700 |
| 9 | Persian | Tajikistan | 2,700 |
| 10 | Parsi | Sri Lanka | 2,600 |

## Evangelization by Peoples

### Evangelization, 1900–2050

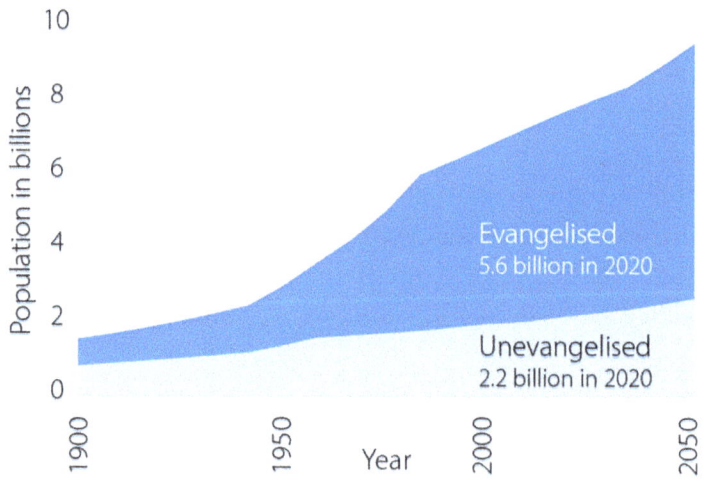

Source: Todd M. Johnson and Gina A. Zurlo, *World Christian Encyclopedia*, 3rd ed. (Edinburgh: Edinburgh University Press, 2019), 33.

Least-evangelized peoples (over 1 million population), 2020

|   | People | Country | % evangelized |
|---|---|---|---|
| 1 | Bakhtiari | Iran | 11.7% |
| 2 | Maaza Bedouin | Egypt | 12.3% |
| 3 | Beja (Beni-Amer) | Sudan | 13.2% |
| 4 | Southern Luri (Lori) | Iran | 14.6% |
| 5 | Laki (Leki, Alaki) | Iran | 14.6% |
| 6 | Dimili Kurd (Southern Zaza) | Turkey | 15.2% |
| 7 | Kanembu | Chad | 15.5% |
| 8 | Southern Pathan | Afghanistan | 15.5% |
| 9 | Tajakant Bedouin | Algeria | 15.7% |
| 10 | Fur (Furawi) | Sudan | 16.5% |

Largest unevangelized peoples (World A), 2020

|   | People | Country | Population |
|---|---|---|---|
| 1 | Han Chinese (Jinyu) | China | 60,308,000 |
| 2 | Bhojpuri Bihari (Deswali) | India | 48,852,000 |
| 3 | Maitili (Maithili, Tharu) | India | 41,400,000 |
| 4 | Han Chinese (Kan, Gan) | China | 41,280,000 |
| 5 | Han Chinese (Hunanese) | China | 40,722,000 |
| 6 | Awadhi (Baiswari, Bagheli) | India | 27,600,000 |
| 7 | Sindhi | Pakistan | 25,977,000 |
| 8 | Algerian Arab | Algeria | 25,560,000 |
| 9 | North Korean | North Korea | 25,533,000 |
| 10 | Braj Bhakha (Antarbedi) | India | 24,201,000 |

Largest evangelized non-Christian peoples (World B), 2020

|   | People | Country | Population |
|---|---|---|---|
| 1 | Han Chinese (Mandarin) | China | 901,447,000 |
| 2 | Japanese | Japan | 123,361,000 |
| 3 | Bengali | Bangladesh | 111,431,000 |
| 4 | Bengali | India | 107,226,000 |
| 5 | Telugu (Andhra, Tolangan) | India | 96,125,000 |
| 6 | Maratha (Maharathi) | India | 93,385,000 |
| 7 | Han Chinese (Wu) | China | 92,532,000 |
| 8 | Western Punjabi (Lahnda) | Pakistan | 89,459,000 |
| 9 | Javanese (Orang Jawa) | Indonesia | 88,173,000 |
| 10 | Tamil (Madrasi, Tamalsan) | India | 86,388,000 |

Largest Christian peoples (World C), 2020

|   | People | Country | Population |
|---|---|---|---|
| 1 | USA White | United States | 124,560,000 |
| 2 | Russian | Russia | 115,205,000 |
| 3 | Brazilian White (Branco) | Brazil | 109,425,000 |
| 4 | Mexican Mestizo | Mexico | 70,538,000 |
| 5 | German (High German) | Germany | 49,221,000 |
| 6 | Brazilian Mulato | Brazil | 46,763,000 |
| 7 | English (British) | United Kingdom | 46,281,000 |
| 8 | African American (Black) | United States | 39,720,000 |
| 9 | Polish (Pole, Silesian) | Poland | 35,799,000 |
| 10 | Ukrainian | Ukraine | 33,169,000 |

## Bible Translation

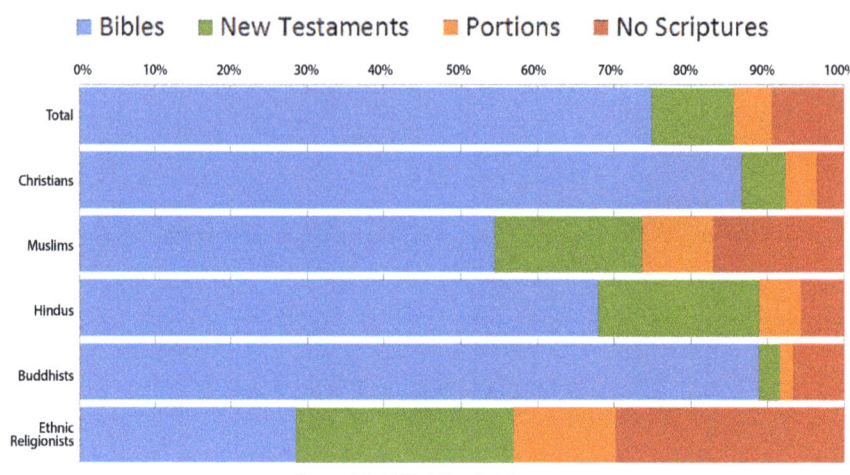

Source: World Christian Database

Largest peoples with own Bible, 2020

|   | People | Country | Population |
|---|---|---|---|
| 1 | Han Chinese (Mandarin) | China | 901,447,000 |
| 2 | USA White | United States | 124,560,000 |
| 3 | Japanese | Japan | 123,361,000 |
| 4 | Russian | Russia | 115,205,000 |
| 5 | Bengali | Bangladesh | 111,431,000 |
| 6 | Brazilian White (Branco) | Brazil | 109,425,000 |
| 7 | Bengali | India | 107,226,000 |
| 8 | Telugu (Andhra, Tolangan) | India | 96,125,000 |
| 9 | Maratha (Maharathi) | India | 93,385,000 |
| 10 | Han Chinese (Wu) | China | 92,532,000 |

Largest peoples with a New Testament (but no full Bible), 2020

|   | People | Country | Population |
|---|---|---|---|
| 1 | Western Punjabi (Lahnda) | Pakistan | 89,459,000 |
| 2 | Egyptian Arab | Egypt | 62,823,000 |
| 3 | Bhojpuri Bihari (Deswali) | India | 48,852,000 |
| 4 | Maitili (Maithili, Tharu) | India | 41,400,000 |
| 5 | Algerian Arab | Algeria | 25,560,000 |
| 6 | Braj Bhakha (Antarbedi) | India | 24,201,000 |
| 7 | Southern Punjabi | Pakistan | 22,390,000 |
| 8 | Bangri (Deswali, Hariani) | India | 20,284,000 |
| 9 | Iraqi Arab | Iraq | 18,806,000 |
| 10 | Northeastern Tai (Isan) | Thailand | 18,497,000 |

Largest peoples with at least one book of the Bible (but no NT), 2020

|   | People | Country | Population |
|---|---|---|---|
| 1 | Upper Egyptian Arab | Egypt | 24,736,000 |
| 2 | Syrian Arab | Syria | 13,544,000 |
| 3 | Southern Pathan | Afghanistan | 11,986,000 |
| 4 | Rajasthani (Jaipuri) | India | 11,785,000 |
| 5 | Tunisian Arab | Tunisia | 10,497,000 |
| 6 | Rangpuri (Rajbansi) | Bangladesh | 10,441,000 |
| 7 | Lombard | Italy | 9,281,000 |
| 8 | Neapolitan-Calabrian | Italy | 7,679,000 |
| 9 | Western Pathan (Afghani) | Pakistan | 6,848,000 |
| 10 | Rajasthani (Mewari) | India | 6,643,000 |

Largest peoples without a single book of the Bible, 2020

|   | People | Country | Population |
|---|---|---|---|
| 1 | Han Chinese (Jinyu) | China | 60,308,000 |
| 2 | Han Chinese (Kan, Gan) | China | 41,280,000 |
| 3 | Han Chinese (Hunanese) | China | 40,722,000 |
| 4 | Deccani | India | 17,325,000 |
| 5 | Northern Yemeni Arab | Yemen | 13,828,000 |
| 6 | Southern Yemeni Arab | Yemen | 12,527,000 |
| 7 | Saudi Arab | Saudi Arabia | 12,249,000 |
| 8 | Saudi Arab Hijazi | Saudi Arabia | 11,335,000 |
| 9 | Tujia (Tuchia) | China | 7,190,000 |
| 10 | Rajasthani (Mewati) | India | 6,400,000 |

Largest peoples without own or second-language scriptures, 2020

|   | People | Country | Population |
|---|---|---|---|
| 1 | Han Chinese (Jinyu) | China | 60,308,000 |
| 2 | Rajasthani (Mewati) | India | 6,400,000 |
| 3 | Mina | India | 4,786,000 |
| 4 | Han Chinese (Huizhou) | China | 4,118,000 |
| 5 | Godwari | India | 3,905,000 |
| 6 | Pahari | Pakistan | 3,369,000 |
| 7 | Bagri (Bahgri, Bagari) | India | 2,564,000 |
| 8 | Central Pathan | Pakistan | 2,430,000 |
| 9 | Anaang (Western Ibibio) | Nigeria | 2,144,000 |
| 10 | Northern Luri (Lori) | Iran | 2,133,000 |

## Cities

### Rural/urban Christians, 1900–2050

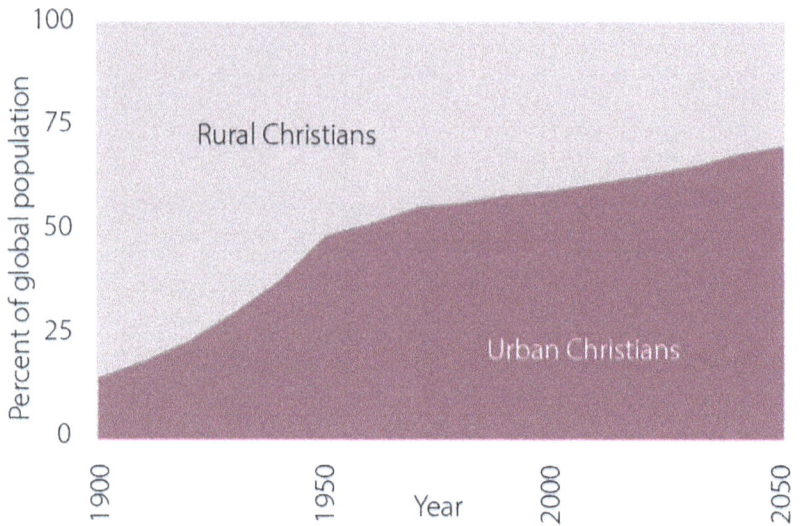

Source: Todd M. Johnson and Gina A. Zurlo, *World Christian Encyclopedia*, 3rd ed. (Edinburgh: Edinburgh University Press, 2019), 30.

### Largest cities, 2020

|   | City | Country | Population |
|---|---|---|---|
| 1 | Tokyo | Japan | 37,393,000 |
| 2 | Delhi | India | 30,291,000 |
| 3 | Shanghai | China | 27,058,000 |
| 4 | São Paulo | Brazil | 22,043,000 |
| 5 | Ciudad de México (Mexico City) | Mexico | 21,782,000 |
| 6 | Dhaka | Bangladesh | 21,006,000 |
| 7 | Al-Qahirah (Cairo) | Egypt | 20,901,000 |
| 8 | Beijing | China | 20,463,000 |
| 9 | Mumbai (Bombay) | India | 20,411,000 |
| 10 | Kinki M.M.A. (Osaka) | Japan | 19,165,000 |

### Cities with the most Christians, 2020

|   | City | Country | Christians |
|---|---|---|---|
| 1 | Ciudad de México (Mexico City) | Mexico | 20,802,000 |
| 2 | São Paulo | Brazil | 19,398,000 |
| 3 | Kinshasa | DR Congo | 13,123,000 |
| 4 | Buenos Aires | Argentina | 13,032,000 |
| 5 | Manila | Philippines | 12,810,000 |
| 6 | Rio de Janeiro | Brazil | 12,247,000 |
| 7 | New York-Newark | United States | 11,282,000 |
| 8 | Moskva (Moscow) | Russia | 10,532,000 |
| 9 | Lagos | Nigeria | 10,345,000 |
| 10 | Lima | Peru | 10,237,000 |

Largest evangelized non-Christian cities, 2020

|   | City | Country | Population |
|---|------|---------|------------|
| 1 | Tokyo | Japan | 37,393,000 |
| 2 | Delhi | India | 30,291,000 |
| 3 | Shanghai | China | 27,058,000 |
| 4 | Dhaka | Bangladesh | 21,006,000 |
| 5 | Al-Qahirah (Cairo) | Egypt | 20,901,000 |
| 6 | Beijing | China | 20,463,000 |
| 7 | Mumbai (Bombay) | India | 20,411,000 |
| 8 | Kinki M.M.A. (Osaka) | Japan | 19,165,000 |
| 9 | Karachi | Pakistan | 16,094,000 |
| 10 | Chongqing | China | 15,872,000 |

Largest unevangelized cities (World A), 2020

|   | City | Country | Population |
|---|------|---------|------------|
| 1 | Kolkata (Calcutta) | India | 14,850,000 |
| 2 | Tehran | Iran | 9,135,000 |
| 3 | Ahmadabad | India | 8,059,000 |
| 4 | Surat | India | 7,185,000 |
| 5 | Baghdad | Iraq | 7,144,000 |
| 6 | Ankara | Turkey | 5,118,000 |
| 7 | Kabul | Afghanistan | 4,222,000 |
| 8 | Tel Aviv-Yafo (Tel Aviv-Jaffa) | Israel | 4,181,000 |
| 9 | Kano | Nigeria | 3,999,000 |
| 10 | Jaipur | India | 3,909,000 |

Least evangelized cities, 2020

|   | City | Country | % Evangelized |
|---|------|---------|---------------|
| 1 | Makkah (Mecca) | Saudi Arabia | 16.9% |
| 2 | Al-Madinah (Medina) | Saudi Arabia | 16.9% |
| 3 | Herat | Afghanistan | 18.0% |
| 4 | Mazar-e Sharif | Afghanistan | 18.0% |
| 5 | Kandahar | Afghanistan | 20.1% |
| 6 | El Aaiún | Western Sahara | 21.1% |
| 7 | Kabul | Afghanistan | 26.1% |
| 8 | Amara | Iraq | 26.1% |
| 9 | Nasiriyah | Iraq | 26.1% |
| 10 | Diwaniyah | Iraq | 26.1% |

## Country Indicators

*These indicators are reported in the World Christian Database, but originally sourced from the United Nations.*

### Socioeconomics, Health, and Gender Inequality in Global Christianity

**Christian distribution of Human Development Index**
Low 35% | Medium 46% | High 19%

**Christian distribution of life expectancy**
<65 Years 18% | 65-75 Years 27% | 75+ Years 55%

**Christian distribution of Gender Inequality Index**
High 11% | Moderate 34% | Low 55%

Source: Todd M. Johnson and Gina A. Zurlo, *World Christian Encyclopedia*, 3rd ed. (Edinburgh: Edinburgh University Press, 2019), 5.

### Highest Human Development, 2020

| | Country | HDI |
|---|---|---|
| 1 | Norway | 95.3 |
| 2 | Switzerland | 94.4 |
| 3 | Australia | 93.9 |
| 4 | Ireland | 93.8 |
| 5 | Germany | 93.6 |
| 6 | Iceland | 93.5 |
| 7 | Sweden | 93.3 |
| 8 | Hong Kong | 93.3 |
| 9 | Singapore | 93.2 |
| 10 | Netherlands | 93.1 |

### Lowest Human Development, 2020

| | Country | HDI |
|---|---|---|
| 1 | Niger | 35.4 |
| 2 | Central African Republic | 36.7 |
| 3 | South Sudan | 38.8 |
| 4 | Chad | 40.4 |
| 5 | Burundi | 41.7 |
| 6 | Sierra Leone | 41.9 |
| 7 | Burkina Faso | 42.3 |
| 8 | Mali | 42.7 |
| 9 | Liberia | 43.5 |
| 10 | Mozambique | 43.7 |

### Highest GDP per capita, 2020

| | Country | GDP p.c. |
|---|---|---|
| 1 | Qatar | $117,000 |
| 2 | Luxembourg | $94,300 |
| 3 | Singapore | $85,500 |
| 4 | Brunei | $71,800 |
| 5 | Ireland | $67,300 |
| 6 | United Arab Emirates | $67,300 |
| 7 | Kuwait | $65,500 |
| 8 | Norway | $64,800 |
| 9 | Switzerland | $57,400 |
| 10 | San Marino | $56,900 |

### Lowest GDP per capita, 2020

| | Country | GDP p.c. |
|---|---|---|
| 1 | Central African Republic | $660 |
| 2 | Burundi | $700 |
| 3 | Liberia | $750 |
| 4 | DR Congo | $810 |
| 5 | Niger | $930 |
| 6 | Mozambique | $1,100 |
| 7 | Malawi | $1,100 |
| 8 | Eritrea | $1,200 |
| 9 | Madagascar | $1,400 |
| 10 | Togo | $1,400 |

Highest corruption, 2020

| | Country | Corruption index |
|---|---|---|
| 1 | Somalia | 90.0 |
| 2 | Syria | 87.0 |
| 3 | South Sudan | 87.0 |
| 4 | Yemen | 86.0 |
| 5 | North Korea | 86.0 |
| 6 | Sudan | 84.0 |
| 7 | Afghanistan | 84.0 |
| 8 | Guinea-Bissau | 84.0 |
| 9 | Equatorial Guinea | 84.0 |
| 10 | Burundi | 83.0 |

Lowest corruption, 2020

| | Country | Corruption index |
|---|---|---|
| 1 | Denmark | 12.0 |
| 2 | New Zealand | 13.0 |
| 3 | Sweden | 15.0 |
| 4 | Switzerland | 15.0 |
| 5 | Singapore | 15.0 |
| 6 | Finland | 15.0 |
| 7 | Norway | 16.0 |
| 8 | Netherlands | 18.0 |
| 9 | Canada | 19.0 |
| 10 | Luxembourg | 19.0 |

Highest education percent, 2020

| | Country | Education % |
|---|---|---|
| 1 | Canada | 100.0% |
| 2 | Austria | 100.0% |
| 3 | Finland | 100.0% |
| 4 | Estonia | 100.0% |
| 5 | Luxembourg | 100.0% |
| 6 | Iceland | 100.0% |
| 7 | Uzbekistan | 99.9% |
| 8 | Czechia | 99.8% |
| 9 | Slovakia | 99.3% |
| 10 | Latvia | 99.3% |

Lowest education percent, 2020

| | Country | Education % |
|---|---|---|
| 1 | Chad | 5.5% |
| 2 | Niger | 6.6% |
| 3 | Burkina Faso | 8.5% |
| 4 | Burundi | 9.3% |
| 5 | Bhutan | 9.6% |
| 6 | Guinea | 11.7% |
| 7 | Papua New Guinea | 12.2% |
| 8 | Mali | 13.1% |
| 9 | Tanzania | 14.3% |
| 10 | Ethiopia | 15.8% |

Highest adult literacy, 2020

| | Country | % literate |
|---|---|---|
| 1 | United States | 100.0% |
| 2 | Japan | 100.0% |
| 3 | Germany | 100.0% |
| 4 | United Kingdom | 100.0% |
| 5 | France | 100.0% |
| 6 | Ukraine | 100.0% |
| 7 | Canada | 100.0% |
| 8 | Uzbekistan | 100.0% |
| 9 | North Korea | 100.0% |
| 10 | Australia | 100.0% |

Lowest adult literacy, 2020

| | Country | % literate |
|---|---|---|
| 1 | Western Sahara | 10.0% |
| 2 | Niger | 15.5% |
| 3 | Chad | 22.3% |
| 4 | Somalia | 25.0% |
| 5 | South Sudan | 26.8% |
| 6 | Afghanistan | 31.7% |
| 7 | Guinea | 32.0% |
| 8 | Sierra Leone | 32.4% |
| 9 | Benin | 32.9% |
| 10 | Mali | 33.1% |

Highest Internet user percent, 2020

| | Country | % Internet users |
|---|---|---|
| 1 | Iceland | 98.2% |
| 2 | Luxembourg | 98.1% |
| 3 | Liechtenstein | 98.1% |
| 4 | Bahrain | 98.0% |
| 5 | Andorra | 97.9% |
| 6 | Norway | 97.3% |
| 7 | Denmark | 97.0% |
| 8 | Monaco | 95.2% |
| 9 | United Kingdom | 94.8% |
| 10 | Qatar | 94.3% |

Lowest Internet user percent, 2020

| | Country | % Internet users |
|---|---|---|
| 1 | North Korea | 0.0% |
| 2 | Eritrea | 1.2% |
| 3 | Somalia | 1.9% |
| 4 | Guinea-Bissau | 3.8% |
| 5 | Central African Republic | 4.0% |
| 6 | Niger | 4.3% |
| 7 | Madagascar | 4.7% |
| 8 | Chad | 5.0% |
| 9 | Burundi | 5.2% |
| 10 | DR Congo | 6.2% |

### Highest physicians per 10,000, 2020

|   | Country | Physicians per 10,000 |
|---|---|---|
| 1 | Cuba | 75.2 |
| 2 | Monaco | 66.5 |
| 3 | San Marino | 63.6 |
| 4 | Greece | 62.6 |
| 5 | Austria | 52.3 |
| 6 | Georgia | 47.8 |
| 7 | Portugal | 44.3 |
| 8 | Norway | 43.9 |
| 9 | Lithuania | 43.8 |
| 10 | Switzerland | 42.5 |

### Lowest physicians per 10,000, 2020

|   | Country | Physicians per 10,000 |
|---|---|---|
| 1 | Niger | 0.19 |
| 2 | Malawi | 0.19 |
| 3 | Ethiopia | 0.22 |
| 4 | Tanzania | 0.22 |
| 5 | Liberia | 0.23 |
| 6 | Sierra Leone | 0.24 |
| 7 | Burundi | 0.28 |
| 8 | Somalia | 0.29 |
| 9 | Chad | 0.44 |
| 10 | Guinea-Bissau | 0.45 |

### Highest life expectancy, 2020

|   | Country | Life expectancy |
|---|---|---|
| 1 | Hong Kong | 85.3 |
| 2 | Japan | 85.0 |
| 3 | Macao | 84.7 |
| 4 | Switzerland | 84.2 |
| 5 | Liechtenstein | 84.2 |
| 6 | Singapore | 84.1 |
| 7 | Italy | 84.0 |
| 8 | San Marino | 84.0 |
| 9 | Holy See | 84.0 |
| 10 | Spain | 84.0 |

### Lowest life expectancy, 2020

|   | Country | Life expectancy |
|---|---|---|
| 1 | Central African Republic | 54.4 |
| 2 | Chad | 55.2 |
| 3 | Lesotho | 55.6 |
| 4 | Nigeria | 55.8 |
| 5 | Sierra Leone | 55.9 |
| 6 | Somalia | 58.3 |
| 7 | South Sudan | 58.7 |
| 8 | Cote d'Ivoire | 58.7 |
| 9 | Guinea-Bissau | 59.4 |
| 10 | Equatorial Guinea | 59.8 |

### Highest infant mortality per 1,000, 2020

|   | Country | Infant mortality per 1,000 |
|---|---|---|
| 1 | Central African Republic | 71 |
| 2 | Sierra Leone | 70 |
| 3 | Chad | 67 |
| 4 | Somalia | 63 |
| 5 | DR Congo | 60 |
| 6 | South Sudan | 59 |
| 7 | Equatorial Guinea | 58 |
| 8 | Mali | 57 |
| 9 | Pakistan | 56 |
| 10 | Nigeria | 55 |

### Lowest infant mortality per 1,000, 2020

|   | Country | Infant mortality per 1,000 |
|---|---|---|
| 1 | Iceland | 1.01 |
| 2 | Hong Kong | 1.17 |
| 3 | Singapore | 1.42 |
| 4 | Finland | 1.42 |
| 5 | Japan | 1.56 |
| 6 | Slovenia | 1.58 |
| 7 | Norway | 1.71 |
| 8 | Estonia | 1.71 |
| 9 | Sweden | 1.72 |
| 10 | South Korea | 1.80 |

### Highest water access percent, 2020

|   | Country | % water access |
|---|---|---|
| 1 | Germany | 100% |
| 2 | United Kingdom | 100% |
| 3 | France | 100% |
| 4 | Italy | 100% |
| 5 | Romania | 100% |
| 6 | Chile | 100% |
| 7 | Netherlands | 100% |
| 8 | Belgium | 100% |
| 9 | Greece | 100% |
| 10 | Sweden | 100% |

### Lowest water access percent, 2020

|   | Country | % water access |
|---|---|---|
| 1 | Eritrea | 19% |
| 2 | Papua New Guinea | 37% |
| 3 | Uganda | 39% |
| 4 | Ethiopia | 39% |
| 5 | Somalia | 40% |
| 6 | Angola | 41% |
| 7 | DR Congo | 42% |
| 8 | Chad | 43% |
| 9 | New Caledonia | 45% |
| 10 | Niger | 46% |

### Highest HIV adults per 1,000, 2020

|   | Country | HIV adults per 1,000 |
|---|---|---|
| 1 | Eswatini | 272 |
| 2 | Lesotho | 250 |
| 3 | Botswana | 219 |
| 4 | South Africa | 189 |
| 5 | Namibia | 138 |
| 6 | Zimbabwe | 135 |
| 7 | Zambia | 124 |
| 8 | Mozambique | 123 |
| 9 | Malawi | 92 |
| 10 | Uganda | 65 |

### Highest malaria per 1,000, 2020

|   | Country | Malaria per 1,000 |
|---|---|---|
| 1 | Mali | 460 |
| 2 | Burkina Faso | 423 |
| 3 | Rwanda | 393 |
| 4 | Guinea | 387 |
| 5 | Niger | 379 |
| 6 | Togo | 360 |
| 7 | Nigeria | 350 |
| 8 | Central African Republic | 312 |
| 9 | Mozambique | 308 |
| 10 | Sierra Leone | 304 |

### Highest % female, 2020

|   | Country | % female |
|---|---|---|
| 1 | Nepal | 54.2% |
| 2 | Hong Kong | 54.1% |
| 3 | Sint Maarten | 54.0% |
| 4 | Caribbean Netherlands | 54.0% |
| 5 | Curacao | 54.0% |
| 6 | Martinique | 54.0% |
| 7 | Latvia | 53.9% |
| 8 | Turks & Caicos Is | 53.9% |
| 9 | Guadeloupe | 53.9% |
| 10 | Dominica | 53.9% |

### Lowest % female, 2020

|   | Country | % female |
|---|---|---|
| 1 | Qatar | 24.8% |
| 2 | United Arab Emirates | 30.9% |
| 3 | Oman | 34.0% |
| 4 | Bahrain | 35.3% |
| 5 | Maldives | 36.6% |
| 6 | Kuwait | 38.8% |
| 7 | Saudi Arabia | 42.2% |
| 8 | Equatorial Guinea | 44.4% |
| 9 | Bhutan | 46.9% |
| 10 | Djibouti | 47.5% |

### Highest gender gap, 2020

|   | Country | Gender gap |
|---|---|---|
| 1 | Yemen | 0.57 |
| 2 | Afghanistan | 0.37 |
| 3 | Pakistan | 0.25 |
| 4 | Chad | 0.22 |
| 5 | Central African Republic | 0.22 |
| 6 | Syria | 0.21 |
| 7 | Guinea | 0.19 |
| 8 | Mali | 0.19 |
| 9 | Niger | 0.19 |
| 10 | Togo | 0.18 |

### Lowest gender gap, 2020

|   | Country | Gender gap |
|---|---|---|
| 1 | Qatar | -0.03 |
| 2 | Latvia | -0.03 |
| 3 | Lithuania | -0.03 |
| 4 | Mongolia | -0.02 |
| 5 | Belarus | -0.02 |
| 6 | Russia | -0.02 |
| 7 | Estonia | -0.02 |
| 8 | Barbados | -0.02 |
| 9 | Uruguay | -0.01 |
| 10 | Namibia | -0.01 |

### Highest gender inequality, 2020

|   | Country | Gender inequality |
|---|---|---|
| 1 | Yemen | 83 |
| 2 | Papua New Guinea | 74 |
| 3 | Chad | 71 |
| 4 | Mali | 68 |
| 5 | Central African Republic | 67 |
| 6 | Cote d'Ivoire | 66 |
| 7 | Liberia | 66 |
| 8 | Afghanistan | 65 |
| 9 | DR Congo | 65 |
| 10 | Niger | 65 |

### Lowest gender inequality, 2020

|   | Country | Gender inequality |
|---|---|---|
| 1 | Switzerland | 3.9 |
| 2 | Denmark | 4.0 |
| 3 | Sweden | 4.4 |
| 4 | Netherlands | 4.4 |
| 5 | Belgium | 4.8 |
| 6 | Norway | 4.8 |
| 7 | Slovenia | 5.4 |
| 8 | Finland | 5.8 |
| 9 | Iceland | 6.2 |
| 10 | South Korea | 6.3 |

# Acknowledgments

*Les chiffres sont les signes de Dieu—Statistics are signs from God.*

Roger Schütz ("Brother Roger," 1915–2005)
founder of the Taizé Community

Like all projects of the Center for the Study of Global Christianity, this book represents the efforts of a team. Peter Crossing, our data analyst, helped envision the contours of this Festschrift from its inception and is the master behind all the data that appear in this book. Chris Guidry, designer, expertly desktop published this manuscript, as he has done for every major publication of the Center since the 1990s. I'd also like to thank Center research assistants Shela Chan, Noah Karger, and Grace Zhao for assisting with various parts of the manuscript and for keeping it a surprise from Todd for many months.

This book includes contributions from only 32 people that have interacted with Todd in the past three decades. There are thousands more who have worked with him closely, gleaned from his wisdom, and have been influenced by his work tracking trends in global Christianity, world religions, and mission. His faithfulness, attention to detail, and emphasis on collaboration have encouraged so many people to thoughtfully engage in research worldwide and make good decisions based on relevant data. Special thanks to all those who have supported Todd's research over the years, including large foundations, mission organizations, local churches, and individuals.

Finally, I'd like to thank Todd's family. His wife, Tricia, and their three daughters, Laura, Claire, and Valerie, have been constant supporters of him and his work, and by extension, our longstanding research legacy. As the reflections in this book describe, the Johnson family provide the foundation of love, encouragement, and strength to persevere in times of joy and times of struggle. This volume is to honor Todd Johnson on his 65th birthday in 2023, and in doing so acknowledges a lifetime of faithful ministry, partnership, and service to the church around the world.

# Contributors

UCHENNA D. ANYANWU (PhD, Fuller Theological Seminary) served with his spouse, Dolapo, in cross-cultural ministry with Calvary Ministries (CAPRO) in West and North Africa. He currently volunteers with Frontier Fellowship as a mission specialist. Uchenna is an ordained minister in the Anglican Church. His research focused on staurocentric theology for peacebuilding in Nigeria's context of acute violence.

JOSEPH BYAMUKAMA (MDiv, Gordon-Conwell Theological Seminary) was born and raised in Ibanda District in Western Uganda. He is pursuing his PhD in New Testament Studies at Ridley College, Australia, under Brian Rosner. Byamukama is married to Daphne, and together they have two sons, Abaho and Abaasa. The Byamukamas live in Kampala, Uganda, and serve with Veracity Fount, a ministry that aims toward researching and resourcing the Ugandan church for its renewal.

JANE CHUN (MDiv, Gordon-Conwell Theological Seminary) is the youth/English-speaking pastor of North Boston Korean United Methodist Church in Andover, MA. Born and raised in New York, she was called to the New England area after God changed her life during college. She received a Pastoral Study Project from the Louisville Institute to study English-speaking second-generation Korean experience and is also a research specialist at the Center for Urban Ministerial Education in Boston, MA.

PETER F. CROSSING (DipTh, Australian College of Theology) gained computer mapping and database expertise through work at the Sydney Centre for World Mission, the National Church Life Survey, and Mapinfo Australia. These positions led to a role as data analyst for the *World Christian Database*, from which came the *World Christian Encyclopedia*, *World Christian Trends*, and the *Atlas of Global Christianity*. He is married with two daughters and a son and lives near Sydney, telecommuting daily to the Center for the Study of Global Christianity.

JAMES MARION DARLACK (MSLIS, Drexel University) served as Library Director at Gordon-Conwell Theological Seminary's Goddard Library in South Hamilton, Massachusetts. He is currently serving as the Senior Director of Vanguard University's O. Cope Budge Library in Costa Mesa, California, and completing a Doctor of Ministry degree concentrating on Global Christianity and Development.

**Darrell Dorr** is Communication Coordinator for Frontier Ventures, a missionary order focused on frontier mission in least-reached peoples. He has served as an editor with various publications during the past 40 years, including the fifth edition of the *Operation World* prayer handbook, the *Atlas of Global Christianity*, and the third edition of the *World Christian Encyclopedia*.

**Sharon Ellis** (MAR, Gordon-Conwell Theological Seminary) is a photographer and storyteller who has worked in Africa, Europe, Asia, and North America. As a Canadian who grew up in South Asia she was exposed to a global perspective from a young age and has continued to function in a global context throughout her life.

**Jarrett Fontenot** (MDiv, Gordon-Conwell Theological Seminary) is a priest in the Anglican Church in North America and serves as Rector of Holy Cross Anglican Church in Baton Rouge, LA.

**Michael Hahn** (MDiv, Gordon-Conwell Theological Seminary) has been a Research Associate with the Center for the Study of Global Christianity since 2018. A graduate of the MFA in Writing program at Pacific University, Michael also writes essays, short fiction, and literary criticism.

**David A. Hannan** (MAOT and MABL, Gordon-Conwell Theological Seminary) is a PhD student in Ancient Near Eastern Studies at Harvard University. While completing his master's degrees at Gordon-Conwell, he worked as a research assistant at the Center for the Study of Global Christianity and a Hebrew teaching assistant. His primary research interests are the intersection of comparative methodologies, ritual theory, historiography, and ancient Near Eastern literatures, focusing on ritualized acts of warfare, cultic objects, and their literary representation in the Hebrew Bible. He has presented papers at the Oxford Postgraduate Conference on Assyriology, the American Academy of Religion, the Society of Biblical Literature, American Society of Overseas Research.

**Richard Haney** (PhD, Oxford Centre for Mission Studies and Middlesex University) is the Executive Director of Frontier Fellowship, on staff since 2014 after serving as a missions pastor, new church development pastor and interim pastor for over 35 years. He also currently serves as adjunct faculty at Gordon-Conwell and teaches history lessons for the Perspectives course. He and his wife, Pam, have three grown daughters and nine grandchildren.

BERT HICKMAN (MAR, Gordon-Conwell Theological Seminary) is Director of Research for RUN Ministries. While a student at Gordon-Conwell he interned at the Center for the Study of Global Christianity, where following graduation he spent 10 years as a research associate and senior research associate. He is associate editor of the Edinburgh Companions to Global Christianity (Edinburgh University Press) and was an associate editor for the *Atlas of Global Christianity* and the *World Christian Encyclopedia*, 3rd edition. Prior to his life in mission research, he worked in the fields of public health and intellectual property.

DARYL R. IRELAND (PhD, Boston University School of Theology) is Research Assistant Professor of World Christianity and Associate Director of the Center for Global Christianity and Mission at Boston University.

S. KYLE JOHNSON (PhD, Boston College) is a theologian and college instructor, as well as a passionate advocate for pedagogical innovation in higher education. Currently, he consults in the intersections of technology and education at the Center for Digital Innovation in Learning at Boston College. He is also a part-time instructor of theology at Boston College, where he has taught several interdisciplinary courses in the areas of religious studies, theology, and international politics. He is developing a book manuscript that explores the intersections between Christian demonology, coloniality, and anti-Blackness. His research has been published in *Spiritus: A Journal of Christian Spirituality*, and online at The Conversation.com and ReadingReligion.com.

PATRICK JOHNSTONE is a former missionary in South Africa with Dorothea Mission. He is the originator of *Operation World*, first as a 32-page booklet on 40 countries with prayer points, and now one of the most sought-after prayer guides for Evangelicals around the world. Over 2.5 million copies have been printed in 12 languages.

GRACE JI-SUN KIM (PhD, University of Toronto) is a professor of Theology at Earlham School of Religion. She is the author or editor of 21 books, most recently, *Spirit Life, Invisible* and *Intersectional Theology*. Kim is a Series Editor for Palgrave Macmillan Series, "Asian Christianity in the Diaspora" and has served on the American Academy of Religion's Board of Directors. Kim writes for *Baptist News Global, Sojourners,* and *Faith and Leadership* and has published in *TIME, The Huffington Post, Christian Century, US Catholic Magazine* and *The Nation*. She is the host of Madang podcast which is hosted by the Christian Century and is an ordained Presbyterian Church (USA) minister.

FERUZA KRASON (MA, Gordon-Conwell Theological Seminary) is a Bible Translation and a Scripture Engagement consultant with SIL Eurasia Area. She served in the Northern Uzbek Bible translation project as one of the mother tongue translators for 22 years.

SANDRA S.K. LEE (MDiv, Gordon-Conwell Theological Seminary) is a wife, mother, and ordained pastor. She is a regional administrator for the Evangelical Covenant Church, overseeing the credentialing of ministers and conference ministries for over 90 ministries and over 200 pastors from Virginia to Maine. She is managing editor of the *Atlas of Global Christianity* (Edinburgh University Press) and co-authored articles with Todd M. Johnson published by William Carey Library, the *International Bulletin of Missionary Research*, ISPCK, and at the World Christianity Group at the American Academy of Religion. Her ongoing passion is studying African, Asian, and Latin American history, culture, diaspora, and theology for the purpose of shepherding and equipping ministers.

JUSTIN LONG (MA, William Carey International University) has been involved in missions research for nearly 30 years. He presently serves as Director of Research for Beyond and editor of the 24:14 Movement Database. He and his wife Heidi have four children and live in the United States.

JASON MANDRYK (MA, Providence College and Theological Seminary) sensed that God was putting in him a more global calling to see the big picture, to analyze the trends, and to communicate the global challenge to the church. Jason coauthored the sixth edition of *Operation World*, released in 2001, with Patrick Johnstone. A regular speaker at mission events, Jason specializes in mission mobilizing, focusing on the biblical basis for mission and weighing strategic considerations for mission today and in the future.

BRIAN MCATEE served as a Global Field Personnel for the Cooperative Baptist Fellowship among international students in Athens, Georgia (1996–1997) and at Boston University (1997–2004). After his time with the Center for the Study of Global Christianity (2004–2008), Brian served refugees from the Chin State in Myanmar and the Nuba Mountains in central Sudan as Missions Minister at the First Baptist Church of Oklahoma City until April 2014. Brian now serves a state government role and lives with his wife, Kristin, in the Oklahoma City area.

BRYAN NICHOLSON (MS, University of Georgia) is a cartographer/geographer working on the design team at the Center for the Study of Global Christianity. His studies focused on cartography, geographic information systems (GIS), and cultural geography. He has designed maps and data visualizations for many organizations and publications through his project, cartoMission. He also teaches as an adjunct geography instructor in Colorado Springs, CO.

SUJIN PARK (MDiv, Gordon-Conwell Theological Seminary) is the founder and director of Singing Diary Ministries since 2005 as well as a Korean American singer-songwriter, worship minister, and also formerly an arts missionary with A.C.T. International. She has worked with various musicians and artists around the world in musical productions and recording projects, for performance in musical and missional scenes, and as producer and director for various conferences and concerts. For over 15 years, she shared her life and songs anywhere she was led to go, including Korea, Japan, United Kingdom., Germany, the Philippines, China, India, Israel, Egypt, Indonesia, the USA, and Canada. She studied Music Composition and Theology.

EVA PASCAL (PhD, Boston University) is an Assistant Professor of Religious Studies at St. Michael's College in Vermont. From 2006–2010, she taught classes on Christianity and Buddhism, world religions, and theology at Payap University in Chiang Mai, Thailand. Her research interests include the history of Christianity in Asia and encounters with other religions, especially Buddhism. Her second area of research explores the intersection of religion and development, and she oversees the multimedia site Old & New in Shona Religion at Boston University School of Theology.

KENNETH R. ROSS is Professor of Theology and Dean of Postgraduate Studies at Zomba Theological University in Malawi. He is also Visiting Professor at several African Universities, Series Editor of the *Edinburgh Companions to Global Christianity* (Edinburgh University Press), and Advisor to the World Council of Churches Commission on World Mission and Evangelism. Among his recent books are *Mission, Race and Colonialism in Malawi: Alexander Hetherwick of Blantyre* (Edinburgh University Press, 2023) and, co-edited with Asiyati Lorraine Chiweza and Wapulumuka O. Mulwafu, *Beyond Impunity: New Directions for Governance in Malawi* (University of Cape Town Press, 2022).

**Justin Schell** (MA and MAR, Gordon-Conwell Theological Seminary; MBA, EDHEC Business School) serves as the director of executive projects for the Lausanne Movement (www.lausanne.org) as well as the US director for Union (www.theolo.gy). He is author of *Come and See: A History and Theology of Mission* as well as the forthcoming *The Mission of God in the Short Studies in Biblical Theology* series by Crossway Publishing. He is husband to Megan and daddy to Henry and Evie. They are members at Evergreen Church in Tulsa, OK.

**Jennifer Lee Shin** (ThM, Gordon-Conwell Theological Seminary) is currently a PhD student in Old Testament at Wheaton College.

Benjamin Thomas (DMin, Gordon-Conwell Theological Seminary) is a co-founder and CEO of B2THEWORLD and the leader of Kigali International Community School in Rwanda. He is a New Yorker, the son of Indian immigrants to the USA, a husband, and a father of four. He enjoys spending time with his family and being present as a dad and a husband. He currently serves in Rwanda and is passionate about global leadership, global education, and global missions. He is also an advocate for children in post-conflict countries.

**Charles Tieszen** (PhD, University of Birmingham) is a scholar studying the history and theology of Christian-Muslim relations. He is a section editor for the multi-volume project, Christian-Muslim Relations: A Bibliographical History (Brill). He was elected a Fellow of the Royal Historical Society in 2019. His most recent book is The Christian Encounter with Muhammad: How Theologians have Interpreted the Prophet (Bloomsbury, 2022). He lives with his family in northern California.

**Molly Wall** is a researcher and editor with Operation World, which she co-directs with author Jason Mandryk. She is an editor of *Operation World* (IVP Books, 7th Ed), and the advising editor of *Pray for the World* (IVP Books). Prior to serving with Operation World, Molly served as a researcher and curriculum developer with the US Center for World Mission (now Frontier Ventures). She is the editor of *The Blessing: God's Promise, Our Purpose*(Institute for International Studies), and assisted with editorial work on *Perspectives on the World Christian Movement* (William Carey Library, 4th Ed). Molly and the Operation World team are based at the All Nations Christian College near London in the UK.

CINDY M. WU (MAR, Gordon-Conwell Theological Seminary) is an author, missions mobilizer, and ordained minister. She and her husband are co-founders of Mosaic Formation, a ministry focusing on the spiritual formation of leaders serving diverse and underserved communities. She is co-author of *Our Global Families: Christians Embracing Common Identity in a Changing World* (Baker Academic, 2015) with Todd M. Johnson, and author of *A Better Country: Embracing the Refugees in Our Midst* (William Carey Publishing, 2017).

KENNETH YOUNG (MAR and MA, Gordon-Conwell Theological Seminary) is a native of Sylvester, Georgia. At Gordon-Conwell he was a Michael Haynes Scholar, Byington Scholar, and member of the Theta Alpha Epsilon Honor Society. He is pastor of Calvary Baptist Church in Haverhill, MA, as well as Associate Director of the Massachusetts Council of Churches. He is married to Adrianne D. Gladden-Young and has two daughters.

GINA A. ZURLO (PhD, Boston University) is Co-Director of the Center for the Study of Global Christianity. She is author of *Global Christianity: A Guide to the World's Largest Religion from Afghanistan to Zimbabwe* (Zondervan 2022) and *Women and World Christianity: Building and Sustaining a Global Movement* (Wiley-Blackwell 2023). She is also co-editor, with Todd Johnson, of the *World Christian Database* (Brill) and co-author of the *World Christian Encyclopedia*, 3rd edition (Edinburgh University Press). She was named one of the BBC's 100 most inspiring and influential women of 2019 for her work in quantifying the religious future.

www.ingramcontent.com/pod-product-compliance
Lightning Source LLC
Chambersburg PA
CBHW061206070526
44583CB00025B/3137